*The essence of optimism is that it takes no account of the present, but it is a source of inspiration, of vitality and hope where others have resigned; it enables a woman to hold her head high, to claim the future for herself and not to abandon it to her enemy.*

Dietrich Bonhoeffer (1906-45), German Protestant theologian

# Surviving Financial Disasters

The Ultimate Guide to: Bankruptcy, Foreclosure, Auto Repossession, Eviction, and Excessive Debts
and more

Tiffany R. Love

Petra Publishing and Company
385 S. Lemon Street, #E314
Walnut, CA 91789
www.PetraPublishingCompany.com

Shaun & Cheryl:
Best wishes on your
Best Seller!!! Looking forward
to seeing you on Oprah!
Tiffany R. Love

Cover design by Michael McBride
Bar Code supplied by Dave Evers

©2004 by Petra Publishing and Company/ Tiffany R. Love

First edition, version I
Printed in the United States of America

Petra Publishing and Company
385 South Lemon Avenue, Suite E314
Walnut, CA 91789-2727
www.petrapublishing.com


Library of Congress Cataloging in Publication Data

Love, Tiffany R., 1971-
 Surviving Financial Disasters: Bankruptcy, Foreclosure, Auto Repossession, Eviction, Excessive Debt and more/Tiffany R. Love, --1st
Ed.
        p.cm.
Includes bibliographical references and index.

Printed in the United States of America

ISBN 0-9712429-5-X

This book is dedicated to my friend Abizar,
for bringing me back to life.


And for my beloved dog Rasta (1991-2003).

# Table of Contents

## FORECLOSURE                                                          **67**

# Acknowledgments

*Believe, when you are most unhappy that there is something for you to do in the world. So as you can sweeten another's pain, life is not in vain.*

Hellen Keller

I had always been the independent self-contained type who often chose to avoid trouble unless being forced to meet it head on. During my unpleasant financial experiences I discovered the best approach to conquering adversity is to face it without fearing an adverse outcome. As a result I've become confident in my ability to *persevere* despite the consequences. I feel invincible in respect to solving problems within my power. I also learned that the longer my head stayed underneath the blanket and the bills piled inside the mailbox the worse my situation became. By greeting challenges I find it less intimidating to express myself despite the listener. However, facing difficult financial situations can humble the strongest spirit, and I too was reminded of my humanity. Many times I could have been embarrassed had it not been for the maturity, professionalism and understanding of many people working for and against me. My financial crisis is over; however, I'm continually learning how to integrate what I want and what others need from me into my new perspective. My state of self-containment is broadening to include others I would have never before enjoyed. Although, I would not want to endure such crisis in the future, I'm thankful for what I learned from this experience.

The most challenging aspect to surviving any threat is remaining encouraged during disappointments. It takes determination to avoid succumbing to defeat; I appreciate myself and those who sincerely love me for not giving up. I'm also thankful for the silent applauses I've received.

When I think of how to thank my special friend, who supported me during every difficult day to help elevate my happiness, I feel overcome with indebtedness. He provided the quote on the opening page, when I couldn't see any way out of my predicament. After reading it, I felt empowered to take another step for my defense and it worked. That day changed my outlook and approach to sustain me during each arduous day that followed. What I'll never forget is how Abizar patiently listened thousands of miles away while I described my living hell. When I demanded to know why he bothered to talk to me, he would lovingly answer. When I complained, he acknowledged my distress, and when I felt better he was happy too. Thank you Abizar, I know it wasn't easy, but you made me feel then like the person I am today.

Thanks to my family for your continual support especially my mother, father and siblings, who always encourage me even when they have doubts. I thank my animal friends Nacolbie, Shanook, *Rasta*, and Delilah as well as their caregivers. And a special thank you to all the people at Jade Escrow in Rowland Heights, California, especially Kim for your example of patience and focus.

And thanks to all those who help to make me feel special. You're names may not be listed in this book, but they are embedded in my heart. Your images will always be with me even into eternity!

# Introduction

*Courage is as often the outcome of despair as hope; In one case we have nothing to lose, in the other everything to gain.*

Diane De Pottiers

After authoring a resource book on getting through life situations, I never would have imagined I would need many of the resources I provided to readers.

Writing is a *creative* profession, known to cause financial strain until a big break occurs. I knew the risks involved, but I was willing to do almost anything to see my dream come to fruition. Had I known then what I know now, I would have carefully planned my course.

Although I had maintained employment while I wrote the majority of the book, I didn't anticipate sudden unemployment. During the final months of pre-publication, in August 2002, I received a notice from my lender that my home was in foreclosure. Like so many people I fretted, then buried the letter underneath a stack of papers in hope it would simply go away, at least until the Oprah Show® called.

I owned a home in California, which I knew could be worth something to someone, but how much I did not know. Having had unpleasant experiences with unaccountable real estate agents in the past, I was reluctant to call an agent to assist me with the sale of my home. In fact, I did not need to call; nearly every other person I met sold real estate. In October, I completed my book and received the first prints. A huge success for me, I

*So what do we do? Anything. Something. So long as we just don't sit there. If we screw it up, start over, try something else. If we wait until we've satisfied all the uncertainties, it may be too late.*

Lee Iacocca

thought, but my house was weeks away from being sold by the lender and I needed to stop this right away. I did what so many people do; I panicked and filed for bankruptcy. A mistake if you have a significant amount of equity in your home, or you have steady income (details about negotiating with your lender/creditors as alternatives to filling for bankruptcy are covered in this book). Conversely, I was able to prevent the sale of my home with the bankruptcy courts protection.

The lessons I learned from interacting with my lender, attorneys, bankruptcy court and others are compiled in this book. But it's not limited to information. Stories representing different life lessons are included to inspire readers who would not have ordinarily contemplated behavioral patterns which led to financial disaster and other difficulties. Much of the information is personal as to what I experienced. What I did not experience, I interviewed experts and performed research.

It is my desire that you find this book informative as well as inspirational. It's filled with sound hints, samples, and forms as well as lighthearted comments to help ease your mind. As I've learned, everyone experiences some form of difficulties. Being able to remove the urgency in order to calmly respond can save time, money and energy. By being informed you can easily see a way out of *temporary* problems. Hopefully, it's not as disastrous as it seems.

By no means do I attempt to diminish the seriousness of the issues by adding humor or a fresh outlook. I wrote the book in this manner because many people, including myself, are overwhelmed with fear of losing all they've worked for. The threat of losing property is not a new experience, and I've written this book to help.

## About This Book

This book is a compilation of information gathered from different experiences that I either faced first hand, interviewed experts or researched from various sources. Throughout the chapters I communicate what I learned, to provide readers with a broader scope of alternatives. My mistakes are shared as well as my successes. Those struggling with difficult financial situations should find this book a comfort.

Someone summarized the idea for my book as *gorilla law*. It provides a true first hand account (not from a gorilla, rather a determined person) of how resources work for those reliant on them as well as providing detailed information on how to work through difficulties. Each chapter begins with an empowering quotation. Phrases I recited to retain a positive and hopeful outlook are also included.

## About the Stories Included in This Book

I'm a conceptual thinker as many of my problems are solved within my head. In fact, most of the stories included in this book were images, like movies before my eyes, birthed to sort out inner pains I experienced at different periods in my life. The stories weren't

*necessarily* generated by the experiences covered in this book, rather other life challenges; thereby making their application universal. I've relied on them to encourage me regardless of the circumstances and I hope they do the same for you.

## Rescue Me!

This book is effective if you're honest about your financial problems. Most will need to abandon the desire to be rescued by super lotteries, casinos, and relatives. It's rare people have such luck, yet it does happen for a few. By eliminating expectations for being rescued your opportunities become evident. When a part-time job at the supermarket taken to pay a few bills turns into a new career in management, you can easily congratulate yourself for taking initiatives to improve your condition. Those who have yet to learn how to confront problems should take time to evaluate their circumstance before reading any further. The information provided should be put to use. It's vital for readers to be honest with yourself to get the most out of this book.

Someone asked me what about people who are simply living the *American Dream* by owning a home, driving a nice car, sending children to nice schools, and working long hours at a company yet not generating enough income to pay their bills. I believe that our quest to live the *American Dream* includes moments of living beyond our means. If these *moments* occur frequently, it can easily cause financial ruin. It doesn't take an accounting degree to ascertain if you can afford the purchase or not. When we can't, we finance and finance and finance until we're deep in debt. The *American Dream* easily becomes the *American Nightmare*.

## Prescription For Troubled Times

The list below has been compiled to encourage readers who encounter challenges:

- **Maintain a positive outlook**: Get as much information about your situation as possible. Good information can change perceptions for nearly any predicament.

- **Exercise**: take long bike rides, walks, jogs, scenic drives, etc. Take your dog(s) for a walk or drive your children to the park for playtime. Time spent dwelling on problems can cause you to feel hopeless. Work through your cares with activities.

- **Meditate**: Take time to relax and center your thinking. Meditation helps to balance urgent cares with ultimate life goals such as being happy and peaceful. Tapes and books are available at many music stores; if meditation tapes are not in your budget try your local library they may have rental copies available.

- **Read a good book**: Through many of my difficult days I relied on the passages from the Language of Letting Go by Melanie Bettie (see notation below). If you need extra strength or a positive balanced outlook, this book is a must have.

- **Don't beat yourself up**: We all tend to defeat ourselves before we begin. Even disappointing situations can develop a greater self worth. Don't sell yourself short, you can get through this challenge.

-☼- *Language of Letting Go, by Melanie* Bettie. ©1996. Hazelden Information Education. $16.00 (USD).

## Take It One Day At A Time

Each one of us has overcome some form of adversity where it initially felt easier to simply quit. Don't give up. If you made it through that experience, you can certainly get through this one. It took a great deal of determination to preserve, and you certainly have what it takes to overcome this challenge. Go for it, you can do this too!

## The Disclaimer

Although the author and publisher have exhaustively researched all sources to ensure the accuracy and completeness of the information contained in this book, we assume no responsibility for errors, inaccuracies, omissions, or any inconsistency herein. Any slights of people or organizations are unintentional.

Readers should use their own judgment or consult an expert in given profession for specific remedies. The author <u>is not</u> an attorney and is not engaging in legal practice by writing this book. This book contains examples of documents filed in court by the author and responses to her filings. Because each state, county and city operates uniquely it is the reader's responsibility to comply with local laws.

At the time of publishing, all links contained in this guide are active and all agency names and addresses were verified. Agencies and companies change locations and telephone numbers frequently. When contacting a company, please verify that the information is accurate.

We would like to know if you were unable to locate a resource, and/or if you would like us to consider a resource for our next edition. Please contact us at:

Petra Publishing and Company
385 South Lemon Avenue, Suite E314
Walnut, CA 91789-2727
www.petrapublishing.com

## Limitations of This Book

Each person has unique circumstances, which contribute to the outcome of their case. As a non-attorney, I am unable to predict or include resources for each circumstance. However, included throughout this book are resources to help readers find additional information.

## About the Resources Contained in This Book

The book, web site, and agency references contained in this book are not paid advertisements. Neither the author nor publisher received payments, monetary or otherwise from agencies for inclusion in this book. The author performed common research techniques to obtain all resources. Neither the author nor publisher bears any responsibilities for the agency actions or lack thereof. For expert referrals, consult a professional in the pertinent field.

Thousands of nationwide resources are available for any given subject matter. Consult with your local and state elected officials for locating alternative resources within your community.

# Help Is On The Way

Once upon a time in a far away land lived a king. During a ceremony celebrating his reign, the king felt disappointed with his life. As he watched the crowd from the stands high above, he couldn't help feeling alone in his thoughts. Not being able to bear watching the celebration any longer he set out to the desert where he toiled day and night to build a home in the shape of a silo for total shelter. Remaining discontent with his life he called the desert home. A small peep-hole through the mortar was his only view to the outer world.

One day during the king's nap he was awaken by a loud thunderous sound. The king immediately ran to see the cause of this noise. He thought it was a thunderstorm from far off; however, there weren't any clouds as far as his eyes could see. As he continued to look he noticed a cloud of dirt billowing from the air. After the dirt settled there appeared the sight of a vast army. With arrows and cannons fired directly at the silo, the king's home collapsed.

On the ground amongst the rubble he bent over with his face between his knees, and cried to himself, *why? Who would want to do this to me?* When he lifted his eyes, he noticed the army was his own. The king ran to his commander and exclaimed, *why are you tying to kill me?! Why did you do this to me? This is my home that I built with my two hands.* The commander gently dismounted the horse and softly approached the king. He removed his hat and knelt before his majesty. He spoke, *dear king we were not trying to kill you, we're only trying to free you.*

# Bankruptcy

*One of man's finest qualities is described by the simple word "guts" –*
*The ability to take it. If you have the discipline to stand fast when*
*your body wants to run, if you can control your temper and remain*
*cheerful in the face of monotony or disappointment, you have "guts" in*
*the soldiering sense.*

Colonel John S. Roosman

Some of us have stories about *bad* habits we developed to enter bankruptcy, for others it's a matter of circumstance, but for most it's a combination of both. I can remember when I was 19 years old I went to the bank to withdraw all the money in my savings account. After the teller handed the money to me she said, *what good is money when it's in the bank, money should be enjoyed.* Certainly this is bad advice if you have bills to pay, but for me it occasionally became a proverb used to justify spending rather saving. Years later when I recovered from being severely ill, I practiced the tellers saying to the fullest. I found it useless to save an excessive amount of money which would have been enjoyed by others if I had died, so I enjoyed every dollar I earned no matter how much or little money I was earning. This lasted until the day I was found unexpectedly out of work; which eventually caused my financial disaster. I think every person should enjoy their lives to the fullest. Hopefully, you have food, water, shelter and more. However, the thought that they maybe in jeopardy is what brings us to bankruptcy and this section is designed to inform debtors as they migrate through *real life* bankruptcy situations.

If you are reading this book, chances are you have decided to personally defend your rights. Good for you! I welcome you to the *gorilla law* club. There will be difficult days, but don't give up. I know that you can make it through this experience; you will be much stronger than what you could have ever imagined if you are well informed. Carefully read this chapter to plan your course of action. You may choose to hire an attorney after reading, as there are many variables in bankruptcy. An attorney maybe a wise choice for most people; however, I encourage everyone filing for bankruptcy to familiarize themselves with available options to help keep your attorney *honest.* The more you know of your choices the easier it will be to communicate with your legal counsel.

## I'm In Trouble Now, So What Should I Do?

Read sections in this book that offer alternatives to filing for bankruptcy. If you need to file, read this chapter to determine which bankruptcy chapter is best for you and then file your petition. Those who need extra time to complete the bankruptcy forms should file an emergency petition, which could be depending on the court, only the non schedule forms. This will allow you to complete the schedules at a later time. Review the paperwork carefully to ensure they are accurately completed and all creditors, to your knowledge, are listed.

When you enter bankruptcy determine how you want to get out of it. Do you need a discharge, protection to sell your house, or time to repay your debts? Once you've decided on a course, let your actions and documents support your stance. You can always change your mind later, but don't enter bankruptcy oblivious to your desires.

Guard your sanity by not taking the *oftentimes* unprofessional actions of certain court and trustee office staff too personally. They will not be in your life forever, just for a period of time. Don't respond to their conduct by being equally rude; maintain your dignity. Although, I found the clerk's office extremely helpful and even the attorney for the trustee's office a wealth of information, although she didn't provide any legal advice it was oftentimes *implied*. Be clear about you what to accomplish. Always take notes and research your position before acting.

## How Bankruptcy Works

In bankruptcy there is the bankruptcy judge, trustee, estate and debtor. The judge is the ultimate decision-maker for the estate. The trustee is also employed by the Federal government to oversee the estate. They are not necessarily neutral as they are hired to represent your assets and not you. If the trustee goes along with your motion good chances are the judge will also. It's best to keep the trustee on your side, as your creditors will attempt to do the same. Estate is everything you own, owe, and what's owed to you. The person seeking protection from creditors is called the debtor, that's us. We file bankruptcy for different reasons. When you enter bankruptcy do so with an exit plan, so that no matter what your creditors file against your case, it doesn't deter you from reaching your objective. For example, if you file to have your debts discharged then make sure you remain focused on preparing the necessary paperwork to discharge your debts.

In addition to the enormous amount of paperwork there are meetings which debtors must attend, payment plans, hearings, etc. These are covered in more depth throughout this chapter.

## Overview of Bankruptcy

Bankruptcy is divided into chapters. Chapter 7 & 13 are most commonly utilized by individual debtor(s) (in bankruptcy your new name becomes debtor) who need the protection of the court to stay (or halt) creditors from collecting against you. Each chapter in bankruptcy has different requirements, for this book, I will cover chapters 7 & 13 only as they apply to individual debtors. Once you file for bankruptcy the court takes control of your estate. Meaning any and all assets and debts incurred, and listed in your schedules, are under the protection of the courts. The court appoints a trustee to administer the estate. In order to receive court protection for the duration of your case, you must have an estate worth protecting (each court operates differently so the requirements may vary). For example, those filing for chapter 7 discharges that have steady income are evaluated on their ability to pay their debts. Likewise, people filing for chapter 13 who do not have any income are evaluated on their ability to pay monthly trustee fees and creditors payments.

## Bankruptcy Costs

Bankruptcy is not free. It costs approximately $185 to file for chapter 13, and $200 to file for chapter 7. Fee waivers are not easily granted and money (either cash or money order) must be presented at the time of filing.

## The Difference Between Chapter 7 & 13

In chapter 7 the debtor's nonexempt (property creditors can go after that is not protected by state exemptions – for more information on your state's exemptions contact the bankruptcy clerk's office), if any exists, is liquidated to pay as much, if not all, the debtor's creditors, while in most chapter 13 cases only a portion of the debtor's income is used to pay creditor's. Under chapter 7 the debtor loses all or most of his/her nonexempt property and receives a chapter 7 discharge (see Discharging Debts in Chapter 13), which releases the debtor from liability for most debts.

Under chapter 13, the debtor usually retains his/her nonexempt property, must pay off as much of his/her debts as the court deems feasible, and receives a chapter 13 discharge, which is broader than a chapter 7 discharge as it could release the debtor from liability of several types of debts not dischargeable under chapter 7. However, a chapter 13 case normally lasts much longer, up to five years, than a chapter 7 case and is usually more expensive for the debtor as payments to creditors and the trustee must be made.

## Chapter 7 Bankruptcy

Chapter 7 bankruptcy involves the liquidation of all your assets to pay creditors and a discharge of debts to provide the debtor with a *fresh start*. The chapter 7 trustee takes complete control of your estate (everything you own or are entitled to) and sells nearly everything of value to pay your creditors. They also discharge allowable debts on your behalf. Chapter 7 is straight forward. Creditors may object to debtors discharges, and debtors file responses supporting the validly of the discharge.

If you have significant amount of assets, the trustee's office considers this a high priority. He/she will aggressively manage your case as they receive a percentage of all liquidated assets.

## Basic Procedure for Chapter 7 Bankruptcy

Enclosed in the petition packages (forms) is a sworn list of creditors, schedule of assets and liabilities, list of exempted property, schedule of current income and expenditures, statement of financial affairs and intent regarding consumer debts secured by property of the estate. Upon filing the petitions, you surrender, to the trustee, all property of the estate (11 U.S.C. 521). The automatic stay is in full effect granting relief from pursuing creditors. This prohibits creditors from pursuing debtors outside the bankruptcy court.

The courts send notice to all creditors listed on the sworn list of creditors that you are in bankruptcy (11 U.S.C. 342). Within approximately 30 days debtors are required to attend an informal meeting with the trustee called the *meeting of the creditors*. Debtors and creditors meet with the trustee to question the debtor about his/her ability to repay debts. The meeting typically consists of the trustee, debtor, debtor's attorney and creditor's attorney (if one is retained). The debtor must attend this meeting. If you do not attend, the trustee could file a motion to have your case dismissed. Should you file a response to the trustee's motion to dismiss your case, you must have a good reason and documentation to support your statements. It's common for people to suddenly become ill prior to the first meeting of creditors. Attempt to take good care of yourself as an illness may not be excused. During the meeting your attorney can answer questions for you. The debtor is sworn in by the trustee who may tape the meeting. The trustee determines which creditor's you can pay and which will be discharged. The trustee will also assess the validity of your bankruptcy. If your case is best suited for chapter 13, the trustee may file a motion with the court requesting the conversion of your case.

During the meeting of the creditors, your attorney doesn't *object* to questions asked by your creditors, most likely, he/she will answer certain questions on your behalf or clarify your statements. Debtors are required to answer questions in *good faith* (11 U.S.C 341).

Creditors often times will file a proof of claim within 90 days after the first date set for the meeting of creditors. At the end of the case, if a surplus remains after all claims are paid in full, the court may grant an extension of time for filing of claims not filed during the initial 90 day period. The trustee and debtor can object to any creditor's proof of claim (*see sample of opposition to proof of claim found at the end of this chapter*).

## My Experiences In Chapter 13

After I completed my petition forms, I filed them at the Central District Bankruptcy Court in California (downtown Los Angeles). Initially, I petitioned the court with tears in my eyes for a fee waiver, but it was not granted. My first lesson seldom does that bankruptcy court grant fee waivers. I scrapped up $185.00 and filed an emergency case, which meant I had another 15 days to complete the schedules. In the Chapter 13 petition package, it explains what documents must be immediately filed and the proper order. Take time to carefully read the petition package. The total time I spent completing the emergency forms was less than 4 hours, including photocopying of documents.

For the central district, one original and four copies must be filed (a total of 5 complete sets). Courts often have copy centers located within the building or nearby for those who have not made the correct amount of copies. Remember to bring enough money, as the centers charge per page. Another requirement for the central district is *blue backs*, a blank blue sheet of paper that must be attached to the backside of the original document (an additional cost of $0.35).

Within a few days, I received a notice to file the remaining documents within 15 days or my case could be dismissed. The total time it took me was 13 hours. Completing the schedules is the most laborious task in bankruptcy. As the hours past, I half typed pages and hand wrote the others and later filed the missing schedules to complete my bankruptcy petition.

The next day I made an important decision, when I had money again, I would manage it more carefully. It was obvious that my disorganization and lack of planning was the fuel that accelerated me into bankruptcy.

> Obtain a copy of your credit report and list every item you owe. Accurately complete schedules and avoid slight omissions, as the petition is a sworn legal document.
>
> Remember that chapter 13 petitioners agree to pay the trustee's office a percentage, typically 3-10% (most likely 10%), of your total payments to creditors.

Within one week after my filing, I received notice of the first meeting of the creditors. My emergency filing occurred December 5th and the first meeting of the creditors was held January 29th.

I referred to the following book for assistance in preparing my schedules:

*Chapter 13 Bankruptcy Repay Your Debts* by Attorney Robin Leonard © 2002 Nolo Press. $34.99 (USD).

Not everyone will have the extra funds to pay for a book. Spend a few hours at the bookstores where copies of the desired titles are on hand. Remember to take your schedules with you. Before I purchased this book I completed my schedules inside the book store in pencil, and then later I typed over my original markings.

## Representing Yourself

Depending on your finances, you may have no other choice but to represent yourself. Petitioners without legal representation are solely responsible for the management of their case. Bankruptcy court can have additional pressures than local courts, because the powers of the trustees and judges are broad, they tend to act more intimidating towards petitioning parties. Those who look beyond the intimidation can do quite well. Certainly self representation is your right, which when exercised correctly it can be rewarding.

You will begin to feel comfortable the more you learn about the federal and local bankruptcy laws. The entire bankruptcy code is available online at: http://www4.law.cornell.edu/uscode/11

Read as much pertinent information as you need, the more you know the more confident you'll become. Most public law libraries (many courts have law libraries inside) have the entire federal bankruptcy code, as well as local codes, sample motions, tactical procedures and forms. Don't attempt to memorize the vast amount of information; take notes and rehearse what you've learned.

There will be information that you simply will not understand, but that happens to everyone. Always articulate what you want, in brief statements to the trustee and judge.

Stay current with the developments of your case. Respond by deadlines and attend required meetings. Paralegals and attorney's can offer support to those who need knowledgeable eyes to review forms prior to filing. There is a fee for this service, but is maybe worth to cost to avoid future problems.

> The Latin word *Pro Se*, meaning *for oneself.* The word *In Pro Per* is a title that also maybe used by individuals representing choosing to represent themselves.

## Hints For Pro Se Petitioners

To be effective at self-representation you must detach your feelings from the case. Your creditor's portrayal of you doesn't matter. They will attempt to depict you as a deadbeat loser who refuses to pay his/her bills. When they file motions against your case, particularly those in chapter 13, it's not you they are attacking; just the case and an image they've created.

Those choosing to represent themselves must detach personal feelings and focus on facts; thereby creating an image before the court of a responsible person willing to repay his/her debts.

## More Bankruptcy Hints

When you arrive at hearings, meetings or court dates (with the judge or trustee) always dress professionally. Your appearance speaks volumes about you: take time to look neat and polished. Even if you borrow clothes, never arrive to court wearing street clothes such as jeans, shorts, T-shirts, etc. Perfume & cologne can cause allergies to erupt so it's best to avoid wearing them.

Once I sat in court and watched people lose their homes and other property. Each one of the debtors was dressed in casual clothing and did not carefully listen to the judge. In contrast, the attorneys representing creditors where professionally clothed. During my first court appearance I requested the clerk move my case down from number one to number three and I watched others who went before the court. I was thankful that my appearance measured up to that of my creditors and I had the extra time to study the judge's manner. This added to my confidence, which tremendously helped me.

Once again, ensure that forms are thoroughly and accurately completed. The court will dismiss your case if your forms are not correctly completed.

I didn't know before I filed my petition, the courts could dismiss my case, but thankfully the forms were nearly properly completed (minor errors were sorted out later in bankruptcy).

## I Want To Hire An Attorney, How Do I Find One?

Referral to an attorney is most recommended. Family, friends, and co-workers can provide first hand information about their attorney's behavior and knowledge of bankruptcy laws. A tip I learned from an attorney is to call several attorney offices and ask the receptionist if the attorney is any good. You may inquire about their work load. If they have a negative relationship with their staff, you certainly don't want their service. From my experience, I attempt to locate people who can answer my questions without being offended that I asked. They should also educate you on what is happening with your case. If they can't teach you, they probably don't know or possess the confidence in their skills to teach. In addition, a knowledgeable attorney should inform you of the pros and cons for each available option.

Like others, I've retained lawyers who did not effectively represent me. This was due to my feelings of urgency to act on my defense. When my creditor's attorneys filed motions in court I panicked and quickly sought the aid of unproductive counsel who were quick to charge and slow to act. In turn, I learned how to express my dissatisfaction with them before I dismissed their services. This allows the person to *get on the ball* or risk not being paid for their work.

The following are resources for locating an attorney:

*The Best Lawyers In America* by Naifeh, Steven, & White. © 2003. Woodward/White Inc. $200.00 (USD).
*This is an expensive book, but it could be worth the costs if you desperately need to find reputable legal counsel. Check with your local library for a copy to review or look online for a used copy to purchase.*

**The American Bar Association**
www.abanet.org

**NACBA (National Association of Consumer Bankruptcy Attorneys)**
2300 M. Street, NW Suite 800
Washington, DC 20037
(202) 331-8005
http://nacba.com

**Other Web Resources**

http://www.lawyers.com
http://www.abcworld.org/abchome.html
http://www.bankruptcyaction.com
http://www.attorneyfind.com
http://www.legallawhelp.com

## I Need To File Bankruptcy Now, Which Chapter Should I Choose

Many legal professionals file for chapter 7 on their client's behalf before filing for chapter 13. In chapter 7 most nonsecured debts (debts not backed by any collateral such as real property) can be discharged, for those who cannot financially meet their obligations. After their debts are discharged, the debtor can exercises his/her *one time* right to convert their case to chapter 13 and commence payment of non-dischargable debts, such as mortgages, auto loans, school loans, taxes, etc. This practice is known as chapter 20. Like chapter 13, the automatic stay is in effect (however, once you file for chapter 7 your mortgage lender will more than likely file a motion from relief of the automatic stay). Before you attempt this on your own, pay for a consultation with a knowledgeable attorney or paralegal as you don't want your case dismissed before you convert to another chapter.

Everyone's needs are unique; only you can determine your best interest. If you don't have many nonsecured debts (such as credit cards); you may want to file for chapter 13 to begin payment arrangements, considering you are able to make trustee payments as well as payments to creditors, or you may have enough equity (or other assets) to pay off debts. If you are in need of money and you do not own valuable property, chapter 7 maybe a good option to eliminate debts and begin a *fresh start*.

## I Have Enough Information, How Do I File?

Bankruptcy courts have the required petition forms available online and in the clerk's office. To obtain forms online, locate the court and web site in Appendix G (and provided on the CD ROM at the back of this book). Click the desired chapter and download the desired forms. Those who do not own a personal computer can visit the bankruptcy court clerk's office to obtain forms or locate copies at law libraries. You can use public computers to download forms (even copy centers have computers connected to the internet). Some libraries charge a fee

for printing, so bring money to pay printing fees.

People who do not feel confident their abilities to complete the forms can hire a knowledgeable attorney or paralegal that specializes in bankruptcy law to review the petitions for accuracy. Most likely they will charge a fee, usually less than if they were representing you in court. However, it maybe worth the cost, as your case could be dismissed if the forms are improperly completed.

> Remember to file your documents in the required proper order. If your files are out of order and/or incomplete the court could dismiss your case.
>
> It's important to accurately list information in your petitions. Each state has additional laws as to how much a debtor can exempt. Exemption information can be obtained online or at the bankruptcy clerk's office. This information may also be included inside your petition package and online.
>
> Furthermore, the trustee can object to your exemptions. They will do so within 30 days after the meeting of creditors.

## Emergency Filing

Preparing the required documentation for bankruptcy is time consuming. Depending on your bankruptcy court rules, you maybe allowed to file a select amount of forms to start your bankruptcy case. Additional time is granted, such as two weeks, to file the remaining petition forms. This incomplete package is referred to as an emergency filing. If you are seeking immediate protection of the courts, commence with the emergency filing and then file remaining documentation before the court's expiration date. The emergency package typically consists of forms that aren't schedules (*see Appendix G*), which occupy the most time to complete as they require detailed financial information. Unless you have been granted a fee waiver, you must bring cash or a money order for the entire filing fee; these fees are expected at the time of filing the emergency petition.

## The First Meeting Of The Creditors

The meeting of the creditors allows everyone you owe to question your ability and intention to repay your debts. It may seem scary to face your creditors, but it's not as bad as what it seems. Before you enter take time to breathe and relax. This meeting is a thorough evaluation of your financial situation. If you have an attorney he/she will be along. Answer questions honestly and to the best of your ability. Should you represent yourself, do not be afraid. Take notes, ask for clarifications when needed, and don't feel embarrassed. Some trustee offices offer classes for pro se petitioners. Contact your trustee office for more information prior to the first meeting.

When you arrive, present two forms of identification such as a valid driver's license and your social security card. Those receiving an income must present proof. Chapter 13 petitioners are expected to have their mortgage payments from the date you filed for bankruptcy in addition to your plan payment to the trustee's office.

Within 60 days following the first meeting of the creditors objections to general discharges are filed. After 60 days, if no motion to dismiss or objections are pending the court automatically grants the discharge. The trustee can grant a discharge without a court hearing if all of the debtor's paperwork is in order. Remember, each trustee's practices vary.

People filing for chapter 13 must have payments to the trustee if not they are at risk of having their case dismissed; however you can respond to the trustee motion to dismiss your case and bring payments to the hearing before the judge along with a good reason why payments were not made to the trustee. If no good reasons exits, assure the courts that this problem will not occur again in the future.

The motions to dismiss is a request to the judge to close [or dismiss] your case. Motions are not set in stone, only requests to the court. When the judge signs the order it's official, but this occurs at, or shortly after, the hearing date.

## Discharging Debts in Bankruptcy (chapter 7 & 13)

Discharge eliminates personal liability debtor's have [to pay] on a claim or debt. The debtor's goal in any chapter 7 is to have as many debts discharged to obtain a *fresh start*. Customarily all debts created before the bankruptcy filings are discharged with some exceptions covered in the following section. In essence you are not obligated to pay and creditors are not allowed to pursue collection. Creditor's who have pursued civil litigation in state court must dismiss their actions if a federal bankruptcy judge discharges the debt. In fact, a creditor must cease telephone calls, letters and personal contacts.

## Non-Dischargeable Debts

As stated in the previous sections, creditors can object to a discharge at any time if it falls within the provisions of 11 U.S.C. 523. Section 523 covers ten categories sorted into two areas. The two areas address debts that cannot be discharged (non-dischargeable) due to wrongful conduct and public policy. A claim must fall within one of the following exceptions to be found non-dischargeable.

Debts not discharged due to the debtor's misconduct include:
- intentional torts,

- fraud,
- larceny,
- embezzlement,
- fiduciary violations,
- drunk driving

Debts not discharged due to public policy include:
- alimony and child support,
- taxes and customs duties,
- government fines
- penalties and forfeitures
- educational loans
- unscheduled debts (not listed in the schedules so that a creditor could file a proof of claim) and certain debts surviving a prior bankruptcy case

Under bankruptcy rule 4007; 11 U.S.C. 523 a creditor can object within 60 days of the first date of the meeting of the creditors if :
- the debt is a consumer debt created close to the debtor's filing for bankruptcy,
- is a result of willful and malicious injury to a person or property of another

> A creditor seeking to prove fraud must show that there was a false, material representation of fact made by the debtor that the debtor knew was false at the time he/she made it. In addition, the claim must have been made with the intention of deceiving the creditor. Some courts have held that when a credit card is used, the debtor *implicitly* represents the ability and intention to pay for the goods and services charged. Courts find that some credit card debt is non-dischargeable under the fraud exception.

Yes, those who charge their credit cards to the maximum before filing for bankruptcy maybe charged with fraud. Under section 523, certain consumer debt created right before filing a chapter 7 is non-dischargeable. This is applicable to items loosely defined as *luxury goods or services* purchased within 40 days before filing, owing to a single creditor aggregating more than $500. Likewise, cash advances taken 20 days before filing bankruptcy for more than $1,000 extended by a creditor under an open end credit plan can be considered fraud.

Any credit extended based on false financial statements is subject to exception from discharge. Statements made in financial statements have to be materially false with the intent to deceive the creditor to fall within the exception.

> Credit applications ordinarily do not qualify as a *financial statement* if it does not require a disclosure of debts.

Further worry to debtors, the trustee or a creditor can motion the court (under U.S.C 727) to disallow a final discharge of all debts, of whatever nature, if the debtor has done the following:

(1) destroys or conceals his/her property within one year before filing or after the date of filing, with the intent to hinder, delay or defraud a creditor;
(2) conceals, destroys, falsifies or fails to preserve records of his financial condition;
(3) knowingly in a bankruptcy case makes a false account, oath or claim;
(4) gives, offers, receives, or attempts to obtain money, property or an advantage for acting or forbearing to act;
(5) withholds forms from an officer of the estate records related to his property or financial affairs;
(6) fails to satisfactorily explain any loss of assets; or
(7) refuses to obey court orders or refuses to respond to questions posed by the court

The court may dismiss a bankruptcy case if the debtor:

(1) unreasonably delays the proceedings to the creditor's prejudice;
(2) fails to pay necessary fees or payments; or
(3) fails to file his schedules.

## When Does The Discharge Occur

The timing of the discharge varies, depending on the chapter under which this case is filed. In a chapter 13 the court may discharge as soon as practical after the debtor completes all payments under the plan. This could take up to three years since most chapter 13 plans provide for payment up to 36 months. In a chapter 7 (liquidation) case, for example, the court usually grants the discharge promptly on expiration of the time fixed for filing a complaint objecting to discharge and the time fixed for filing a motion to dismiss the case for substantial abuse (60 days following the first date set for the meeting of creditors). Typically, this occurs about four to eight months after the date the debtor files the petition with the bankruptcy court.

Although, debtor's filing for chapter 13 generally receive a discharge after they've completed their payments according to their plan, they may also apply for a *hardship discharge*. The courts may grant a *hardship discharge* if the debtor's failure to complete payments under his/her plan is due to circumstances beyond their control. This occurs prior to the completion of their bankruptcy. Similar with a chapter 7 discharge, a *hardship discharge* has exemptions from discharge.

## Obtaining A Discharge

A discharge is a permanent order releasing debtors from personal liability for certain types of debts. A discharge doesn't immediately happen, it can take several months (for chapter 7 cases, typically 4 months if no objections are filed) before the debtor receives notice of discharge. However, once a debtor is granted a discharge, creditors must refrain from collection activities including legal action. In addition, they are not to contact the debtor (which includes telephone calls, letters, and personal visits). The court has determined that the debtor is no longer required to pay discharged debts. Discharges can be obtained in chapter 7 as well as Chapter 13 cases.

In chapter 7 (*fresh start*), if there are no objections, debtors will automatically receive a discharge after the time provided for creditors to file an objection. Within the order of discharge creditors are warned not to communicate with the debtor, if so they can be subject to punishment for contempt even in cases where the creditor claims they haven't received the order for discharge, the debtor's protection remains in effect.

In chapter 13 debtors typically receive a discharge after all plan payments have been made, which can take several years, typically 4 years. Exceptions are hardship discharges discussed in the next section. As with chapter 7 cases, the discharge can take several months to receive after plan payments have been made. This is so because a chapter 13 bankruptcy case can last up to five years.

Creditors and the trustee can object to debtor's discharge. Creditors will file a complaint called *adversary proceeding* with objections falling within the categories described in the section Non-Dischargeable debts. If a debtor receives a discharge based on false information the courts, after investigating the legitimacy of the discharge, can revoke the discharge.

## Hardship Discharges

Debtors, in chapter 13, experiencing inordinate circumstances beyond their control can petition the court for a hardship discharge. Courts view hardships as *circumstances for which the debtor should not justly be held accountable*. The court can grant a hardship discharge even in cases where plan payments have not been made. Prior to granting a hardship discharge, the courts will *impel* debtors to modify their plan. In cases where this is not feasible, a hardship discharge is considered.

## Motion For Relief From The Automatic Stay

Relief from the automatic stay removes the protection (*of the automatic stay*) debtors have from pursuing creditors. Motions for *relief* are not limited to mortgage lenders, as any creditor can file a motion to relieve the automatic stay protection; however, it doesn't mean the court will automatically grant their request as they must have solid ground for requesting *relief*. Chapter 13 debtors who can prove the creditor's interest is protected, either by equity or income can successfully fight a motion from relief. Chapter 7 debtors should attempt to convince the trustee's office that the assets are protected. It's possible for the chapter 7 trustee to caution creditors who attempt to take action when it's known that the estate is adequately protected.

When I received a motion for relief from the automatic stay from my lender I panicked. I thought I was protected from foreclosure in bankruptcy, but then I had this new threat. My emotions where erratic and I eventually hired an attorney that I would have otherwise not selected. Should you receive a notice don't be frighten. Losing control of your emotions can cause more harm than good.

Creditors have the right to petition the court for relief from the automatic stay. This enables them to continue with actions outside of the bankruptcy court. This is a serious issue if you need the bankruptcy court's protection. Debtors should file a response within the time frame specified on the motion and serve all parties, including the trustee. Creditor's will oftentimes file such motions if they believe there isn't enough collateral to secure their interests. Debtors should prove to the courts their ability to repay their debts and assure the courts the creditor's interests are protected.

Some creditors will enter into an agreement with debtors called an *Adequate Protection Order*. This protects the creditor should the debtor fail to make payments.

> An Adequate Protection Order (APO) is an agreement between two parties that the debt will be repaid. It states the amount to be paid over a period of time and the commencement date. The agreement oftentimes states that if the debtor does not satisfy the terms of the agreement they will automatically be granted relief from the automatic stay. Bankruptcy judges will sign this agreement as well as representatives for the creditor and debtor. APO's provide another alternative for debtors to remain in bankruptcy; however, it will be on the creditor's terms. Creditors will cease pursing relief from the automatic stay once this document is filed with the courts. However, failure to abide by this agreement will cause action on the part of the creditor to obtain relief.

## Answer To Motions From Relief of the Automatic Stay

When your creditor petitions the courts for relief from the automatic stay, debtors should file a response before the deadline. In many cases the response is due 14 days before the date of the hearing (i.e., if the court hearing is set for June 1st the answer is due 14 days before June 1st).  Even if a response is late, be sure to file one prior to the date of the hearing. Samples of responses to motions from relief of the automatic stay are provided. The answer should refute the lender's accusations that the property isn't adequately protected, if that is the creditor's claim. A show of good intention would be to hand over delinquent payments due since the bankruptcy filing or prove they have been made.

Furthermore, assure the court that sufficient equity exists. If it does, provide documentation to support your claim. Proof of equity could be an appraisal report and a pending sale (escrow documentation are considered gold, for those who want to sell their homes). If your property is in escrow, provide a copy of the escrow instructions (at least the first page) showing the lenders interest are secured. The web site, Lawyer Assist (http://lawyerassistant.com/freeforms) provides free templates for various petitions, forms and letters. The trustee's office may also be of assistance for obtaining necessary forms.

Those who do not have equity in the property to protect your creditor's interest can show the courts that sufficient income exits to repay debts. Not all motions from relief of stay involve private creditors. Landlords can file a motion from relief of stay to continue with eviction proceedings. The outcomes of these cases are dependent on the landlord's willingness to accept payments or continue with the eviction process.

## Willful Violation of the Automatic Stay

The debtor's main protection in bankruptcy is the automatic stay imposed by section 362 of the bankruptcy code (see *Automatic Stay* provided at the end of this chapter). Once a bankruptcy petition has been filed creditors are stayed from most collection actions against the debtor and the property of the estate. In most circumstances, the creditor cannot sue, repossess or foreclose, obtain judgments, liens, continue collection actions, contact the debtor or send notices under the protection of the bankruptcy court.

The bankruptcy code has a procedure for creditors to obtain relief from the automatic stay in certain situations. Should creditors ignore the courts to engage in actions against debtors, litigation can be pursued within bankruptcy for debtors to pursue compensation. This process is known as *Willful Violation of The Automatic Stay.*

Section 362 (h) of the bankruptcy code provides an individual injured by a willful violation of the automatic stay is entitled to recover damages including costs and attorney fees, and in appropriate circumstances punitive damages.

## More Comments On Bankruptcy

Exercise all your options prior to filing for bankruptcy. It's worth the effort to find alternative solutions to prevent the bureaucracies and emotional challenges experienced in bankruptcy. My journey through bankruptcy was exhausting, and devastating. Certainly a learning experience I will never want to repeat.

If I can offer any solace, everyone attempts to live up to their job descriptions. The longer you stay in bankruptcy the easier it is to understand this process is not personal. When negotiating, attempt to create two winners, however, this can only happen if you know what you want.

Being a nice person doesn't mean abandon your good senses. That's when people are taken advantage of. Retain your character, don't compromise your principals, and never be afraid to try. No matter what the outcome, the degree of disappointment felt is within your power. You have the ability to not allow any of this to emotionally destroy you. If you react to every situation, soon you'll begin to question your sanity. Trust yourself and be open to other ideas.

## Converting Your Bankruptcy Case

As previously mentioned, debtors can convert their bankruptcy case from one chapter to another (i.e., a chapter 7 petitioner can convert to a chapter 13 and vise versa). Section 706 (a) in the bankruptcy code allows for a *one time* conversion of your case, as long as the case has not been previously converted. Courts may have forms for debtors to complete who desire to convert their case.

During my bankruptcy, I converted my case twice. At the first meeting of the creditors I converted from a chapter 13 to chapter 7, then later discovered I could resume with the mortgage payments. The attorney I hired reconverted the case from chapter 7 back to chapter 13.

Each time the case was converted I received a notice from the court of the new meeting of the creditors hearing. It was held 30 days from the date the court approved the conversion.

The sample of the conversion I initially used to convert from chapter 13 to chapter 7 is provided at the end of this chapter.

## Opposing Proofs of Claims

Creditor's who believe money is owed to them can file a *Proof of Claim* which is served on the debtor, usually via the mail. The creditor must prove that money is in fact owed to them, which experienced creditors attach proof with their claims.

Debtors who oppose the *proof of claim* in whole or part can file an *opposition to proof of claim*. In

my case I filed several. A sample is provided at the end of this section. In one case the creditor, the Internal Revenue Service, withdrew their claim.

One opposition I filed against a creditor, caused them to reduce the amount originally claimed I owed. By opposing a proof of claim, debtors reduce and/or eliminate debts.

## Ex-Parte Motions

Ex-Parte motions are those to be herd by the judge the same day it's filed. In bankruptcy court I found that the judge didn't necessarily hear the motions the same day. However, if you have an urgent matter adding *Ex-Parte* before the title of your motion signals that the matter is a priority.

## Reaffirming Debts

In bankruptcy debtors can take personal responsibility for debts under reaffirmation. In this case the debtor assumes personal liability for repayment; however, the debt is no longer subject to discharge. Debtors wanting to keep certain property that could otherwise be liquidated or subject to liens can find this a benefit, but only if it doesn't pose any hardships to the debtor or their dependants. Creditor's oftentimes make arrangements to modify payments in exchange for debtors reaffirming the debts.

The reaffirmation agreement is signed by the judge if approved. However, courts are cautious about approving these agreements unless it's certain the debtor understands his/her rights.

## Exiting Bankruptcy

Debtor's can exit bankruptcy once their case has been dismissed or discharge occurs. When you file for bankruptcy, think of how you would like your case to progress and conclude. Once you've developed a plan, proceed with accomplishing your goal. This can be a great learning experience, so remain open minded yet steadfast. During my case I vacillated between making monthly mortgage payments and selling my home although the later is what I truly wanted. Save yourself unnecessary grief, research a choice, then choose a path and stick with it. Your first choice is usually the best, as I've learned.

## Having Your Case Dismissed

Debtor's, in chapter 13, can voluntarily file a motion to dismiss their case at anytime. Chapter 13 petitioners can automatically dismiss their case if the case has not been previously converted. Usually, if there are no serious concerns, the court will agree to the dismissal. Chapter 7 petitioners can file a motion to dismiss however, a hearing maybe held to determine the outcome. Type a simple statement as to why you want your case dismissed. That's all you need. As with all filings, ensure that you have served all interested parties.

Should the trustee file a motion to dismiss your case, you can and should file a response. The case isn't dismissed until the judge approves the order. Remember your case can be dismissed if all schedules are not filed. Remember to act responsibly in terms of completing all required documentation. If the courts believe you are attempting to abuse the bankruptcy court's they can bar you from filing future bankruptcy petitions.

## Selling Property In Bankruptcy (Chapter 13)

Those who have fled to the protection of bankruptcy court have another opportunity to sell their property. Bankruptcy allows debtors to sell their property by obtaining permission from the courts or petitioning the trustee to abandon the property. It's best to locate a buyer and have the property in escrow before

petitioning the courts for permission to sell. If the property is set to close within a short period of time, the courts will set a short notice hearing to rule on your motion. If you want to sell the property, but have not located a buyer, complete and file the necessary forms as it can take several weeks, if not months, before the court conducts a hearing on your motion.

Property with equity to pay some if not all debts could require permission from the courts. In cases where debtors have insignificant belongings that do not exceed a set amount (contact the trustee's office for this amount) the trustee may not have any interest in the proceeds. If the property does not have any equity to pay creditors it's best to request the trustee abandon the property (*see below*). Those with equity should contact the trustee's office to obtain court approved forms, if any. I encountered several weeks of delay because I was unaware the trustee office had the court approved forms for me to complete. The trustee maybe required to comment on the debtor's request before the motion is filed. In these cases, the debtor completes all forms and forwards a copy to the trustee's office. When I filed my motion I overlooked this step, however, the trustee's office forwarded their response to the courts and me.

Attached to my motion to sell residential property (see samples at the end of this chapter) was the first page of the escrow instructions, and estimated closing statement. Because the property was set to close shortly after I filed the motion, the court set a *shorten notice* hearing to respond to objections or concerns from others. In this case the lender did not object to my motion, however, my former attorney did. The court overlooked her objection and continued forward with allowing me to sell the property. I appeared representing myself for the hearing. Before the hearing began, the legal counsel for my former mortgage lender explained his position. I explained mine and he encouraged me to discuss the discrepancies with the judge, which I did. The entire time was less than 10 minutes and we were done with my motion granted. The lender was asked to prepare the order, as I'm not an attorney.

## Trustee's Abandonment of Property

If you have property you want the trustee to abandon, meaning, remove from the protection of the court, you can file a motion or the trustee may choose to abandon their interest. This section of the code is straight forward; I've provided the exact wording below:

**11 USC § 554. Abandonment of property of the estate.**

(a) After notice and a hearing, the trustee may abandon any property of the estate that is burdensome to the estate or that is of inconsequential value and benefit to the estate.

(b) On request of a party in interest and after notice and a hearing, the court may order the trustee to abandon any property of the estate that is burdensome to the estate or that is of inconsequential value and benefit to the estate.

(c) Unless the court orders otherwise, any property scheduled under section 521(1) of this title not otherwise administered at the time of the closing of a case is abandoned to the debtor and administered for purposes of section 350 of this title.

(d) Unless the court orders otherwise, property of the estate that is not abandoned under this section and that is not administered in the case remains property of the estate.

## Will This Ever End?

By now you maybe are wondering if anyone could ever love you. That's a sign that the most difficult parts are almost over. Remain encouraged. Keep your promises and adhere to dates set by the trustee's office. It's good to have someone in your life who objectively listens to you. Try to find a stable compassionate person you can talk over your problems with. Yes this will end, so don't give up.

## How To Find Information Not Covered In This Chapter

Those who choose to represent their interest, whether or not an attorney is utilized should know where to find the entire bankruptcy code. It's conveniently located online and in most public law libraries. For those who enjoy the easy access of the Internet, simply use the table at the end of this section to locate the desired topic. The web site listing the bankruptcy is provided at the end of this section. Log onto the website and perform a search for the desired bankruptcy title.

## What You'll Need To File Motions and Other Documents In Court

In most cases when a motion is filed certain documents should accompany the filing. The following checklist is provided for those filing motions and other pleading in court:

- Proof of Service (Every document you file should be accompanied by a proof of service. This informs the court that other parties are aware of your motion).

- An Order. When you want the judge to respond, an order must be attached that delineates what the court is agreeing to do.

The terminology in the bankruptcy code is fairly straight forward, however, the interpretations vary by court and jurisdiction. Retaining the services of a knowledgeable attorney or paralegal can help should you need *insider* information on how your local court (or judge) rules on certain issues.

- 
- Depending on the motion and court a 15 or 20 day notice must be accompanied. This lets the court know that you have given all the parties severed adequate time to respond.

- Mailing List. This informs the court that the listed parties have been served.

## Bankruptcy Resources

**American Bankruptcy Institute**
www.abiworld.com
info@abiworld.com (Email address)

**NACBA (National Association of Consumer Bankruptcy Attorneys)**
2300 M. Street, NW Suite 800
Washington, DC  20037
(202) 331-8005
http://nacba.com

**Other useful web sites**

http://bankrutpct.com
www.law.cornell.edu/topics/bankruptcy.html

# Partial Outline For Title 11 of the United States Bankruptcy Code

The entire bankruptcy code is available online at http://law.cornell.edu/topics/bankruptcy.html
Sections pertaining to Chapter 7 and Chapter 13 bankruptcy are outlined below. To find what the
bankruptcy law says about the information below, log onto the above web site and follow the links
under title 11 to locate the desired section number.

| Section No. | Title |
|---|---|
| 109 | Who may file for which type of bankruptcy |
| 110 | Nonattorney bankruptcy petition prepares |
| 302 | Who qualifies for filing joint cases |
| 341 | Meeting of the creditors |
| 342 | Giving notice of the meeting of the creditors |
| 343 | Examination of the debtor at the meeting of the creditors |
| 347 | Property the trustee does not want |
| 348 | Converting from one type of bankruptcy to another |
| 349 | Dismissing a case |
| 350 | Closing and reopening a case |
| 361 | Providing adequate protection to a secured creditor |
| 362 | The automatic stay |
| 365 | Executory contracts and unexpired leases |
| 366 | Continuing or reconnecting utility service |
| 501 | Filing proofs of claim |
| 502 | Establishing the amount of a creditor's claim |
| 506 | Determing secured claims and avoiding liens |
| 507 | Claims having priority |
| 522 | Exemptions |
| 523 | Nondischargeable debts |
| 524 | Reaffimation of debts |
| 525 | Prohibited post-bankruptcy discrimination |
| 541 | Property of the Estate |
| 547 | Preferences |
| 548 | Fraudulent transfers |
| 553 | Setoffs |
| 554 | Trustee's abandonment of property |
| 722 | Avoiding liens that impairs exemption; redemption |
| 726 | Distribution of the property of the estate |
| 727 | Discharge |
| 1301 | Codebtor Stay |
| 1304 | Debtor engaged in business |
| 1305 | Postpetition claims |
| 1306 | Property of the estate (for chapter 13) |
| 1307 | Converting or dismissing a Chapter 13 case |
| 1322 | Contents of the Chapter 13 plan |
| 1323 | Modifying the plan before confirmation |
| 1325 | Confirming hearing |
| 1326 | Making plan payments |
| 1327 | Rights and obligations after confirmation |
| 1328 | Discharge |
| 1329 | Modifying the plan after confirmation |

1

UNITED STATES BANKRUPTCY COURT

2

CENTRAL DISTRICT OF CALIFORNIA

3

4   Tiffany R. Love

5

6   Pro Se

7

8   In re:                                    ) Case No.:
                                              )
9   Tiffany R. Love,                          ) The Honorable Barry Russell
                                              )
10          Debtor.                           ) Chapter 13
                                              )
11                                            ) OPPOSITION TO MOTION FOR RELEIFE FROM
                                              ) THE AUTOMATIC STAY; DECLARATION OF
12                                            ) DEBTOR IN SUPPORT THEREOF; and
                                              ) Exhibits
13  F & A FEDERAL CREDIT UNION,               )
                                              )
14          Movant,                           )
                                              )
15                                            ) DATE: July 22, 2003
                                              )
16      Vs.                                   ) TIME: 2:00 PM
                                              )
17  Tiffany R. Love                           ) CTRM: 1668
                                              )
18  Nancy Curry, Chapter 13 Trustee          ) FLOOR: 16TH

19

20

21      Now comes the Debtor, TIFFANY R. LOVE who objects to F&A Federal Credit
    Union (herein referred to as F&A) Motion of Relief from Stay and ask that
22  said Motion be overruled for the following:

        1. As evidenced by the attached declaration, debtor will be filing a
23         complaint for the willful violation of the automatic stay against F&A,
24         Wills and Simms, et.al., does 1 to 100.

        2. As evidenced by that attached declaration, debtor has the funds for the
25         post petition car note payment due since March 2003, when F&A closed


                    Opposition to Motion For Relief of Stay - 1

debtor's savings account. Payments will be tendered on or before the scheduled hearing date.

3. Debtor has equity in the subject real property as evidenced by F&A's & their attorney's proof of claim for the value of the vehicle.

**WHEREFORE** the Debtor pray as follows:

1. That movant's motion be denied;

2. If movant's motion is not denied then in the alternative an Order for Relief with Adequate Protection be entered allowing the automatic stay to remain in effect providing debtor remains current with her car payments.

3. For such other relief as this court may deem just and proper.


Respectfully submitted,


_____

Tiffany R. Love

Pro se


Opposition to Motion For Relief of Stay - 2

**CERTIFICATE OF SERVICE**

3

4     The undersigned certifies that a copy of the foregoing was served upon

5  the following:

6  Ralph L. Simms

7  Law Offices of Winn and Simms

8  110 E. Wilshire Avenue, Suite 212

    Fullerton, CA 92832

9

10  Nancy Curry

11  Chapter 13 Trustee

12  606 S. Olive Street

13  Suite 1850

14  Los Angeles, CA 90014

15

16  F&A Federal Credit Union

    P.O. Box 30831

17

    Los Angeles, CA 90030-0831

18

19  This 20 day of June, 2003, by regular, postage pre-paid, U.S. Mail.

20

21

22                          _____

23

24

25

Opposition to Motion For Relief of Stay - 3

# Tiffany R. Love

May 7, 2003

Olivia Berlanger
F & A Federal Credit Union
2625 Corporate Place
Monteray Park, CA 91754-7631

> Re:    **Tiffany R. Love**
>        **Chapter 13, Case No.**
>        **Account No's.** :

To Olivia Berlanger:

Please be advised that the above-referenced person has filed a Chapter 13 bankruptcy with the United States Bankruptcy Court in December 2002, Central District Court, in which the F & A Federal Credit Union was included. All accounts, Saving, Car Loan, and Credit Card was included in the Bankruptcy filing.

Since that filing F & A has threaten legal action against me, including legal fees and interest , made attempts to repossess my vehicle, hired an attorney to file a law suite against me (law offices of Winn and Sims), closed my savings account, and taken other harassing collection attempt towards me.

**Please cease sending any notices and/or statements and cease all collection activity in connection with the above-referenced account.** As I have been receiving notices from your company in regards to the above-referenced account. Even a letter stating that your will pursue legal action although I have not been served with legal papers.

The filing invokes Section 362 of the Bankruptcy Code, which provides in pertinent part:

**Section 362.  Automatic Stay**

(a) ... a petition filed under Section 301, 302, or 303 of this title ... operates as a stay, applicable to all entities, of --

> (1)    the commencement or continuation, including the issuance or employment of process, of a judicial, administrative, or other action or proceeding against the debtor that was or could have been commenced before the commencement of the case under this title,

or to recover a claim against the debtor that arose before the
commencement of the case under this title;

(2)

(2)     the enforcement, against the debtor or against the property of the
estate, of judgment obtained before the commencement of the case under
this title;

Thank you for your courtesy and cooperation in this matter.

Sincerely,


Tiffany R. Love


Cc: Law offices of Winn and Sims


**Sent by fax and certified mail**

FILED

# United States Bankruptcy Court
## Central District of California 23 AM 11:30

In re:                              | Case No.:

Tiffany R. Love,                    | Chapter 13

       Debtor.              | The honorable Barry Russell United
                                    | States Bankruptcy Judge

### *Opposition To Proof of Claim*

COME NOW debtor TIFFANY R. LOVE opposes the request for fees submitted by

Internal Revenue Service (hereunto referred to as IRS). Debtor claims that

all debts owed to IRS were paid during the filing of her tax returns and no

outstanding debts are owed to the IRS.

Dated this 23th day of June, 2003

Tiffany R. Love
Pro Se

Opposition To Proof of Claim - 1

FORM B10 (Official Form 10)(4/01)                                                                        ch-13

| UNITED STATES BANKRUPTCY COURT __CENTRAL__ DISTRICT OF __CALIFORNIA__ | PROOF OF CLAIM |
|---|---|

| Name of Debtor | Case Number |
|---|---|
| TIFFANY R LOVE | |

NOTE: This form should not be used to make a claim for an administrative expense arising after the commencement of the case. A "request" of payment of an administrative expense may be filed pursuant to 11 U.S.C. § 503.

02 DEC 19 PM 2:37

| Name of Creditor (The person or entity to whom the debtor owes money or property): | ☐ Check box if you are aware that anyone else has filed a proof of claim relating to your claim. Attach copy of statement giving particulars. |
|---|---|
| Department of the Treasury - Internal Revenue Service | |

CLERK, U.S. BANKRUPTCY COURT
CENTRAL DISTRICT OF CALIFORNIA

BY _____
DEPUTY CLERK

| Name and addresses where notices should be sent:<br>Internal Revenue Service<br>300 N. Los Angeles St. Room 4062<br>Stop 5025<br>LOS ANGELES, CA 90012<br><br>Telephone number: (213) 576-4501   Creditor #:10 | ☐ Check box if you have never received any notices from the bankruptcy court in this case.<br>☐ Check box if the address differs from the address on the envelope sent to you by the court. |
|---|---|

THIS SPACE IS FOR COURT USE ONLY

| Account or other number by which creditor identifies debtor:<br><br>see attachment | Check here ☐ replaces<br>if this claim ☐ amends  a previously filed claim, dated: _____ |
|---|---|

**1. Basis for Claim**

☐ Goods sold
☐ Services performed
☐ Money loaned
☐ Personal injury/wrongful death
☒ Taxes
☐ Other _____

☐ Retiree benefits as defined in 11 U.S.C. § 1114(a)
☐ Wages, salaries, and compensation (fill out below)
Your SS #: ____ ____ ____
Unpaid compensation for services performed
from _____ to _____
         (date)              (date)

| 2. Date debt was incurred:   see attachment | 3. If court judgment, date obtained: |
|---|---|

**4. Total Amount of Claim at Time Case Filed:**   $ ____2,079.79____

If all or part of your claim is secured or entitled to priority, also complete Item 5 or 6 below.
☒ Check this box if claim includes interest or other charges in addition to the principal amount of the claim. Attach itemized statement of all interest or additional charges.

| **5. Secured Claim.** | **6. Unsecured Priority Claim.** |
|---|---|
| ☐ Check this box if your claim is secured by collateral (including a right of setoff).<br>Brief Description of Collateral:<br>☐ Real Estate  ☐ Motor Vehicle<br>☐ Other _____<br><br>Value of Collateral:  $ _____<br><br><br><br><br><br>Amount of arrearage and other charges at time case filed included in secured claim, if any:  $ _____ | ☒ Check this box if you have an unsecured priority claim<br>Amount entitled to priority $ _2,079.79_<br>Specify the priority of the claim:<br>☐ Wages, salaries, or commissions (up to $4,650),* earned within 90 days before filing of the bankruptcy petition or cessation of the debtor's business, whichever is earlier - 11 U.S.C. § 507(a)(3).<br>☐ Contributions to an employee benefit plan - 11 U.S.C. § 507(a)(4).<br>☐ Up to $2,100* of deposits toward purchase, lease, or rental of property or services for personal, family, or household use - 11 U.S.C. § 507(a)(6).<br>☐ Alimony, maintenance, or support owed to spouse, former spouse, or child - 11 U.S.C. § 507(a)(7).<br>☒ Taxes or penalties owed to governmental units - 11 U.S.C. § 507(a)(8).<br>☐ Other - Specify applicable paragraph of 11 U.S.C. § 507(a)(___).<br>*Amounts are subject to adjustment on 4/1/04 and every 3 years thereafter with respect to cases commenced on or after the date of adjustment. |

**7. Credits:**  The amount of all payments on this claim has been credited and deducted for the purpose of making this proof of claim.

**8. Supporting Documents:**  *Attach copies of supporting documents*, such as promissory notes, purchase orders, invoices, itemized statements of running accounts, contracts, court judgments, mortgages, security agreements, and evidence of perfection of lien. DO NOT SEND ORIGINAL DOCUMENTS. If the documents are not available, explain. If the documents are voluminous, attach a summary.

**9. Date-Stamped Copy:**  To receive an acknowledgement of the filing of your claim, enclose a stamped, self-addressed envelope and copy of this proof of claim.

THIS SPACE IS FOR COURT USE ONLY

| Date<br>12/17/2002 | Sign and print the name and title, if any, of the creditor or other person authorized to file this claim (attach copy of power of attorney, if any):<br>_____ Insolvency Manager | A PAGE 2 OF 2 |
|---|---|---|

Penalty for presenting fraudulent claim: Fine of up to $500,000 or imprisonment for up to 5 years, or both. 18 U.S.C. §§ 152 and 3571.

```
 1 │ DEBRA W. YANG
   │ United States Attorney
 2 │ EDWARD M. ROBBINS, JR.
   │ Assistant United States Attorney
 3 │ Chief, Tax Division
   │
 4 │
   │
 5 │
   │ RON S. CHUN
 6 │ Special Assistant United States Attorney
   │
 7 │
   │
 8 │
   │ Attorneys for the United States of America
 9 │
```

**UNITED STATES BANKRUPTCY COURT**

**CENTRAL DISTRICT OF CALIFORNIA**

| | | |
|---|---|---|
| In re | ) | Case No. |
| | ) | |
| | ) | Chapter 13 |
| | ) | |
| TIFFANY R. LOVE, | ) | **WITHDRAWAL OF CLAIM OF THE** |
| | ) | **INTERNAL REVENUE** |
| Debtor. | ) | **SERVICE AND RESPONSE TO** |
| | ) | **OBJECTION TO CLAIM** |
| | ) | |
| | ) | DATE: July 23, 2003 |
| | ) | TIME: 10:00 A.M. |
| | ) | CTRM: 1668 |

TO THE HONORABLE BARRY RUSSELL, UNITED STATES BANKRUPTCY

JUDGE, CHAPTER 13 TRUSTEE, DEBTOR IN PRO PER:

The **United States of America**, on behalf of its agency,

the Internal Revenue Service ("Service"), withdraws the

Service's prepetition estimated claim in the amount of

$2,079.79 (filed on December 19, 2002) with respect to the

above-referenced case. A copy of a letter withdrawing the

above-referenced claim and the claim are attached hereto as

1  Exhibit A.  Based upon the withdrawal of claim, the objection

2  to claim should be moot.

3

4  DATED: July 11, 2003              Respectfully Submitted,

5                                    **DEBRA W. YANG**
                                     United States Attorney

6
                                     **EDWARD M. ROBBINS, JR.**
7                                    Assistant United States Attorney
                                     Chief, Tax Division

8

9                                    _____
                                     RON S. CHUN
10                                   Special Assistant United States
                                     Attorney
11                                   Attorneys for United States of
                                     America

12

13

14

15

16

17

18

19

20

21

22

23

24

25

26

27

28

                                    2

1

2

3

4    Tiffany R. Love
     Pro Se
5

6

7

8    In re:                              ) Case No.:
                                         )
9    Tiffany R. Love,                    ) The Honorable Barry Russell
                                         )
10                      Debtor.          ) Chapter 13
                                         ) Motion/
11                                       ) ORDER FOR DISBURSEMENT OF FUNDS
                                         )
12                                         SHORTENED NOTICE

13

14   Now comes the Debtor, TIFFANY R. LOVE, respectfully requests the

15   disbursement of funds to be paid to her through the closing of her escrow,

     set at any time the debtor can move from her residence at

16                        California. Debtor is unable to relocate out of state

17   without having funds to secure an apartment, security deposit, moving

     fees, etc in New York. Debtor is the only family member who resides in the

18   state of California and is unable to locate alternative housing, without

19   sufficient funds, for herself and two large dogs.

20   The deadline for proofs of claims passed on May 28, 2003. Without

21   including oppositions the total of proof of claims is approximately

                    . The net proceeds from the sale of the home, minus all proofs

22   of claims and escrow fees, is                 (although debtor is opposing

     proofs of claim filed by Sunita Sood and the Internal Revenue Service).

23   Debtor request             to be paid through escrow to her, Tiffany R.

24   Love, Social Security number                .

25   On June 2, 2003, debtor Motion to Sell Residential Property was granted.

     However, debtor was unaware her motion should have contained an Order for

                      Opposition to Motion For Relief of Stay - 1

1 Disbursement of Funds. Since that time the debtor has successfully brought
2 her escrow to near close and must vacate the property so that all
3 creditors can be paid.

4
                              Respectfully submitted,
5

6
7                             Tiffany R. Love
8                             Pro se
9
10
11
12
13
14
15
16
17
18
19
20
21
22
23
24
25

Opposition to Motion For Relief of Stay - 2

**United States Bankruptcy Court**

**Central District of California**

In re:                                    ) Case No.:
                                          )
Tiffany R. Love,                          ) Chapter 13
                                          )
              Debtor.                     ) The Honorable Barry Russell, United
                                          ) States Bankruptcy Judge

                                          Motion To Sell Residential Property

### MOTION TO SELL RESIDENTIAL REAL ESTATE

Now comes TIFFANY R. LOVE, Debtor, who respectfully requests the Court to allow the sale of her residential real estate pursuant to 11 U.S.C. 363 and Local Bankruptcy Rule 6.2.

                              Respectfully submitted,



                              Tiffany R. Love

                              Pro se

Motion To Sell Residential Property - 1

MEMORANDUM IN SUPPORT

Debtor's home, located at _____ was set forth in the schedules. The Debtor now seeks to sell her home for at least _____ . Attached, as an exhibit hereto, is the first page of escrow instructions for real estate. **(Exhibit A).**

As shown by the Debtor's Estimated Closing statement **(Exhibit B)**, Debtor should net approximately _____ (according the Countrywide Home Loans Inc. Proof Of Claim, **Exhibit C).**

From this, Debtor claims her exemption under Ohio Revised Code Section 2329.66(A)(1). Debtor needs _____ exemption paid to her in order to take care of her transition expenses, including moving expenses, as well as apartment and utility deposits. The remainder shall be paid to the Chapter 13 Trustee for the purposes of accelerating completion of the plan.

Based on the contract in the Good Faith statement, we estimate that approximately _____ will be paid to the Chapter 13 Trustee. Any arrears that were to be paid through the plan on account of any mortgage shall be satisfied by the mortgage pay-off at closing.

Debtor submits that sufficient monies are being paid to satisfy all liens, encumbrances and closing costs. Debtor understands that the Trustee needs to be furnished with a copy of a final closing statement. Even though there will be no need to continue conduit payments after closing, Debtor shall still continue her total payment to the Trustee unchanged.

Motion To Sell Residential Property - 2

WHEREFORE, Debtor respectfully requests the court to issue an Order allowing the sale as described.

Respectfully submitted,

_____

Tiffany R. Love

Pro se

### Fifteen DAY NOTICE (pursuant to LBR 9013-1)

If the relief sought is opposed, a response must be filed with the Bankruptcy Clerk and served upon Debtor's attorney within fifteen (15) days of the date set forth in the Certificate of Service. The Court is authorized to grant the relief requested without further notice should a timely response not be filed.

Motion To Sell Residential Property - 3

1    Tiffany R. Love

2

3    In Propria Persona

4

5

6              UNITED STATES BANKRUPTCY (

7               DISTRICT OF LOS ANGELES

8

9    Tiffany R. Love,                          )    Case No.:

10                   Debtor,                    )    Chapter 13
                                                )
11                                              )
                                                )
12                                              )

13

14       **MOTION TO CONVERT CHAPTER 13 TO CHAPTER 7**

15

16   1.   On December 5, 2002 debtor Tiffany R. Love, filed a voluntary petition for the relief

17        under Chapter 13.

18   2.   The debtor has reassessed her financial obligations and income to determine that Chapter

19        7 is the best course of action and hereby exercises her one-time right to convert to

20        Chapter 7 In good faith .

21

22   3.   Pursuant to local bankruptcy rul 1017-1, the debtor hereby motions to convert this

23        Chapter 13 to a case under Chapter 7.

24   4.   Debtor swears that her case has not been previously converted under Section 1112, 1208,

25        or 1307 of title 11.

26

                              1
                    Love, Tiffany R. Case                    t

**UNITED STATES BANKRUPTCY COURT**

**CENTRAL DISTRICT OF CALIFORNIA**

| | |
|---|---|
| In re: | ) Case No.: |
| | ) |
| Tiffany R. Love, | ) Chapter 13 |
| | ) |
| Debtor. | ) Judge Honorable Barry Russell |
| | ) |

---

## MOTION TO VACATE ORDER GRANTING MOTION FOR RELIEF FROM THE AUTOMATIC STAY

### (REAL PROPERTY)

Now comes TIFFANY R. LOVE, debtor, who respectfully moves the Court to issue an Order Vacating the Motion for Relief from the Automatic Stay filed on May 6, 2003 by Countrywide Home Loans, Inc. Debtor, TIFFANY R. LOVE, who contends that estate in which the Bankruptcy court administers has an adequate equity cushion to protect all creditors including Countrywide Home Loans, Inc. Debtor has an open escrow with Jade Escrow for the sale of the property for                    set to close on June 6, 2003 if not sooner once permission from the court is granted; thereby allowing sufficient equity to adequately protect the interest of Countrywide Home Loans, Inc (see **exhibit A**). Countrywide Home Loans, Inc. claims debtor owes approximately

(see **exhibit B**) leaving an excess                    to the estate.

On April 28, 2003 debtor filed a motion to sell residential property and is acquiring the correct forms to approval of the Chapter 13 trustee.

FURTHERMORE, the buyers of this property are fully qualified and closing of escrow is scheduled for June 6, 2003 if not sooner (**see exhibit A**). Debtor has retained the services of Bradmont realty to facilitate the sale in a reasonable time. Debtor moves the court to vacate the order granting relief from the automatic stay.

Debtor is filing this motion independent of counsel, Sunita Sood, after receiving letters and telephone calls from counsel stating that she will be

MOTION TO VACATE ORDER GRANTING MOTION FOR RELIEF FROM THE AUTOMATIC STAY - 1

1  filing a Motion to Withdraw as Attorney, while debtor was recovering from a
2  small bowel obstruction. Debtor has no reason otherwise to believe that
   Sunita Sood has not filed such motion.
3      Furthermore, Debtor is unaware of agreements made between Sunita Sood
4  and Countrywide Home Loans as debtor had no reason to believe that Sunita
   Sood's offices was representing her. The Law Offices of Sunita Sood was aware
5  of the pending escrow and the equity in the property to defend motion against
6  relief from the automatic stay. On April 28, 2003 debtor filed a motion to
   continue hearing set for on April 28, 2003 with Countrywide Home Loans and a
7  Motion to Sell Residential Property for
8      Additionally, debtor appeared May 1, 2003 at schedule creditors hearing
   of which Sunita Sood was not present, instead another counsel. The counsel
9  did not have any documentation to show the Chapter 13 Trustee counsel and
10 hearing was continued to June 12, 2003. However, counsel did show debtor a
   motion to Withdraw as Attorney, but she refused the debtor's request to
11 retain a copy.
12     Debtor has consistently demonstrated her desire to pay debts to
   Countrywide Home Loans, and moves the court to grant motion to vacate order
13 granting automatic stay to allow for the sale of property at
14     in order for debtor to repay Countrywide and other creditors.
15
16                         Respectfully submitted,
17
18
19
20                         Tiffany R. Leve
21                         Pro se
22
23
24
25

MOTION TO VACATE ORDER GRANTING MOTION FOR RELIEF FROM THE AUTOMATIC STAY - 2

## MEMORANDUM IN SUPPORT OF MOTION

Bankruptcy Rule Procedure under section 362(d)(2), the creditor seeking relief from the automatic stay initially bears the burden of showing that the debtor has no equity in the secured property. See Anderson v. Farm Credit Bank of St. Paul (In re Anderson), 913 F 2d 530, 532 (8th Cir. 1990); In re Fenske, 96 B.R. 244,247 (Bankr. D.N.D. 1988) (citing United Sav. Ass'n v. Timbers of Inwood Forest Assocs., 454 U.S. 365 (1988)); see also 11 U.S.C. § 362 (g)(1) (1994) ("In any hearing under subsection (d)... of this section concerning relief from the stay ... the party requesting such relief has the burden of proof on the issue of the debtor's equity in the property; and ... the party opposing such relief has the burden of proof on all other issues."). Once the creditor sustain that burden, the burden of proof then shifts to the debtor to show that the property is necessary to an effective reorganization. See Anderson, 913 F.2d at 532.

Attached hereto is the escrow documents confirming sale of the property at            and a Proof of Claim submitted by Countrywide Home Loans for            (Exhibits A & B).

For the reasons stated above, the Debtor respectfully moves the Court to issue an Order vacating the Motion to Remove Stay.

Respectfully submitted,

_____

Tiffany R. Love

Pro se

MOTION TO VACATE ORDER GRANTING MOTION FOR RELIEF FROM THE AUTOMATIC STAY - 3

```
 1                    UNITED STATES BANKRUPTCY COURT

 2                    CENTRAL DISTRICT OF CALIFORNIA

 3

 4

 5   In re:                              )  Case No.:
                                         )
 6   Tiffany R. Love,                    )  Chapter 13
                                         )
 7            Debtor.                     )  The Honorable Barry Russell, United
                                         )  States Bankruptcy Judge
 8

 9   _____

10

11    MOTION TO VACATE ORDER GRANTING MOTION FOR RELIEF FROM THE AUTOMATIC STAY

12                            (REAL PROPERTY)

13        This matter comes before the Court on the Motion to Vacate Order

14   Granting Motion For Relief from The Automatic Stay filed by the Debtor on May

15   12, 2003, 2003.

16        This Court finds that all parties in interest have been served and

17   there has been no objections filed.

18        IT IS THEREFORE ORDERED that the Motion to Vacate Order Granting Motion

19   For Relief from The Automatic Stay is granted.

19        IT IS SO ORDERD.

20

21   Dated:_____             _____

22                                       The Honorable Barry Russell

23                                       U.S. Bankruptcy Judge

24   _____

25



     MOTION TO VACATE ORDER GRANTING MOTION FOR RELIEF FROM THE AUTOMATIC STAY - 4
```

**UNITED STATES BANKRUPTCY COURT**

**FOR THE CENTRAL DISTRICT OF CALIFORNIA**

| | |
|---|---|
| Debtor, Tiffany R. Love | ) Case No.: |
| Chapter 13 Trustee, Nancy Curry | ) |
| | ) Chapter 13 |
| Vs. | ) |
| | ) The honorable Barrry Russell, United |
| F&A Federal Credit Union, | ) States Bankruptcy Judge |
| Wills & Simms, | |
| CRS Recovery Services, does 1 to 100, | |
| et.al. | |

**COMPLAINT FOR DAMAGES AND SANCTIONS for WILLFUL VIOLATION OF THE AUTOMATIC STAY**

COME NOW debtor TIFFANY LOVE, respectfully moves the court to impose punitive damages for violations of the automatic stay against F&A Federal Credit Union (hereunto referred to as F&A) and Wills & Simms law firm of F&A Federal Credit Union, and CRS Recovery Services, repossession agent to F&A. In addition to punitive damages, Debtor requests that the maximum actual and punitive damages be awarded due to egregious and retaliatory behaviors of F&A, Wills & Simms, CRS Recovery Services, does 1 to 100 et.al.

*Debtor will provide additional supporting documentation at the time of hearing. Debtor has sold her residence and is relocating causing documentation to not be one location.*

**Factual Background**

Debtor initially filed for bankruptcy protection in November of 2002, of which F&A was listed as a creditor. Debtors, fee waiver was not granted, and Debtor filed another petition listing F&A as a

Willful Violation Of Automatic Stay - 1

1    creditor throughout her schedules and in her plan. On Janurary 28, 2003 debtor converter her

2    case to Chapter 7. On or around March 24, 2003 debtor's case was converted back to Chapter

3    13. Debtor listed F&A as a creditor on each of her bankruptcy filings. She continued to pay her

4    car note and adhere to requests of F&A.

5

6    F&A Federal Credit Union is a lender of signature, automobile, home, equity and general credit

7    loans. F&A Federal Credit Union uses a bankruptcy notification service to identify if borrowers

8    have filed for bankruptcy to protect their interests due to the variety of loans they offer. They

9    have sufficient funds of a half billion dollars to pay punitive damages.

10

11    On February 12, 2003 debtor contacted F&A after she was not able to access funds in her

12    account (F&A commonly places a hold on the debtor's savings account to keep her credit card

13    and car loan account current). An unidentified person from F&A stated that her car note was

     past due. The debtor authorized the transfer of funds to cover delinquencies. The F&A

14    representative confirmed they had received information regarding her bankruptcy from the

15    chapter 7 trustee's office and they were not going to transfer funds to cover credit card

     payments at that time. However, the debtor continued to receive credit card statements from

16    F&A (exhibits to be provided at the time of hearing). During the same time debtor began

17    receiving telephone calls from parties listed in schedules, the Chapter 7 trustee had contacted

     them for information regards to debtors accounts and status.

18

19    On or around February 24, 2003 debtor received a check in the amount of $5,000. Debtor

20    deposited the check into her savings account with F&A. On March 18, 2003 debtor's account

     was placed on hold to not allow for any transactions. Debtor discovered the hold, the same day

21    it was issued and contacted F&A and spoke with Olivia Berlanga (hereunto referred to as

22    Olivia). Olivia informed debtor there had been a check returned NSF (Non sufficient Funds), and

23    asked debtor when could she have the funds to cover this debt. Debtor informed Olivia that she

     was flying out of town on the 21st and she would return the following week to resolve the matter.

24    She instructed Olivia that is was not intentional and would contact the author of the check to

25    remedy the situation. In fact, debtor was successful locating the intermediary person the author

     of the check used to communicate on the 20th and informed her of the NSF problem to be

Willful Violation Of Automatic Stay - 2

resolved when the debtor returned. Upon debtor's return from out of state, she could not easily locate the intermediary person. Once contact was made, she stated that the funds would be covered, but she wasn't certain of details how. Debtor provided account numbers and methods of how the funds could be transferred to her account. Debtor contacted F&A and left a message informing them that funds would be transferred. Within days of contact with the intermediary person, debtor learned, her savings account had been closed blocking the method she commonly used for depositing and transferring funds.

Debtor called F&A and spoke with Olivia to inquire why the account had been closed. Olivia was only interested in obtaining the debtor's home telephone number and stated it was out of her control to open the account; thereby refusing to mitigate damages the debtor was incurring by not have funds available. Debtor inquired of Olivia whose control was it to open the account. Olivia provided another name. Debtor called the manager of the department and left a message that she was upset the account had been closed, wanted the account opened to allow for the transfer and informed them that she was in bankruptcy and it was their best interest to work out a solution rather than incur additional costs for both parties. Debtor faxed a letter to F&A's management on April 8, 2003 expressing her outrage (as debtor has experienced retaliatory treatment from F&A in the past) and demanded that account be immediately opened to allow for the check author to transfer the funds. The debtor successfully located the author of the check and funds could be deposited thereby remedying the problem and providing access to funds for debt payments, and living expenses such as food.

Debtor received a response from F&A, stating that all communication should be directed to their attorneys at Wills & Simms. In addition, debtor began receiving letters from F&A, sent to an old address, which took several weeks to reach the debtor. F&A also ordered the repossession of her vehicle (proof they knew her home address), which frighten the debtor, as she lives alone. Two large men frequently appeared at her door (pictures will be provided at time of hearing) and walked around her property at various hours of the day and night. Debtor also noticed men traveling behind her when she drove her car contributing to her frequent vomiting and emotional distress. Debtor has a known potentially debilitating condition (mechanical small bowel obstruction), which stress can cause adverse side effects. These acts also prohibited the debtor from using her vehicle for work. Men arriving at her door and following her put the debtor in a hostile situation. Adding to the egregious retaliatory and vengeful actions of F&A and their attorneys Wills and Simms. F&A could have avoided putting the debtor through such tactics by

Willful Violation Of Automatic Stay - 3

opening the account and allowing for the transfer to mitigate theirs and debtors damages. Having knowledge of the debtors bankruptcy filing, F&A did not get the permission from the court to proceed with legal actions, repossession, or the closing of her accounts.

Debtor received letter from the law firm of Wills and Simms, this time at the correct home address, requesting full payment of the overdraft amount and threatening a law suit within 30 days of she did not respond. The law firms of Wills and Simms, subsequently filed the lawsuit within the 30 day period before waiting for the debtor response. They did not serve the debtor at her home (as they have the correct address), and she has no information as to the location of the lawsuit in order to respond. Her knowledge of their legal action was known through a solicitation she received in the mail from a law firm asking to represent her. Debtor faxed and mail a notice to Willis & Simms and F&A reminding them of her bankruptcy filing and citing the her legal protection as she had done in the past to stop the illegal actions of F&A, see below.

Debtor has experienced hostile and retaliatory treatment from F&A in the past when she disputed their charges in violation of Federal and State laws. In July of 2001, debtor informed F&A of erroneous charges to her credit card. F&A did not act nor did they perform an investigation into the legitimacy of her claim. In fact, F&A began to charge fees to her savings account for charges incurred, by their negligence, of managing her credit card account. This practice continued for several months until debtor refused to pay charges, and threaten a lawsuit if these behaviors did not stop. F&A failed to comply with Federal Debt Collection Practices Act, as debtor wrote to F&A to dispute the charges on several occasions. After five months of incurring excess charges, enduring blocked access to her account, and verbal assaults by their collection staff debtor was successful at getting the charges reversed; however there was no compensation to the debtor for enduring such malicious tactics by F&A.

**Request for Punitive Damages**

Although the debtor filed for bankruptcy she continued to make payments to F&A. Upon notification from F&A the Chapter 7 trustee had contacted them about her account she continued to make payments for her automobile loan. F&A, being a lender of home and other loans, had multiple methods of knowing the debtor had filed for bankruptcy, including direct contact with the debtor. F&A has a history of retaliating against the debtor and the automatic

Willful Violation Of Automatic Stay - 4

stay provision posed no obstruction for their vengeful actions. The debtor is requesting the maximum dollar amounts in punitive damages to deter their egregious behaviors.

Due to F&A, Wills and Simms, etc conduct, sophistication, and motives the debtor moves the court to impose the highest amount of punitive damages as they have the ability to pay and have access to technology that could have prevented their revengeful actions.

**Request for Actual Damages**

Due to the actions of F&A and their representatives, the debtor was not able to remedy the NSF overdraft, although she made repeated attempts to do so; thereby causing the debtor to not have access to funds to pay Chapter 13 trustee, cover utility bills, pay maintenance workers, cover food and other living costs. Furthermore, she was not able to use her vehicle causing her significant financial damage as debtor is a freelance writer who was employed.

**Summary**

F&A has a history of acting in a hostile manner toward the debtor. They have taken to extremes rather than follow laws that protect their customers. F&A has previously acted outside the constraints of the laws to *punish* the debtor and the actions described in this complaint is only a summary of the anguish the debtor has sustained due to their actions. F&A and their agents violated the stay by 1) closing debtor's savings and credit accounts, 2) Hiring attorneys Wills & Simms 3) Pursing a lawsuit against the debtor in state court while having knowledge the debtor is in bankruptcy, 3) Sending accounts to collection while debtor is in the protection of the court 4) Acting to have debtor's vehicle reposed. All these actions were taken without first obtaining relief from stay, Section 362 (a)(3). Including any additional acts the court may find. Had F&A and their agents informed the bankruptcy court they would have discovered the property was adequately protected with equity from the debtors home sale, as they subsequently learned from Sunita Sood's office and they later filed a proof of claim.

Despite their actual knowledge of the bankruptcy filing through one or more of these means, (the debtor, Chapter 7 trustee, and their Bankruptcy Notification Service) F&A, Wills & Simms, et. al did not reverse their actions and restore the status quo, as they were required to do. Infact

Willful Violation Of Automatic Stay - 5

1  the debtors savings account is closed. Instead they proceeded with the law suits, repossession,
2  and closing debtors accounts. These actions clearly represent willful actions and entitlement of
3  the debtor to receive damages.

4

5

6  ## Memorandum of Points and Authorities
7

8

9  11 U.S.C. § 362. Automatic stay
10  Section 362 provides, inter alia, that:
   (a) Except as provided in subsection (b) of this section, a petition filed under section 301, 302,
11  or 303 of this title, or an application filed under section 5(a)(3) of the Securities Investor
12  Protection Act of 1970, operates as a stay, applicable to all entities, of–
   (2) the enforcement, against the debtor or against property of the estate, of a judgment obtained
13  before the commencement of the case under this title[.]
14

15  (h) An individual injured by any willful violation of a stay provided by this section shall recover
16  actual damages, including costs and attorneys' fees, and, in appropriate circumstances, may
   recover punitive damages.
17

18

19  The scope of the automatic stay is "undeniably broad." It stays the "commencement or
   continuation . . . or other action or proceeding against the debtor that was or could have been
20  commenced before the [filing of the bankruptcy]," as well as the enforcement of a pre-petition
21  judgment against the debtor or property of the estate. The stay as to actions against a debtor
   continues until the case is closed, dismissed, or a discharge is granted or denied.
22  It also stays actions to "obtain possession of property of the estate or of property from the
23  estate or to exercise control over property of the estate." The stay remains in effect until such
24  property is no longer property of the estate. "Property of the estate" is also very broadly defined
25  to include all of the debtor's legal and equitable interests in property as of the commencement of
   the case, wherever located and by whomever held. Whether a debtor has a legal or equitable

Willful Violation Of Automatic Stay - 6

---

interest in property is determined by state law. The determination of whether the automatic stay applies to any given activity or property is to be made in the first instance by the bankruptcy court, not by a creditor or its attorney. Actions taken in violation of the automatic stay are void and of no force or effect, even when there is no actual notice of the existence of the stay. In addition, an " individual injured by any willful violation of a stay provided by this section *shall* recover actual damages, including costs and attorneys' fees, and, in appropriate circumstances, may recover punitive damages."

Dated this 12th day of June, 2003

Tiffany R. Love
Pro Se

Willful Violation Of Automatic Stay - 7

# Hang In There

Once upon a time there lived a rabbit whose life long ambition was to become the fasted running jack rabbit in the land. Morning, noon, and night he practiced for the major upcoming race. Sacrificing time with family and friends, he was determined to become number one. As luck would have it, the night before the national race the rabbit suffered an injury so severe one hind leg required amputation. The rabbit was devastated. Phantom pains of lost dreams far outweighed those of the missing limb. All he'd worked for, all the sacrifices were lost.

During a somberly quiet midday, the rabbit remembered that he'd wanted to teach years before he began practicing for the race. Although he couldn't tolerate returning to the track, he knew one subject equally well – multiplication. During his days as a teacher the rabbit daily forced himself against painful memories into the classroom. At the end of the semester one former struggling student announced, *I'm certainly happy you lost your leg.* This startled the rabbit, *Why are you happy that I lost my leg* he inquired. The class turned to face the student, and the rabbit stared intently into his eyes as he spoke, *because if you had continued with your former life, I would have never known how to force myself to learn.*

# Foreclosure

> *Being unready and ill equipped is what you have to expect*
> *in life. It is the universal predicament. It is your lot as a*
> *human being to lack what it takes. Circumstances are*
> *seldom right. You never have the capacities, the strength, the*
> *wisdom, the virtue you ought to have. You must always do*
> *with less than you need in a situation vastly different from*
> *what you would have chosen.*
>
> Charlton Osburn Jr.

Sudden unemployment and illness can turn an ordinary life upside down. The threat of losing a home is not the end of the world, but it can feel like it. Each day thousands of people receive notices that their homes are in jeopardy of being sold by lenders. If you have received a notice of default, you are not alone. Remain as calm as possible. It's not the time to kick your dog, smack the kids and leave your spouse. It's time to relax, think rationally and attempt to stay sober, at least most days, in order to develop solutions for getting yourself and family through these rough waters. I know you are afraid of losing your home; it's not predestined that you will lose the house. I think you can keep your home until you're ready to move and begin a fresh life filled with new joys and pleasures (albeit there maybe pressure for you do it sooner rather than later). By not panicking you can see avenues to explore negotiations with your lender that may save your home. Avoid making rush decisions that may immediately benefit you but can cause an avalanche of financial problems in the future. Remember, lenders have a vested interest for borrowers to keep their homes; your attempts are worthwhile.

During my crises, I hit the panic button and filed for bankruptcy. Every attorney I met afterwards said it was a huge mistake and now I understand why. I desperately wanted out of that house, but I didn't know where I was going to move with two huge dogs. Like many, I too didn't have much cash on hand, and I was unsure of the future. That's why it's important to determine your objective while you're in control of the property. You can plan your future even when you don't have available cash in your hands. Had I decided earlier that I wanted to sell the home; I could have avoided bankruptcy, attorney fees and unnecessary stress by selling my home months earlier. Bankruptcy has its merits, if you loathe telephone calls from your creditors, but it's not the only way out. This chapter has information, options and hints to build upon. Take time to explore the different options, and personalize the information to suit your needs.

## I'm In Trouble Now, So What Should I Do?

Don't worry. Even this situation can turn out good. You have several options to carefully consider. If the lender has filed a *deed in lieu of foreclosure* you only have a short amount of time to act, less than 20 days. Bankruptcy can halt the foreclosure. Filing a wrongful foreclosure action with a lis pendes will also stop the foreclosure process. Entering into a forbearance agreement with your lender will also save the home if arrangements are kept. Another practical option is selling the property, which maybe wisest choice if you want out.

Certainly, don't fear. Carefully evaluate the choices provided in this chapter and pursue them to the fullest. Maintain self-control and this experience can be overcome.

Those who are working will find a forbearance agreement the easiest method to saving the house. Also those who are expecting money can enter into a forbearance agreement.

*Keep strong if possible; in any case keep cool.*

Sir Basil Liddell Hart

## How Foreclosures Are Typically Conducted

While the manner in which a foreclosure occurs is unique to each state, there are some standard practices such as the lender must notify the borrower of the default. If delinquent payments (or payment arrangements) are not made the lender provides notice of the date and time of the foreclosure sale. Notice is provided twenty-one days prior to the sale. The law states that foreclosure sales of real-property be held the first Tuesday of each month between 10:00 a.m. and 4:00 p.m. The sale is conducted at the courthouse in the county where the property is located.

Typically a notice of pending sale or cure default is posted on the property to be sold. The notice typically allows for no less than 21 days to cure the default before the property is sold at auction. Notification is made to residents in the home and mailed to the last known address of the borrower and any co-borrowers. In addition, a copy of the notice is filed in the county clerk's office and published in a newspaper.

> Should the notice of foreclosure sent via mail be returned by the post office, the lender has no further duty to notify the borrower(s). Proof of the mailing to borrowers is sufficient in most courts.

Once the twenty-one day waiting time period expires the property sale is conducted, at a courthouse where interested parties bid on the property.

The following procedure is typically followed for Power of Sale foreclosures:

(1) Default notice.

(2) An opportunity to cure defaults.

(3) A notice of intent to *accelerate* the note if not brought current. The outstanding principal balance plus any accrued and unpaid interest and expenses are currently due and payable.

(4) Notice of acceleration of the note.

(5) Notice of the date and place of the foreclosure sale.

## Types of Foreclosures

The foreclosure process and procedures are determined by the laws where the property is located and federal statutes that protect homeowners.

In the US there are four primary methods of foreclosure; (1) Judicial foreclosure (2) Power of Sale, (3) Strict foreclosure and (4) Entry and Possession. Each is defined in this chapter.

Borrowers have the opportunity to raise procedural (such as the lender did not follow the foreclosure process according to laws and/or contracts) and substantive (such as the lender engaged in fraud or deception) defenses.

In addition to procedural and substantive defenses the borrower can also raise technical defenses such as improper parties, lack of jurisdiction, insufficiency of service or process and improper pleading. For additional information see the *Wrongful Foreclosure* section in this chapter.

## Judicial Foreclosure

As the name implies, *judicial foreclosures* occur by directly obtaining a court order. Half of the states use judicial foreclosure. Lenders holding a mortgage file an action in court to obtain a judicial decree authorizing the foreclosure sale. After considering all of the defenses, the court can conclude that the lender has a right to foreclose. The courts will determine the amount owed and may set a deadline for redemption (the date and time the lender can take possession of the property), if available. Should the borrower fail to pay the delinquency by the date set by the court, foreclosure will proceed according to local rules and/or state statutes.

In the lawsuit the lender must prove that there is a valid mortgage, the borrower defaulted on the terms of the mortgage, and all proper procedures have been followed.

In most states the sale has to be reviewed and confirmed by the court. Sheriff's or a public officer will typically conduct the foreclosure sale.

## Power of Sale

*Power of sale* allows the lender to conduct a sale of the property, in default, if the lender notifies the borrower of the delinquent payments. Lenders do not have to file a lawsuit to foreclose.

Standardized mortgages issued by Freddie Mac, Fannie Mae, and Ginnie Mae require the homeowner to grant the bank the power to sell the property at public action in cases of default. States that allow *power of sale* can find the clause in the loan documents and deed.

## Strict Foreclosure

*Strict foreclosures* allow lenders to obtain a court order that transfers the title of the home from the borrower to the lender. Courts will set the time in which the borrowers have to pay the balance of the loan. If the balance is not paid by the set time, the borrowers loose the property. Strict foreclosure allows the lender to become the owner of the property. Connecticut, Vermont and Maine are three states currently conducting *strict foreclosures*.

After regaining title by legal means, the lender could sell the property at a later date. Lenders could receive any excess from the sale over and above what the borrower owed on the loan. Alternatively, the lender could simply keep the property and rent it out. To become the owner through strict foreclosure, however, the lender must follow some specific procedures. The lender must obtain possession of the property and hold it throughout the redemption period, which is one year on pre-1975 mortgages and three months on post-1975 mortgages.

In Maine, there are three methods for the lender to regain possession as part of the strict foreclosure process:

1.  A lender can obtain a writ of possession (which authorizes the sheriff to throw the borrower out) from a court by filing a lawsuit that asks for the writ as part of a conditional judgment.

2.  The lender can enter the property and take possession if the borrower consented to it in writing.

3.  The lender may enter the premises peacefully, openly and without opposition, in the presence of two witnesses.

It's possible for lenders to foreclose on the property without regaining possession at the time of foreclosure by arranging to sell the borrower's property. Initially, the lender files a lawsuit to obtain a judgment stating the borrower owes the money. The lender must wait until the end of the redemption period. At the end of the redemption period, the lender will sell the property by a special procedure.

The lender publishes public notice of the impending foreclosure for three successive weeks in a newspaper of general circulation in the county where the property is located. The notice should state the lender is claiming the property due to a breach of the mortgage conditions (such as nonpayment of the loan) and give a description of the property, the date of the mortgage and the nature of the breach. A copy of the printed notice and the name and date of the newspaper in which it was last published must be recorded with the county clerk's *office (or according to state laws)* within 30 days of the last publication of the notice. Alternatively, an attested (sworn) copy of the printed notice maybe served on the borrower by the sheriff, and a copy of the notice and the sheriff's return (indicating that it was served) maybe recorded within 30 days after service.

The foreclosure sale must take place no less than 30 days and no more than 45 days after the initial publication of notice. The property must be sold at public sale to the highest bidder, which maybe the lender or anyone else. At the end of the sale, the sales costs are deducted and the lender must disburse the remaining money in accordance with the foreclosure judgment. Other lien holders should already have been joined when the foreclosure suit was first filed, so they may receive some portion of the proceeds. Any surplus proceeds from the sale must be paid to the borrower. The borrower may contest the accounting within 30 days after the sale, but the high bidder at the foreclosure sale will still retain title.

A strict foreclosure does not involve a judicial sale of the property. Instead, individuals or entities which hold an interest in the property being foreclosed are assigned *Law Days*. Law Days are assigned in inverse order of priority. This means that the last creditor has the first opportunity to redeem the property. Law Days give each owner of an interest in the property an opportunity on a specific date to come forward and pay the entire debt due the lender. If the holder of an interest in the property does not pay the entire debt on its Law Day, it forfeits its interest in the property, and the next prior creditor has the opportunity to redeem the property by paying the lender in full on the next business day. This process continues until the lender is paid in full, receives absent payments, or takes title to the property.

> Borrower's residing in the state of Maine have a waiver procedure that could adversely affect lenders, but it could be helpful to borrowers. If the lender accepts money or anything of value on the mortgage debt after the foreclosure has begun and before the redemption time period has expired, then the lender *waives* the foreclosure procedure. However, the lender may receive income from the property after properly taking possession without inciting a waiver.

## Entry and Possession

If you think *Strict Foreclosure* is cruel, *Entry and Possession* allows lenders to physically enter the property and take *constructive* possession. Although the lender may not physically reside in the property they take title and are considered the property owners. Entry and possession could and is often times used in conjunction with other types of foreclosures.

> With any of the types of foreclosures, the lender will charge fees attributed to selling the property. If equity exists in the property to sufficiently cover the costs associated with paying off the home and fees, the borrower is entitled to the remaining balance. In most cases the lender will attach fees to consume any overage which could be given to borrowers.

## Avoiding Foreclosure

The least expensive and most effective method for saving your home is to make payment arrangements with your lender. Banks are in the business of loaning money, not selling property. It's in the best interest of banks to keep the borrower in the loan as long as possible. Every effort should be made to communicate with your lender. Particularly during tough economic times as most lenders will offer feasible arrangements to avoid foreclosing.

> On average, it takes three to six months to complete a foreclosure.

Attempt to contact bank representatives who are willing to explore solutions. In a perfect world the agents will be willing to help, but some of us experience unnecessary stress if the agent is only interested in belittling borrowers to feel good about themselves. Certainly do not be deterred from this behavior, continue to seek out solutions with other agents rather than quitting.

Most major lenders have departments (or contract with local organizations) dedicated to troubled loans. Agents assist borrowers with loan repayment plans, forbearance, reamortization, along with other options available to the borrower. It's in the best interest of borrowers to take these attempts seriously before considering bankruptcy or foreclosure.

In some cases, there is help available from sources other than your lender. These organizations work with financially troubled borrowers to devise solutions for keeping them in their homes.

If your delinquency is due to illness, contact you homeowners insurance to inquire if illness or unemployment mortgage protection insurance is included in your plan. In most cases, this type of insurance is purchased separately; however, some mortgage brokers encourage borrowers to purchase such insurance at the loan inception.

## Short Sale

*Short sale* is a private sale of real property which is agreed to by the lender and the borrower to avoid foreclosure. Under the short sale scenario, a lender agrees to take less than a full payoff on its mortgage debt. The borrower benefits as a result of foreclosure being avoided. The lender benefits in that it is not required to take on the real property through foreclosure and the costs of resale associated with that property.

## Deed In Lieu Of Foreclosure

A *deed in lieu of foreclosure* is the result of the lender and the borrower agreeing that the borrower will give the lender a deed to the property which secures the loan. The deed in lieu of foreclosure would halt the need for the lender to continue the foreclosure process. Usually, the agreement includes the understanding that the debt is paid in full. Many lenders have *loss mitigation* programs to help borrowers who do not want to endure the stress of resisting foreclosure. Some lenders will offer incentives for borrowers who willfully transfer the deed back to the lender.

*The greatest test of courage on earth is to bear defeat without losing heart*

Robert G. Ingersoll

Those who have not been successful locating any form of assistance to make mortgage payments can transfer the deed of their home to the lender. Borrowers must vacate the residence as it becomes the property of your lender. This is a huge favor to your lender who avoids the foreclosure process. This should be your last resort for obvious reasons, as any rights to the property, including proceeds from sale (if any), are no longer entitled to the borrower.

## Refinancing The Property

If you can refinance your residence, obtain a second mortgage to pay the delinquency or purchase another less expensive property, you're wise to do so sooner than later; carrying out any plan that helps to keep your family safe and stable is the ideal. You maybe able to rent one property while taking out a loan on another. Lenders are more sympathetic to delinquent landlords therefore more willing to extend debts on rental property as opposed to primary residences. For information on locating loans try the following web sites:

www.mortgagemag.com
www.bankrate.com

## Special Forbearance

Lenders frequently make arrangements for repayments of delinquency. The conditions are based on your financial situation and can include a temporary reduction in your mortgage or a temporary suspension of your payments. Those experiencing a reduction in income or increase in living expenses can qualify for a special forbearance. Contact your lender for details. Furnish all necessary documentation that may qualify you for a special forbearance.

## Mortgage Modification

People experiencing difficult financial situations, yet can continue paying their monthly mortgage may qualify for a *mortgage modification*. Examples of modification include spreading the delinquent balance over several months. This will increase your monthly mortgage payments. For example, if your mortgage payment is $1,000 per month and you've missed three months payments (totaling a delinquency of $3,000) your lender can divide the delinquent balance into six monthly payments [of $500] and add it to your monthly mortgage. The new mortgage payment will be $1,500.

This process is also known as a forbearance and repayment. Lenders are willing to enter into a forbearance agreement as long as payment can be made in the near future. Another option is to extend the term of your mortgage by adding the delinquent balance of your loan; known as reamortization. Borrowers will continue to pay their monthly mortgage. Your monthly mortgage payment will most likely increase. Mortgage modification is ideal for those who are recovering from financial disaster. Those generating a monthly income that covers their costs and extras to repay their debts should seriously consider this option.

## Partial Claim

Partial claims allow borrowers to receive a one-time payment from the FHA (Federal Housing Authority) insurance fund to bring your monthly mortgage payment current. You qualify for the *one time* partial claim if your loan is insured by FHA. Loans issued through HUD (Housing and Urban Development) and Freddie Mac is certain to be FHA insured.

The partial claim is filed by your lender. The claim is an interest free promissory note; a lien is placed on the property that must be paid in full. It's due when the mortgage is paid in full or the property is sold. If you are interested in obtaining a partial claim you must be at least four months delinquent in their mortgage payment but no more than 12 months and financially able to begin making monthly mortgage payments.

## Payment Assistance

Programs exist to assist homeowners with meeting their monthly mortgage. The programs vary by institution and state, if any is provided. It is in the best interest of people to research mortgage payment assistance programs in your area. Some churches and other non-profit groups may also offer assistance.

Depending on the amount of assistance a family requires, public agencies can assist with mortgage payments and food purchases. Although the payments may not be sufficient to relive delinquency, as it may take several weeks before a person can begin receiving assistance. In some cases, it maybe less expensive for government agencies to keep a person in the home rather finding alternative housing at a more expensive cost.

## Selling The Property

Obviously the easiest method to avoid foreclosure is selling the property. This can be the best decision if you have equity in the home. It opens the door to a new life, which you may need after enduring months of financial stress. Seriously evaluate your long term goal. If you want to live a simple life with less stress and ease, this could occur within a few weeks away. The best course to relieving yourself of foreclosure threats could be locating to a new area or state, with a lower cost of living. For more information on home selling *see chapter six.*

## Refunding

According to the HUD web site, the Veterans Administration offers Refunding to borrowers. At the VA's desecration they can buy the loan from the holder. The VA becomes your lender. This often occurs when lenders refuse to extend mortgage modification plans with borrowers who can continue making payments. Borrowers should exhaust their options with their lender prior to contacting the VA.

## Hiring An Attorney To Negotiate With Your Lender

Knowledgeable real-estate attorneys can help develop a viable plan of action you can present to your lender. With your permission he/she can contact your lender to negotiate directly on your behalf to potentially stop the foreclosure. Informed attorneys may also offer solutions you didn't consider and work out agreements that you can manage. Before you file for bankruptcy or lose your home, take time to locate a knowledgeable attorney to find the best solution for your need.

## Filing Bankruptcy to Stop Foreclosure

Bankruptcy can abruptly stop foreclosure. Lenders must cease all contact with the borrower and work directly through the trustee and courts. If you are able to continue monthly payments Chapter 13 bankruptcy is a good solution as creditors may not have any choice in accepting your repayment plan. In some cases, borrowers can temporarily cease making portions of their mortgage payment such as interest and tax payments to enable them to meet other necessary obligations. Once you file for chapter 13 bankruptcy you must deliver your monthly mortgage payment to the trustee (chapter 13 debtors are expected to repay their debts). Consult with a knowledgeable attorney or paralegal, as the date you file for bankruptcy could allow you to begin the paying mortgage notes the first month of meeting of the creditors. Delinquencies can be paid overtime, up to the duration of your bankruptcy case. For more information *see chapter one, Bankruptcy*.

## Coping With Negotiations

Negotiations with your lender and coping with the stress of not having enough money to pay your bills are draining, but don't give up. Sometimes it's best to take a breather from the talks to develop new ideas for solving problems. A luxurious vacation in Hawaii, a round of an 18 hold golf game, or a day at the spa is probably out of the budget. Think creatively to find relaxation during these days of stress. Plan for a family picnic at the park, take the dogs to the lake, or share a low budget meal with your spouse. Moments of difficulties can develop an inner strength that lasts long after these days have past. On an occasion you may need to treat yourself to a drink or three, but don't let it become a habit, rather an occasional treat. Remember to keep your mind clear.

When your income source is not reliable or extenuating circumstances prevent you from keeping payment arrangements some, representatives understand while others may not. Avoid being distracted by short sighted people. Remain focused on your goal to save your residence. By relaxing through the stress you can salvage joys brought by a new day. Talk with someone who can offer a fresh outlook or provide useful input. Don't worry about what will occur the following day; trust yourself to make it happen.

*Resources:*
*Stop Foreclosure Now in California* by Llyoyd M. Segal. (c) 1997. Nolo Press. $29.95.
*This book has good ideas that can be used by people residing in any state.*

For a dictionary of foreclosure terms see: www.foreclousres.com/pages/definitions.asp

## When You've Lost Your Home

Foreclosure is not the end of the world. Many people face circumstances where they lose their primary residence and/or investment properties due to various circumstances. I can recall a hand full of people who confided to me that they've lost property in the past. It does feel awful. Like many of the people I've met, you can purchase again or you may choose to rent, but certainly you can continue on with your life. Do not dwell too long on this change. Shift gears and begin to move on. Locate a place or room to rent. Proceed each day with restoring your happiness which is no longer tied to property. Create a new plan of action.

## What Happens After Foreclosure

Your home could possibly be sold the day of the *trustee sale*, if so, the lender will send you a notice to vacate or proceed with an eviction. If you believe the foreclosure is due to wrongful behavior by your lender you can file a *Wrongful Foreclosure* action, *see the following section.* You may have rights to recover your property. However, you most likely will need to hire an attorney.

> Trustee sales are advertised in advance and require an all cash bid from perspective buyers. The sale is usually conducted by a sheriff, a constable or lawyer acting as trustee. This kind of sale, which usually attracts savvy investors, is not for the novice. In a trustee sale, the lender who holds the first loan on the property starts the bidding at the amount of the loan plus costs. Successful bidders receive a trustee's deed. Trustee sales are typically conducted on the first Tuesday of each new month.

After the property is foreclosed borrowers maybe responsible for additional money. The borrower is liable for any difference between the foreclosure sale price and the mortgage balance (frequently referred to as the deficiency). The deficient balance plus fees can be pursued by the lender after the foreclosure sale. Some lenders will avoid further costs by not attempting to collect these fees, although each case is unique.

## Wrongful Foreclosure Actions

Filing a wrongful foreclosure action is potentially the most effective weapon borrower's use against lenders to halt foreclosure. Borrowers do not have to wait until the trustee sale to file a wrongful foreclosure action, in fact, it maybe best to bring this action prior to the foreclosure sale although it can be brought afterwards with an unlawful detainer complaint. However, it's wise to file your complaint while you occupy the property.

A wrongful foreclosure is a complaint filed by the borrower, usually by his/her attorney, against the lender and foreclosing trustee in court (in most states it's filed in superior court). In the complaint the borrower alleges one or more of the following:

- That there was grossly inadequate price, irregularities which tended to contribute to inadequacy of price,

- Illegal, fraudulent or willfully oppressive sale of the property under a power of sale contained in a mortgage or deed of trust.

- The lender failed to give proper notice of accelerations of the proposed sale. *For more information on acceleration see the section titled How Foreclosures Are Typically Conducted at the beginning of this chapter.*

> In addition to bankruptcy and wrongful foreclosure actions, borrowers can sue in equity to rescind the sale. By suing in equity, borrowers who are able to pay off the mortgage at the time he/she appears in court can set aside the foreclosure sale.
>
> Borrowers who can rapidly sale the property may find this a viable alternative to filing for bankruptcy to stay/halt the foreclosure sale.

Wrongful foreclosure actions can also state that the amount stated as due and owing in the notice of default is incorrect for one or more of the following reasons:

- An incorrect interest rate adjustment, incorrect tax impound accounts.

- Misapplied payments.

- A forbearance agreement which was not adhered to by the lender.

- Unnecessary forced place insurance.

- Improper accounting for a confirmed chapter 13 bankruptcy plan.

- The lender accepted partial payments after initiation of the wrongful foreclosure process, and then continues with the foreclosure.

What led the borrower to take legal action (also referred to as *cause of action*) alleged in wrongful foreclosure action may include the following:

- Breach of contract.

- Intentional infliction of emotional distress.

- Negligent infliction of emotional distress.

- Violation of the state's Business and Professions code.

- Quick title.

- Accounting and/or promissory estoppel. *Discuss this matter further with competent and knowledgeable legal counsel.*

Damages can be awarded to successful borrowers in the nature of emotional distress. If the borrower can prove by clear and convincing evidence that the lender or trustee was guilty of fraud, oppression, or malice in its wrongful conduct, punitive damages may also be awarded. Successful borrowers can delay (and even rescind) foreclosure anywhere from 45 days to two years. If borrowers have a valid suit, lenders will attempt to enter into an *offer in compromise* to avoid further litigation.

> A wrongful foreclosure action can be combined with an unlawful detainer action, in cases where borrowers bring the suit after the foreclosure sale.

## Lis Pendens

A notice of pending litigation, referred to in law as lis pendens (which literally means *litigation is pending*), is filed by borrowers or their attorneys. It can bring any sale of the property to a halt. The notice is filed with the county recorder's office. Typically, attorneys file for lis pendens when they open a lawsuit for preventing the sale of real-property (as in wrongful foreclosure actions). Once a lis pendens is recorded no title insurance company will issue a title insurance policy until the lis pendens is removed.

If the borrowers do not have enough evidence to establish their case, the court will grant the order to remove the lis pendens. The penalties for wrongfully recording a notice of pending action vary, however, borrowers could face additional monetary penalties and attorney costs. Lenders will typically aggressively fight for the removal of a lis pendens; depending on your state laws. The court could set a hearing within 30 days to determine validity of the borrower's lawsuit. This hearing does not determine the outcome of the lawsuit, only if it has merit.

*Contact a knowledgeable real-estate attorney for more information, and/or perform additional research on this topic at your local law library.*

## Losing Property To A Spouse

Potentially the most agonizing aspect to a divorce is for one spouse, who has equally (if not more) maintained a vested interest in a property, to hand it over to the other spouse. So many divorces bitterly linger on for years over this issue.

The vacating spouse resents this act, even when voluntarily done. Even if the spouse has remarried and purchased other property in the future, the one they lost seems to haunt their inner being. There is no one solution for recovering from this emotional torture, as the issues seem to stem deeper than the lost property. Instead it's tantamount to betrayal. For some a cure may not exist as their motives are set on revenge. However, for those who can manage their disappointments to appreciate a lovelier life beyond their attachment to the property, peace can be found in due time. Take it one day at a time.

It's possible to pursue litigation against a spouse to recover the property, in no fault divorces, if it was not divided equally and/or equitably. Although if legal action persists, it's best to sell the home rather continue incurring *legal* expenses. Contact a knowledgeable divorce attorney for more information.

## You Can Only Control Yourself

Once you've done everything in your power, let go. It's impossible to dictate the outcome. Feel comfortable in knowing that it's not your job to direct what happens afterwards.

# Three Auto Repossession

*The meaning of things lies not in the things themselves, but in our attitude towards them.*

*Antoine de Saint-Exupery*

Purchasing vehicles beyond your means feeds the automobile repossession industry. According to a former executive in the automobile repossession field, repossessions typically occur within the first year a vehicle is purchased. Your ability to pay the car note becomes evident to your lender within the first six months. Those who have made payments for years may find their lender flexible and more willing to negotiate terms and payment arrangements due to the vehicle's depreciation, possible high mileage, and wear and tear. Although each lender's collection tactics vary, it's best to negotiate with your lender to determine the best solution. Once repossession occurs, the repossession agency will not relinquish the vehicle unless instructed to do so by your lender, or by court order (particularly for bankruptcy and unlawful action(s) cases). Certainly, this does not bring good news if your car is repossessed. However, it's good to know that threatening the *repo man* (commonly referred to as an adjuster) will not return your car. The repossession agency is a contractor of your lender, so they are working under their control and instructions.

All the information for this section was obtained by research and interviews with individuals who either manage repossession agencies or perform repossessions for major automobile dealers in California. Their experience with financial lenders, repossession agents, and borrowers are compiled in this section which has good information if you are affected by automobile repossession. Some details were omitted due to potential abuse by those who would want to cause injury to the *repo man*. During my research I learned that all walks of life have had their vehicles repossessed; attorneys, actors, musicians, doctors, drug traffickers, strippers as well as common working people. The stories are amazing. Most cars repossessed have been purchased by young adults and those who obtain loans from high interest rate *loan sharks* who finance cars for anyone with a driver's license. Only consumers can rid the country of these types by choosing not to take their loans and teaching children to appreciate a low debt life style.

## I'm In Trouble Now, So What Should I Do?

Those who can keep their vehicle by repaying their delinquency or filing for bankruptcy should contact their lender to inform them of the new arrangement. Most lenders will work with borrowers who are delinquent on their loans. Threatening bankruptcy should raise their eyebrows, as in chapter 13 a debtor can retain the property and could possibly have payments reduced or temporarily halted. For chapter 7 the delinquency must be paid or the court will remove the automatic protection (for more information *see chapter one Bankruptcy*). Many lenders will add the delinquent balance to the loan if borrowers are able to resume making payments.

Hiding the vehicle is a **temporary** solution that can be utilized until some other arrangement is made – considering what good is the vehicle if you can't use it. Those without any method to repay the note and the lender is not willing to negotiate should save themselves potential agony by returning the vehicle. We all want revenge for the exorbitant fees and interest rates charged by dishonorable banks, but it's a waste of your precious life to spend even one minute taking revenge. Let go!

*When things go wrong, don't go with them.*

Anonymous

## Types of Repossession

There are three categories of repossessions; self-help, voluntary and involuntary. Self-help repossession occurs when a lender (typically an individual or small private business) attempts to repossess property without contracting a repossession agency to act on their behalf. Voluntary repossession occurs when a borrower returns property to a lender before a physical repossession occurs. Involuntary repossession occurs when a secured party regains the property without the

consent of a borrower. All three categories are covered in this chapter.

## Laws Regarding Repossession

Each state has it own laws regarding repossession. In addition to specific state requirements, the federal government has adopted the Fair Debt Collection's Practice Act, provided at the end of this section, which grants protection to consumers. These guidelines apply to debt collections including repossession and include prohibitions for repossession agencies engaging in certain acts and practices that endanger and threaten debtors and others. The Fair Debt Collection Practices Act is the foundation for state laws.

States may have additional laws above those mentioned in the federal guidelines. The state of California, for example, has adopted the *Collateral Recovery Act*, if you want to learn more about your state laws, contact your state's consumer agency office for more information (*see Appendix E for a list of nationwide consumer agencies*). As I researched information for this chapter I located state laws in the Business and Professional Codes of my state's civil procedure law at their website. Within the sections I found that a licensed repressor is prohibited from using any badge or title, wearing a uniform, using an insignia, identification card or alias, or making any statement with the intent to give an impression that he is connected in any way with the Federal Government, a state government, or any political subdivision of a state government. *For example, they cannot arrive at your door wearing what would appear to be a police uniform or army clothes.* Repossession companies are prohibited from soliciting recovery of vehicles after they have been located, charging unincurred expenses, and using recovered property for their own personal use. There are additional restrictions for repossession. More information can be found on the Internet.

Repossessions are considered a civil matter, unless conducted under court orders. Under this condition, law enforcement members conduct the repossession. Courts allow officers to enter the debtor's property, including breaking into the dwelling, to retrieve the item(s) listed in the order. The lender commences with a civil action by filing a Replevin or Claim and Delivery. This typically occurs at the lenders request, but most lenders do not seek legal action as it often takes longer to recover the property using the court system and it can be costly.

---

If you are reading this section and are facing the threat of having yours or a loved one's vehicle repossessed, it's too late to reconsider buying a less expensive vehicle or locating a lender offering lower interest rates. Even for those who have had their car repossessed, it's imperative to consider the costs of your next vehicle as a deciding factor verses looks and fashion. You may have to drive a non attractive yet functional car until your income justifies a luxurious one. This is especially directed to young adults who find having a nice car a necessity to keeping up a good reputation. Nothing can be more embarrassing than your friends watching your car being towed away by the repo man. Although a good excuse would be that it's broken, the reality is that it's not. You can save yourself a substantial amount of money by purchasing a less expensive car you can enjoy free and clear of liens for the price of an expensive car, which has inflated interest rates that fatten the pockets of lenders. It's certainly worth considering before making another vehicle purchase.

## Hiding Your Vehicle

Those who do not have a garage may find this task challenging. Hiding your car from the *repo man* (adjuster) is one of life's low moments, but you're not alone. Chances are, someone in your neighborhood is doing or has done the same. While you are keeping the vehicle away from your lender, if possible, attempt to negotiate payment terms. It's in your best interest to use the time wisely. When arrangements are made, **get it in writing**. Ask your lender to mail or fax the new arrangement. You may choose to write it down and request that your lender's representative sign the agreement.

Oftentimes people hide their cars at friends or relatives houses. This is not recommended because the *repo man* can and oftentimes will follow you around to locate the vehicle even before you realize it's designated for repossession. Your lender will also visit all the addresses you listed as references on the contract.

Hiding your car may not be necessary, as it can be easy to talk with your lender to make payment arrangements. No bank wants to sell a car that has far depreciated in value. This is not a hard and fast rule as some lenders enjoy threatening customers until they pay. If you have a reasonable person to contact at the bank, do so immediately.

## Negotiating With Your Lender

Believe it or not, your lender wants you to have the car. There aren't too many people who will pay what you did. If you've had the car for more than two years, it's significantly depreciated and God only knows what condition it's in after you discovered the *repo man* is after you.

Chances are the lender is trying to reach you. Make yourself available, and reach an agreement. Repossession is a large industry; you are not alone. If you failed to live up to past agreements, and have funds to pay, try meeting with the lender in person with the payment.

Decide if you want the car or if you simply need transportation. You can buy a vehicle for roughly $1,000 and it's quite possible you can purchase your previously owned vehicle at an auction significantly less than what you owe. Take time to decide if you can afford the car. If not, let go and move on. Truly it's your banks loss.

> ☀ Some cars are sold at dealer's auctions, which prohibit entrance from those not holding valid car dealer credentials. Some people pay dealers a small fee to bid on certain cars on their behalf. Depending on your state laws it can take a small fee to purchase a dealers license.

Lenders are often willing to negotiate payment arrangements with borrowers. If you are more than three months behind, but you can afford one payment your lender may take the one payment and add the remaining payments to the balance of your loan. This will extend the duration of the note, but help retain the vehicle. Some banks refinance vehicle loans, if you have good credit, which can lower payments but will extend the payment duration which costs the borrower more money. The borrower pays little money over a longer period of time. Refinancing a car is beneficial if you're able to reduce your interest rate and pay off the vehicle within the same time, or sooner, than your original loan.

## Skip Tracing

Lenders having difficulty locating delinquent borrowers hire companies to trace their whereabouts. The industry term is *Skip Tracing* (meaning the borrower has skipped out on the loan). An investigator is assigned to the account to locate the borrower (skip tracers are typically contacted when the

borrower is 90 to 120 days late on payments). Lenders supply the investigator with the borrower's personal information such as social security number, last known address, telephone number, relative's names (maiden names), etc. Most of this information was provided by the borrower at the time the loan application was taken. Your contract *should* have a clause permitting the distribution of this information for debt collection.

## Voluntary Repossession (I Don't Want The Car)

Congratulations, you've decided the car isn't worth the expense of your personal happiness. It's time to call the lender and work out arrangements to return the car as a voluntary repossession, request that it's noted on your credit report as having done so, and commence with enjoying your life.

*There are more serious problems in life than financial ones, and I've had a lot of those. I've been broke before, and will be again. Heartbroke? That's serious. Lose a few bucks. That's not.*

Wille Nelson

Don't worry; you will be able to purchase another vehicle, one that you can afford when you're ready. It's not the end of the world, just not one of your better days. On the brighter side, you've closed the door on a nightmare, so put this experience behind you and move on to happier days.

## Involuntary Repossession (What Happens When A Vehicle is Repossessed)

When accounts are more than 45 days late the lender submits an *Order of Repossession* to their selected vendor. For some repossessions, an adjuster arrives at the borrowers residence or work in a *Not for Hire* tow truck. The truck maybe any shape, size or color; it often does not have a company name or insignia.

---

A representative from the repossession agency may attempt to contact you by telephone and they may appear at your residence or place of work to negotiate the return of the vehicle. Some agents use threats and misconstrue their presence to trick borrowers into returning the property, while other agents attempt to be diplomatic.

If negotiations are used and fail, the repossession company will attempt to take the vehicle out of the borrower's presence by either towing or seizure. Most new cars have electronic access chips which make it difficult to repossess cars, unless towing is involved or the dealer has provided the key chip code to the lender.

You may wonder where the *repo man* is hiding – it depends. The agents avoid hiding in locations where you can easily spot them. They find corners or streets where they watch the subject car come and go while attempting to remain inconspicuous. Typically there are two males in a car/truck and a bag with tools they used to seize the vehicle. If you are hiding the car, they return at different hours of the day and night. There are too many cars to repossess to wait all night for your return, but under pressure they will do nearly anything to recover the property.

Cars with kill switches are not safe. Depending on the type, this will not deter the *repo man*. He takes classes in disabling security systems, kill switches, steering wheel locks, etc. Again, for most new cars with security chips, a tow truck is called to take the vehicle.

After the car is repossessed, depending on your state laws, the agent contacts the borrower within a specified period to obtain belongings left inside the vehicle. Promptly retrieve items as the repossession company may (and most likely will) charge storage fees for items kept inside the vehicle. If items are not recovered by borrowers, the repossession agency disposes of items according to state laws.

Once the vehicle is repossessed, it's taken to the repossession yard. The borrower and police department are notified of the repossession; the lender is also notified. Notification typically occurs within the first 24 hours of the repossession. This rule varies according to state and local laws.

At a later time the vehicle is transported to another yard before being sent to a private auction, where it can be sold. As previously mentioned, if the borrower has dealer credentials to enter the auction they can purchase their vehicle in cash. Depending on your state laws, the lender will notify you of the location of the vehicle at every stage on its transportation.

Furthermore, once the vehicle is repossessed your responsibility to pay does not cease. Some lenders choose to sue borrowers for the reaming balance and/or place a *charge off* on the borrower's credit reports.

## Self-Help Repossession (Repossessions by Individuals)

Repossessions by individuals are rare, but the law does grant private parties the right to repossession. The constitution protection of due process does not apply since repossession is not a state action. Some lenders will attempt to repossess under self help repossession laws. The laws do authorize the secured party, after default, to take possession of collateral either through self help, if done without a breach of peace, or through judicial process (U.C.C. 9-609). A concern for most courts is initiating self-help repossession without notifying the borrower. Those who are facing repossession should be notified in writing to cure the default or face repossession. Should you commence with self-help repossession, retain all communications with the borrower. It maybe wise to send notices via certified mail to document the mailing.

## Breach of Peace

Laws have been drafted to protect borrowers during repossession. The main concern during repossession is a dramatic confrontation between the *repo man* and the debtor. If the debtor hasn't already returned the vehicle chances are they want to retain it until payments can be made. However, the creditor is interested in obtaining possession and selling it at minimal expense prior to any damage, deterioration, or further depreciation. This dichotomy creates an environment for possible physical confrontation.

Borrowers can sue repossession companies, financial lenders, and insurers for damages incurred due to breaches attributed to repossession. The most common violation is breach of peace. Regardless of which state you reside, the waiver of a lender's interest to refrain from breach of peace is prohibited. The federal laws vaguely define breach of peace, yet state laws may provide further details.

1. Repossession occurring within a residence without authorization,
2. When the debtor objects to the repossession or request that repossession cease,
3. Repossessions that involve trespass on property of the debtor, whether or not by forced entry
4. Repossession facilitated by trickery.

Financial recovery from violations of breach of peace is determined by court rules. Under the Universal Commercial Code (U.C.C 9-625) *Damages (including for breach of the peace) are those reasonably calculated to put an eligible claimant in the position that it would have occupied had no violation occurred...*

---

☀ The Federal Debt Collection Practices Act (FDCPA) also applies to the confiscation of property. A business who engages in auto repossession may not "[Take or threaten] to take any nonjudicial action to effect

---

dispossession or disablement or property if – there is no present right to possession of the property claimed as collateral through an enforceable security interest..." Section 808 (6) (A), 15 U.C.S.A 1692f. Thus, a repossessor committing a breach of peace in the course of a repossession (even if the debt is owing), or repossessing when the debt is not in default, faces liability under the Act in addition to tort liability for conversion.

Breach of peace is not the only remedy borrowers have against unscrupulous repossession agencies. Borrowers, for example, can pursue damages due to physical damages caused by unlawful repossession tactics.

## I Filed for Bankruptcy and the Lender wants the Car

The vehicle is protected in the automatic stay clause of the bankruptcy code the moment you file for bankruptcy, which means you have agreed to relinquish your estate (property) to the bankruptcy court, including your vehicle. The protection of the bankruptcy courts applies if the vehicle is listed in your schedules. You are responsible for informing your lender of the bankruptcy filing to halt attempts to collect the vehicle. A sample motion is provided at the end of this section for recovery of debtor's property.

In chapter 7, you can keep the vehicle if payments are brought current before the bankruptcy case is completed or before the lender receives permission from the bankruptcy courts to repossess.

In chapter 13, you can cure defaults and/or seek reduced car payments. Regardless of the bankruptcy chapter, the courts can instruct the lender to return the vehicle even if it was repossessed before you filed for bankruptcy.

If you are in bankruptcy and repossession occurs without the courts permission (or your lender has harassed you by sending letters and placing telephone calls to persuade you to pay) you can file a complaint of *Willful Violation of the Automatic Stay* and request the return of the vehicle (*for more information see the sample provided at the end of this chapter and Chapter One Bankruptcy*).

## The *Repo Man* Broke the Law

It's not uncommon for the *repo man* to break the law during repossession. The adjuster receives constant pressure from lenders to recover their collateral. Those who are significantly behind on payments are a top priority for agencies that do nearly anything to earn their commission and keep their customers.

Commonly, the adjuster will confiscate the vehicle behind a locked gate or from a closed garage: certainly this is a violation of consumer rights and most state laws. According to my sources they've been known to move parked cars that block access to the subject vehicle. These companies do break the law. Should this occurs, file a complaint with the local authorities and take pictures of damage vehicles, locks, and other property. Some people choose to retain attorneys to prosecute. Select a knowledgeable credit and debt attorney familiar with adjuster's tactics and who also has experience litigating against lenders, repossession agencies, and insurers.

---

If the vehicle is removed from an open garage with clear access, you most likely do not have any legal recourse as there isn't any breach of peace. Typical breach of peace complaints include, trespass after warning, criminal mischief, breaking or injuring fences, burglary, and personal injury.

---

## The *Repo Man* Struck Me

Most physical altercations occur when people are resisting repossession. If you are resisting,

the *repo man* must not commence in physically striking you, nor must they initiate physical threats. Furthermore, laws restrict them from carrying weapons and appearing as officers of the state or federal government.

Professional repossession agencies thoroughly train their agents to avoid hostile situations at all costs. Should the *repo man* physically attack or threaten borrowers, display a gun, cause bodily harm or injury as a result of repossession, immediately contact the police and an experienced attorney. Again, take pictures of bruises, scars, etc.; if possible, gather witness' statements who may have seen the altercation or heard screams. Retain all medical records resulting from the attack as this information is crucial to supporting your claim.

## I'm Being Stalked By the *Repo Man*

An adjuster's goal is to remain inconspicuous if at all possible. If the borrower notices them, they typically trade the account with another person at the company. Borrowers with sharp eyes can cause the *repo man* to trade accounts several times.

If their presence is noticeable and menacing this could be considered a breach of peace. Gather license plate numbers and take pictures. Log the date, time and location where you noticed the *repo man*. Do not hesitate to contact local authorities with the information if you believe their presence is harassing and/or threatening.

## The *Repo Man* Took Off With My Baby

Some may find driving off with children inside a repossessed vehicle extreme but it has occurred on more than one occasion. Holding children against their will and putting them in risk of serious injury is illegal. Absolutely no repossession company should engage in such practices. However, they may attempt to block the vehicle to prevent moving until an adult arrives. If you have experienced an agent kidnapping your children, immediately contact local authorities.

> I admonish people not to intentionally leave their children inside a car unsupervised, especially if you are aware it maybe repossessed. This potentially endangers their vulnerable lives.

## The *Repo Man* Took off With My Animal

Unlike human beings, animals are not in possession of a vehicle; therefore, the vehicle can possibly be seized. Depending on the breed and size of the animal, the *repo man* will stay clear, until the vehicle is accessible. However, the car maybe hitched to the tow truck until the borrower returns to retrieve the animal. Should the animal suffer during the repossession, contact your local police authorities, animal protection society and a knowledgeable attorney.

> Do not put your animal friends in jeopardy by leaving them in the vehicle. Truly it isn't worth the extreme attempt.

## The *Repo Man* is Talking To My Neighbors

Laws prohibit debt collectors from talking to second and third parties about a debtor's financial status and disclosing personal information about your debts (*see the Fair Debt Collection Practices Act at the end of this section*). Again, most adjusters are not concerned with *fully* obeying the laws. This is to the disgust of borrowers who suffer the embarrassment of their behavior.

Some adjusters will falsely represent themselves and create false scenarios to convince others to disclose information about borrowers and property. If you discover this type of practice notify your lender in writing and the name of the repossession agency. In the notice clearly state that the agency has violated the terms of the Fair Debt Collection Practices Act, and possibly state laws. Instruct them to cease this practice immediately or be subject to legal action.

## Repossessions On Military Bases

With heighten security throughout the nation; the country's military bases are inaccessible to those without authority to enter. Repossession agencies follow strict procedures for confiscating property on military bases. First they submit the *Order of Repossession* to the base legal department as well as additional pertinent documentation. The legal department contacts the borrower's commander. The commander will determine if the borrower can make the payments or the commander will authorize the release of the vehicle.

For military members who are actively engaged in national defense, the Soldiers' and Sailors' Civil Relief Act of 1940 protects them from creditors. The Act is a federal law that gives military members special rights and protections. For example, if someone sues a member and obtains a judgment against them because they failed to respond to a lawsuit, the Act provides a means for the court to delay the proceedings or re-open the default judgment if the failure to appear in court was due to military service.

Other protections of the act includes a six percent cap on interest rates for certain loans and debts incurred before entering the military, protection against foreclosures and, as mentioned, repossessions without a court order, and prospective relief from certain financial obligations members cannot meet because of military service.

The act is also the law that allows military members to keep their state of residence, continue voting, keep a driver's license, and pay or be exempt from taxes in the member's home state while assigned around the world.

Among the act's chief provision is its ability to reduce interest rates on debts incurred before active-duty status, protect service members and their families from eviction, and delay civil court actions.

But it is not automatic. For service members to take advantage of the Act, individual service members should notify their creditors of the active-duty status and their intent to invoke their Civil Relief Act Rights.

---

**Specific rights under the Act include:**

- Limiting interest rates to 6 percent for all debts incurred before beginning active-duty service. This provision includes interest rates on credit cards, mortgages and auto loans. It does not apply to federal student loans.
- Protecting family members from eviction during times of active-duty service, regardless of whether the lease was signed before or after activation. If the monthly lease is $1,200 or less, a landlord must seek a court order to authorize eviction.
- Prohibiting repossessions and foreclosures without court permission.
- Postponing civil lawsuits the service member is a direct party to, such as bankruptcy.
- Extending deadlines to file lawsuits by eliminating time served on active duty from calculating any statute of limitations.
- Protecting active-duty people from taxation by states other than by their state of domicile.
- Prohibiting creditors and insurance companies from making adverse credit reports, denying credit or taking adverse

---

financial action against a service member based solely on invocation of the Act.

## Repossessions on Indian Land

Indian territory is considered sovereign with each tribe maintaining laws that govern their land. These laws may have strict procedures for repossession. The *repo man* will try to confiscate the vehicle even if such laws exist. Should repossession occur, contact the tribe's legal department, police, and a knowledgeable attorney. However, it maybe difficult to retrieve the vehicle once confiscated no matter how flagrantly the laws were broken.

1   Jane Doeheny
    Pro Se
2   123 Main Street
    Nicetown, CA 91777
3

4               **United States Bankruptcy Court**
              **Central District of California**
5

6   In re:                     )  Case No.: No. 12-3-456789-1

7   Jane Doheny,            )  **Plaintiff Complaint to Compel**

8           Plaintiff      )  **Turnover of Certain Property From**
                  )  **Defendant**
9                   )

10   Loan Sharky Auto Lenders   )

11         Defendant      )

12

13   COME NOW plaintiff, Jane Doheny, the above-named chapter 13 debtor alleges
14   and requests as follows:
    (1) That this is an adversary proceeding brought pursuant to FED.R. BANKR.P.
15       7001(1) and 11 U.S.C. § 542(a) to recover a beige 2000 Nissan Maxima GLE
      assertedly reposed by the defendant, Loan Sharky Auto Lenders, prior to
      the commencement of this chapter 13 case.
16     (2) That this Court has jurisdiction under the provision of 28 U.S.C. §§ 1334,
      151 and 157(a).
17     (3) That under that particular facts and circumstances and applicable laws the
      plaintiff is entitled to possess of the above-described property of the
18       estate for "use" as contemplated in 11 U.S.C. § 363.

19   WHEREFORE, plaintiff respectfully prays for an expedited hearing and order
    directing turnover of the above-describe property of the estate from the
    defendant-creditor.
20

21                       Dated this 30th day of November, 2003

22                           Jane Doeheny

23                           123 Main Street
                        Nicetown, CA 91777
24                         Jane Doeheny
                        Pro Se
25

# THE FAIR DEBT COLLECTION PRACTICES ACT
As amended by Public Law 104-208, 110 Stat. 3009 (Sept. 30, 1996)

To amend the Consumer Credit Protection Act to prohibit abusive practices by debt collectors.
*Be it enacted by the Senate and House of Representatives of the United States of America in Congress assembled,*
That the Consumer Credit Protection Act (15 U.S.C. 1601 et seq.) is amended by adding at the end thereof the following new title:

TITLE VIII - DEBT COLLECTION PRACTICES [Fair Debt Collection Practices Act]
Sec.

## § 801. Short Title [15 USC 1601 note]
This title maybe cited as the "Fair Debt Collection Practices Act."

## § 802. Congressional findings and declarations of purpose [15 USC 1692]
(a) There is abundant evidence of the use of abusive, deceptive, and unfair debt collection practices by many debt collectors. Abusive debt collection practices contribute to the number of personal bankruptcies, to marital instability, to the loss of jobs, and to invasions of individual privacy.
(b) Existing laws and procedures for redressing these injuries are inadequate to protect consumers.
(c) Means other than misrepresentation or other abusive debt collection practices are available for the effective collection of debts.
(d) Abusive debt collection practices are carried on to a substantial extent in interstate commerce and through means and instrumentalities of such commerce. Even where abusive debt collection practices are purely intrastate in character, they nevertheless directly affect interstate commerce.
(e) It is the purpose of this title to eliminate abusive debt collection practices by debt collectors, to insure that those debt collectors who refrain from using abusive debt collection practices are not competitively disadvantaged, and to promote consistent State action to protect consumers against debt collection abuses.

## § 803. Definitions [15 USC 1692a]
As used in this title --
(1) The term "Commission" means the Federal Trade Commission.

(2) The term "communication" means the conveying of information regarding a debt directly or indirectly to any person through any medium.

(3) The term "consumer" means any natural person obligated or allegedly obligated to pay any debt.

(4) The term "creditor" means any person who offers or extends credit creating a debt or to whom a debt is owed, but such term does not include any person to the extent that he receives an assignment or transfer of a debt in default solely for the purpose of facilitating collection of such debt for another.

(5) The term "debt" means any obligation or alleged obligation of a consumer to pay money arising out of a transaction in which the money, property, insurance or services which are the subject of the transaction are primarily for personal, family, or household purposes, whether or not such obligation has been reduced to judgment.

(6) The term "debt collector" means any person who uses any instrumentality of interstate commerce or the mails in any business the principal purpose of which is the collection of any debts, or who regularly collects or attempts to collect, directly or indirectly, debts owed or due or asserted to be owed or due another. Notwithstanding the exclusion provided by clause (F) of the last sentence of this paragraph, the term includes any creditor who, in the process of collecting his own debts, uses any name other than his own which would indicate that a third person is collecting or attempting to collect such debts. For the purpose of section 808(6), such term also includes any person who uses any instrumentality of interstate commerce or the mails in any business the principal purpose of which is the enforcement of security interests. The term does not include --

(A) any officer or employee of a creditor while, in the name of the creditor, collecting debts for such creditor;

(B) any person while acting as a debt collector for another person, both of whom are related by common ownership or affiliated by corporate control, if the person acting as a debt collector does so only for persons to whom it is so related or affiliated and if the principal business of such person is not the collection of debts;

(C) any officer or employee of the United States or any State to the extent that collecting or attempting to collect any debt is in the performance of his official duties;

(D) any person while serving or attempting to serve legal process on any other person in connection with the judicial enforcement of any debt;

(E) any nonprofit organization which, at the request of consumers, performs bona fide consumer credit counseling and assists consumers in the liquidation of their debts by receiving payments from such consumers and distributing such amounts to creditors; and

(F) any person collecting or attempting to collect any debt owed or due or asserted to be owed or due another to the extent such activity (i) is incidental to a bona fide fiduciary obligation or a bona fide escrow arrangement; (ii) concerns a debt which was originated by such person; (iii) concerns a debt which was not in default at the time it was obtained by such person; or (iv) concerns a debt obtained by such person as a secured party in a commercial credit transaction involving the creditor.

(7) The term "location information" means a consumer's place of abode and his telephone number at such place, or his place of employment.

(8) The term "State" means any State, territory, or possession of the United States, the District of Columbia, the Commonwealth of Puerto Rico, or any political subdivision of any of the foregoing.

## § 804. Acquisition of location information [15 USC 1692b]

Any debt collector communicating with any person other than the consumer for the purpose of acquiring location information about the consumer shall --

(1) identify himself, state that he is confirming or correcting location information concerning the consumer, and, only if expressly requested, identify his employer;

(2) not state that such consumer owes any debt;

(3) not communicate with any such person more than once unless requested to do so by such person or unless the debt collector reasonably believes that the earlier response of such person is erroneous or incomplete and that such person now has correct or complete location information;

(4) not communicate by post card;

(5) not use any language or symbol on any envelope or in the contents of any communication effected by the mails or telegram that indicates that the debt collector is in the debt collection business or that the communication relates to the collection of a debt; and

(6) after the debt collector knows the consumer is represented by an attorney with regard to the subject debt and has knowledge of, or can readily ascertain, such attorney's name and address, not communicate with any person other than that attorney, unless the attorney fails to respond within a reasonable period of time to the communication from the debt collector.

## § 805. Communication in connection with debt collection [15 USC 1692c]

(a) COMMUNICATION WITH THE CONSUMER GENERALLY. Without the prior consent of the consumer given directly to the debt collector or the express permission of a court of competent jurisdiction, a debt collector may not communicate with a consumer in connection with the collection of any debt --

(1) at any unusual time or place or a time or place known or which should be known to be inconvenient to the consumer. In the absence of knowledge of circumstances to the contrary, a debt collector shall assume that the convenient time for communicating with a consumer is after 8 o'clock antimeridian and before 9 o'clock postmeridian, local time at the consumer's location;

(2) if the debt collector knows the consumer is represented by an attorney with respect to such debt and has knowledge of, or can readily ascertain, such attorney's name and address, unless the attorney fails to respond within a reasonable period of time to a communication from the debt collector or unless the attorney consents to direct communication with the consumer; or

(3) at the consumer's place of employment if the debt collector knows or has reason to know that the consumer's employer prohibits the consumer from receiving such communication.

(b) COMMUNICATION WITH THIRD PARTIES. Except as provided in section 804, without the prior consent of the consumer given directly to the debt collector, or the express permission of a court of competent jurisdiction, or as reasonably necessary to effectuate a postjudgment judicial remedy, a debt collector may not communicate, in connection with the collection of any debt, with any person other than a consumer, his attorney, a consumer reporting agency if otherwise permitted by law, the creditor, the attorney of the creditor, or the attorney of the debt collector.

(c) CEASING COMMUNICATION. If a consumer notifies a debt collector in writing that the consumer refuses to pay a debt or that the consumer wishes the debt collector to cease further communication with the consumer, the debt collector shall not communicate further with the consumer with respect to such debt, except --

(1) to advise the consumer that the debt collector's further efforts are being terminated;

(2) to notify the consumer that the debt collector or creditor may invoke specified remedies which are ordinarily invoked by such debt collector or creditor; or

(3) where applicable, to notify the consumer that the debt collector or creditor intends to invoke a specified remedy.

If such notice from the consumer is made by mail, notification shall be complete upon receipt.

(d) For the purpose of this section, the term "consumer" includes the consumer's spouse, parent (if the consumer is a minor), guardian, executor, or administrator.

## § 806. Harassment or abuse [15 USC 1692d]

A debt collector may not engage in any conduct the natural consequence of which is to harass, oppress, or abuse any person in connection with the collection of a debt. Without limiting the general application of the foregoing, the following conduct is a violation of this section:

(1) The use or threat of use of violence or other criminal means to harm the physical person, reputation, or property of any person.

(2) The use of obscene or profane language or language the natural consequence of which is to abuse the hearer or reader.

(3) The publication of a list of consumers who allegedly refuse to pay debts, except to a consumer reporting agency or to persons meeting the requirements of section 603(f) or 604(3)[1] of this Act.

(4) The advertisement for sale of any debt to coerce payment of the debt.

(5) Causing a telephone to ring or engaging any person in telephone conversation repeatedly or continuously with intent to annoy, abuse, or harass any person at the called number.

(6) Except as provided in section 804, the placement of telephone calls without meaningful disclosure of the caller's identity.

### § 807. False or misleading representations [15 USC 1962e]

A debt collector may not use any false, deceptive, or misleading representation or means in connection with the collection of any debt. Without limiting the general application of the foregoing, the following conduct is a violation of this section:

(1) The false representation or implication that the debt collector is vouched for, bonded by, or affiliated with the United States or any State, including the use of any badge, uniform, or facsimile thereof.

(2) The false representation of --

(A) the character, amount, or legal status of any debt; or

(B) any services rendered or compensation which maybe lawfully received by any debt collector for the collection of a debt.

(3) The false representation or implication that any individual is an attorney or that any communication is from an attorney.

(4) The representation or implication that nonpayment of any debt will result in the arrest or imprisonment of any person or the seizure, garnishment, attachment, or sale of any property or wages of any person unless such action is lawful and the debt collector or creditor intends to take such action.

(5) The threat to take any action that cannot legally be taken or that is not intended to be taken.

(6) The false representation or implication that a sale, referral, or other transfer of any interest in a debt shall cause the consumer to --

(A) lose any claim or defense to payment of the debt; or

(B) become subject to any practice prohibited by this title.

(7) The false representation or implication that the consumer committed any crime or other conduct in order to disgrace the consumer.

(8) Communicating or threatening to communicate to any person credit information which is known or which should be known to be false, including the failure to communicate that a disputed debt is disputed.

(9) The use or distribution of any written communication which simulates or is falsely represented to be a document authorized, issued, or approved by any court, official, or agency of the United States or any State, or which creates a false impression as to its source, authorization, or approval.

(10) The use of any false representation or deceptive means to collect or attempt to collect any debt or to obtain information concerning a consumer.

(11) The failure to disclose in the initial written communication with the consumer and, in addition, if the initial communication with the consumer is oral, in that initial oral communication, that the debt collector is attempting to collect a debt and that any information obtained will be used for that purpose, and the failure to disclose in subsequent communications that the communication is from a debt collector, except that this paragraph shall not apply to a formal pleading made in connection with a legal action.

(12) The false representation or implication that accounts have been turned over to innocent purchasers for value.

(13) The false representation or implication that documents are legal process.

(14) The use of any business, company, or organization name other than the true name of the debt collector's business, company, or organization.

(15) The false representation or implication that documents are not legal process forms or do not require action by the consumer.

(16) The false representation or implication that a debt collector operates or is employed by a consumer reporting agency as defined by section 603(f) of this Act.

## § 808. Unfair practices [15 USC 1692f]

A debt collector may not use unfair or unconscionable means to collect or attempt to collect any debt. Without limiting the general application of the foregoing, the following conduct is a violation of this section:

(1) The collection of any amount (including any interest, fee, charge, or expense incidental to the principal obligation) unless such amount is expressly authorized by the agreement creating the debt or permitted by law.

(2) The acceptance by a debt collector from any person of a check or other payment instrument postdated by more than five days unless such person is notified in writing of the debt collector's intent to deposit such check or instrument not more than ten nor less than three business days prior to such deposit.

(3) The solicitation by a debt collector of any postdated check or other postdated payment instrument for the purpose of threatening or instituting criminal prosecution.

(4) Depositing or threatening to deposit any postdated check or other postdated payment instrument prior to the date on such check or instrument.

(5) Causing charges to be made to any person for communications by concealment of the true propose of the communication. Such charges include, but are not limited to, collect telephone calls and telegram fees.

(6) Taking or threatening to take any nonjudicial action to effect dispossession or disablement of property if --

(A) there is no present right to possession of the property claimed as collateral through an enforceable security interest;

(B) there is no present intention to take possession of the property; or

(C) the property is exempt by law from such dispossession or disablement.

(7) Communicating with a consumer regarding a debt by post card.

(8) Using any language or symbol, other than the debt collector's address, on any envelope when communicating with a consumer by use of the mails or by telegram, except that a debt collector may use his business name if such name does not indicate that he is in the debt collection business.

## § 809. Validation of debts [15 USC 1692g]

(a) Within five days after the initial communication with a consumer in connection with the collection of any debt, a debt collector shall, unless the following information is contained in the initial communication or the consumer has paid the debt, send the consumer a written notice containing --

(1) the amount of the debt;

(2) the name of the creditor to whom the debt is owed;

(3) a statement that unless the consumer, within thirty days after receipt of the notice, disputes the validity of the debt, or any portion thereof, the debt will be assumed to be valid by the debt collector;

(4) a statement that if the consumer notifies the debt collector in writing within the thirty-day period that the debt, or any portion thereof, is disputed, the debt collector will obtain verification of the debt or a copy of a judgment against the consumer and a copy of such verification or judgment will be mailed to the consumer by the debt collector; and

(5) a statement that, upon the consumer's written request within the thirty-day period, the debt collector will provide the consumer with the name and address of the original creditor, if different from the current creditor.

(b) If the consumer notifies the debt collector in writing within the thirty-day period described in subsection (a) that the debt, or any portion thereof, is disputed, or that the consumer requests the name and address of the original creditor, the debt collector shall cease collection of the debt, or any disputed portion thereof, until the debt collector obtains verification of the debt or any copy of a judgment, or the name and address of the original creditor, and a copy of such verification or judgment, or name and address of the original creditor, is mailed to the consumer by the debt collector.

(c) The failure of a consumer to dispute the validity of a debt under this section may not be construed by any court as an admission of liability by the consumer.

## § 810. Multiple debts [15 USC 1692h]

If any consumer owes multiple debts and makes any single payment to any debt collector with respect to such debts, such debt collector may not apply such payment to any debt which is disputed by the consumer and, where applicable, shall apply such payment in accordance with the consumer's directions.

## § 811. Legal actions by debt collectors [15 USC 1692i]

(a) Any debt collector who brings any legal action on a debt against any consumer shall --

(1) in the case of an action to enforce an interest in real property securing the consumer's obligation, bring such action only in a judicial district or similar legal entity in which such real property is located; or

(2) in the case of an action not described in paragraph (1), bring such action only in the judicial district or similar legal entity --

(A) in which such consumer signed the contract sued upon; or

(B) in which such consumer resides at the commencement of the action.

(b) Nothing in this title shall be construed to authorize the bringing of legal actions by debt collectors.

## § 812. Furnishing certain deceptive forms [15 USC 1692j]

(a) It is unlawful to design, compile, and furnish any form knowing that such form would be used to create the false belief in a consumer that a person other than the creditor of such consumer is participating in the collection of or in an attempt to collect a debt such consumer allegedly owes such creditor, when in fact such person is not so participating.

(b) Any person who violates this section shall be liable to the same extent and in the same manner as a debt collector is liable under section 813 for failure to comply with a provision of this title.

## § 813. Civil liability [15 USC 1692k]

(a) Except as otherwise provided by this section, any debt collector who fails to comply with any provision of this title with respect to any person is liable to such person in an amount equal to the sum of --

(1) any actual damage sustained by such person as a result of such failure;

(2) (A) in the case of any action by an individual, such additional damages as the court may allow, but not exceeding $1,000; or

(B) in the case of a class action, (i) such amount for each named plaintiff as could be recovered under subparagraph (A), and (ii) such amount as the court may allow for all other class members, without regard to a minimum individual recovery, not to exceed the lesser of $500,000 or 1 per centum of the net worth of the debt collector; and

(3) in the case of any successful action to enforce the foregoing liability, the costs of the action, together with a reasonable attorney's fee as determined by the court. On a finding by the court that an action under this section was brought in bad faith and for the purpose of harassment, the court may award to the defendant attorney's fees reasonable in relation to the work expended and costs.

(b) In determining the amount of liability in any action under subsection (a), the court shall consider, among other relevant factors --

(1) in any individual action under subsection (a)(2)(A), the frequency and persistence of noncompliance by the debt collector, the nature of such noncompliance, and the extent to which such noncompliance was intentional; or

(2) in any class action under subsection (a)(2)(B), the frequency and persistence of noncompliance by the debt collector, the nature of such noncompliance, the resources of the debt collector, the number of persons adversely affected, and the extent to which the debt collector's noncompliance was intentional.

(c) A debt collector may not be held liable in any action brought under this title if the debt collector shows by a preponderance of evidence that the violation was not intentional and resulted from a bona fide error notwithstanding the maintenance of procedures reasonably adapted to avoid any such error.

(d) An action to enforce any liability created by this title maybe brought in any appropriate United States district court without regard to the amount in controversy, or in any other court of competent jurisdiction, within one year from the date on which the violation occurs.

(e) No provision of this section imposing any liability shall apply to any act done or omitted in good faith in conformity with any advisory opinion of the Commission, notwithstanding that after such act or omission has occurred, such opinion is amended, rescinded, or determined by judicial or other authority to be invalid for any reason.

## § 814. Administrative enforcement [15 USC 1692*l*]

(a) Compliance with this title shall be enforced by the Commission, except to the extend that enforcement of the requirements imposed under this title is specifically committed to another agency under subsection (b). For purpose of the exercise by the Commission of its functions and powers under the Federal Trade Commission Act, a violation of this title shall be deemed an unfair or deceptive act or practice in violation of that Act. All of the functions and powers of the Commission under the Federal Trade Commission Act are available to the Commission to enforce compliance by any person with this title, irrespective of whether that person is engaged in commerce or meets any other jurisdictional tests in the Federal Trade Commission Act, including the power to enforce the provisions of this title in the same manner as if the violation had been a violation of a Federal Trade Commission trade regulation rule.

(b) Compliance with any requirements imposed under this title shall be enforced under --

(1) section 8 of the Federal Deposit Insurance Act, in the case of --

(A) national banks, by the Comptroller of the Currency;

(B) member banks of the Federal Reserve System (other than national banks), by the Federal Reserve Board; and

(C) banks the deposits or accounts of which are insured by the Federal Deposit Insurance Corporation (other than members of the Federal Reserve System), by the Board of Directors of the Federal Deposit Insurance Corporation;

(2) section 5(d) of the Home Owners Loan Act of 1933, section 407 of the National Housing Act, and sections 6(i) and 17 of the Federal Home Loan Bank Act, by the Federal Home Loan Bank Board (acting directing or through the Federal Savings and Loan Insurance Corporation), in the case of any institution subject to any of those provisions;

(3) the Federal Credit Union Act, by the Administrator of the National Credit Union Administration with respect to any Federal credit union;

(4) subtitle IV of Title 49, by the Interstate Commerce Commission with respect to any common carrier subject to such subtitle;

(5) the Federal Aviation Act of 1958, by the Secretary of Transportation with respect to any air carrier or any foreign air carrier subject to that Act; and

(6) the Packers and Stockyards Act, 1921 (except as provided in section 406 of that Act), by the Secretary of Agriculture with respect to any activities subject to that Act.

(c) For the purpose of the exercise by any agency referred to in subsection (b) of its powers under any Act referred to in that subsection, a violation of any requirement imposed under this title shall be deemed to be a violation of a requirement imposed under that Act. In addition to its powers under any provision of law specifically referred to in subsection (b), each of the agencies referred to in that subsection may exercise, for the purpose of enforcing compliance with any requirement imposed under this title any other authority conferred on it by law, except as provided in subsection (d).

(d) Neither the Commission nor any other agency referred to in subsection (b) may promulgate trade regulation rules or other regulations with respect to the collection of debts by debt collectors as defined in this title.

## § 815. Reports to Congress by the Commission [15 USC 1692m]

(a) Not later than one year after the effective date of this title and at one-year intervals thereafter, the Commission shall make reports to the Congress concerning the administration of its functions under this title, including such recommendations as the Commission deems necessary or appropriate. In addition, each report of the Commission shall include its assessment of the extent to which compliance with this title is being achieved and a summary of the enforcement actions taken by the Commission under section 814 of this title.

(b) In the exercise of its functions under this title, the Commission may obtain upon request the views of any other Federal agency which exercises enforcement functions under section 814 of this title.

## § 816. Relation to State laws [15 USC 1692n]

This title does not annul, alter, or affect, or exempt any person subject to the provisions of this title from complying with the laws of any State with respect to debt collection practices, except to the extent that those laws are inconsistent with any provision of this title, and then only to the extent of the inconsistency. For purposes of this section, a State law is not inconsistent with this title if the protection such law affords any consumer is greater than the protection provided by this title.

## § 817. Exemption for State regulation [15 USC 1692o]

The Commission shall by regulation exempt from the requirements of this title any class of debt collection practices within any State if the Commission determines that under the law of that State that class of debt collection practices is subject to requirements substantially similar to those imposed by this title, and that there is adequate provision for enforcement.

## § 818. Effective date [15 USC 1692 note]

This title takes effect upon the expiration of six months after the date of its enactment, but section 809 shall apply only with respect to debts for which the initial attempt to collect occurs after such effective date.

Approved September 20, 1977

## ENDNOTES

1. So in original; however, should read "604(a)(3)."

## LEGISLATIVE HISTORY:

Public Law 95-109 [H.R. 5294]
HOUSE REPORT No. 95-131 (Comm. on Banking, Finance, and Urban Affairs).
SENATE REPORT No. 95-382 (Comm. on Banking, Housing, and Urban Affairs).
CONGRESSIONAL RECORD, Vol. 123 (1977):
Apr. 4, considered and passed House.
Aug. 5, considered and passed Senate, amended.
Sept. 8, House agreed to Senate amendment.
WEEKLY COMPILATION OF PRESIDENTIAL DOCUMENTS, Vol. 13, No. 39:
Sept. 20, Presidential statement.

## AMENDMENTS:

SECTION 621, SUBSECTIONS (b)(3), (b)(4) and (b)(5) were amended to transfer certain administrative enforcement responsibilities, pursuant to Pub. L. 95-473, § 3(b), Oct. 17, 1978. 92 Stat. 166; Pub. L. 95-630, Title V. § 501, November 10, 1978, 92 Stat. 3680; Pub. L. 98-443, § 9(h), Oct. 4, 1984, 98 Stat. 708.

SECTION 803, SUBSECTION (6), defining "debt collector," was amended to repeal the attorney at law exemption at former Section (6)(F) and to redesignate Section 803(6)(G) pursuant to Pub. L. 99-361, July 9, 1986, 100 Stat. 768. For legislative history, *see* H.R. 237, HOUSE REPORT No. 99-405

(Comm. on Banking, Finance and Urban Affairs). CONGRESSIONAL RECORD: Vol. 131 (1985): Dec. 2, considered and passed House. Vol. 132 (1986): June 26, considered and passed Senate. SECTION 807, SUBSECTION (11), was amended to affect when debt collectors must state (a) that they are attempting to collect a debt and (b) that information obtained will be used for that purpose, pursuant to Pub. L. 104-208 § 2305, 110 Stat. 3009 (Sept. 30, 1996).

# Relax - Let Your Hair Down

There once lived a colony of porcupines whose home was nestled in the forest lands near a stream of life for all the creatures to drink. One porcupine observed the creatures on land, air and sea - but he only socialized with porcupines. As he watched other animals play he often longed to be their friend. One day a beautiful butterfly flew circles near the head of this curious porcupine. Ever so excited, he began to speak with this unique visitor his heart longed to meet.

Each day the thrilled porcupine and butterfly would talk with each other; over time they became inseparable. However, once the eager porcupine moved close to the butterfly she would fly away. This angered the porcupine who thought maybe the butterfly was too beautiful to play with him.

Becoming frustrated with the butterfly's willingness to fly away, the agitated porcupine ordered her to leave and never return. He couldn't bear her unique quality any longer. The butterfly was heartbroken at the thought of losing her new friend, she replied, *from the moment we've met I've been flying circles near you in hopes of finding a place to land that would not hurt.*

# Four Eviction

*The last, if not the greatest, of the human freedoms: to choose their own attitude in any given circumstance.*

Bruno Bettelheim

You've been called many names, but unlawful detainer isn't one you should allow. When a landlord decides to evict tenants they do so based one of the following four reasons: 1) you've failed to pay rent as agreed, 2) have caused more problems than what you're worth, 3) occupying the property they want to sell, and 4) illegally occupying the property. Other reasons may exist such as discrimination and repeated complaints about the condition of the property. These accusations occur frequently but your landlord probably will not admit this in court. If you're facing an eviction you have only one worry, where to move. No matter if you're right or wrong, if the landlord wants you out they often will succeed (particularly rentals offered by individual homeowners. Those occupying public housing and apartment rentals may have greater success). For most states it's a straight forward process. Some states have books available in law libraries which help tenants fight an unlawful detainer action. These books contain pleadings (such as motions) to be used by tenants. If you want to fight eviction, become familiar with your state laws, as some landlords use non judicial means for eviction [for cases that do not contain discrimination which are often heard in federal courts]. The more you know in advance can help ease anxieties. Keep in mind, people are asked to leave properties all the time. It's not the end of the world.

The eviction process varies by state and landlord. However, there are federal statutes which protect the rights of tenants. A short list of those rules can be found at the end of this chapter. The *Uniform Residential Landlord and Tenant Act* (adopted by Alaska, Florida, Hawaii, Iowa, Kansas, Kentucky, Montana, Nebraska, New Mexico, Oregon, Rhode Island, South Carolina, Tennessee, and Virginia) and the *Model Residential Landlord-Tenant Code* are two agents used that set the model for state laws.

## I'm In Trouble Now, So What Should I Do?

If you have a case involving retaliation or discrimination, then certainly fight your eviction in federal or superior court. It takes longer to process these types of evictions, plus you have an opprotunity to ensure your rights are evaluated. A knowledgable attonery is helpful, especially if there are additional tenants who are facing similar problems. Those attempting to strech their case into a larger matter should think twice. The unlawful detainer action can be recorded in courthouses (future landlords can research databases to find out if an unlawful detainer action has been filed against you) and it could be added to your credit report. If you're in the process of eviction begin negoting your way out of it. Speak with your landlord's attorney, he/she maybe more reasonable than the landlord. Certianly consider moving. This is the best way out of an horrible situation that only profits the landlord. In most evictions, the tenant is ordered to move, and in some cases forced out by the marshall or sheriff department. Don't allow yourself to be thrown out, move before hand.

Litigatious tenants representing themselves should conduct research at their local law libraies. Although, some states have provided their landlord tenant laws online, the law library may have guides for tenants who are resisting eviction. Standardized motions are provided in these books that can be modified to fit your situation. This can save pro se defendants an enormous amount of reseach time.

## Thoughts on Fighting An Unlawful Detainer Action

Tenants wanting to represent themselves should honestly evaluate their odds of winning an unlawful detainer action, especially if it's warranted such as cases where the rent has not been paid, property has been damaged, and the lease is expired. In these cases it maybe ineffective to *stretch* the laws to bend in your favor. On the other hand, if you have valid reasons why the unlawful detainer action should be resisted, and you can remain in the property after the lawsuit then you are in a good position to fight for your rights.

Some landlords are difficult to deal with, vulgar, rude, and hateful. If this is your experience (as it also had been mine), don't give them anymore of your money – move out of their property. Certainly avoid using the courts as a channel to teach them a lesson. The judge may agree that the person is revolting, but if the landlord is within their rights to evict you, the judge will rule in their favor. I know first hand that this is a difficult pill to swallow, but don't worry because chances are that you'll be able to recover from this experience. In the mean time, find a relative or friend you can rent a room from for a few months until you locate another place to live.

Take whatever money you have and move out the property so you can enjoy your life. Sue for your deposit monies after you've left, or reach an agreement with your landlord that you'll move out right away if they agree to return your deposit the day after you vacate. The courts will look more favorably on your action if you've vacated the property and left it in good condition.

For those with a pet, ask a friend with a back yard to *temporarily* house your animal. Remember to feed and clean up after the pet while you are in transition. Be sure to do this as it can be taxing on a friend to care for your animal.

If you're fighting an eviction you should have good reasons why you're doing it; more than one is best. Consider the person you're trying to convince, a judge. Judges invest money into property so they may tend to be sympathetic to landlords. So have good reasons why you're fighting the eviction. Some property owners can be difficult to communicate with and opposing the action is the only way to secure your two weeks, but consider the stress and energy it will take for the results.

This may not be the information you want to read, but it's from experience. Unless you can bring a discrimination action in federal or superior court or the property owner is a municipality, fighting an eviction can be a waste of energy.

## What Happens During an Eviction

The eviction process varies by state, municipalities, landlords, and contractual agreements. The following is an overview of the eviction process; however this information may not be applicable to your case.

- Landlords will inform the tenant, in writing, to vacate the property by a set date and time. A 3-day (most likely) or 30-day notice to pay rent and/or quit is served on the tenant, the dates vary according to state procedures. This notice is a prelude to the unlawful detainer action. Once you receive this notice you're blood pressure may increase and you may think, *it takes a good 60 to 90 days to get me out – I can save the money or pay.* Many courts give priority to unlawful detainer cases, meaning they are heard within a set period of time. Tenants should use this time to locate another place, or negotiate with your landlord.

- Once the time has elapsed, your landlord will file an unlawful detainer petition against you. Regardless if you're right or wrong, file an answer to their complaint. (In cases of discrimination, for example, the courts may move your case to another authority to protect your civil rights). Some courts may have pre-approved

forms for tenants to complete, while others required the response in the form of a pleading, see samples provided at the end of this chapter. All documents you file in court must be served on opposing parties or their attorney's and a *proof of service* must accompany the complaint. Proofs of service are documents sworn by a person that is not a party to the case stating a person or entity has been sent the document.

> The tenant's answer can be a demur (the defendant/tenant objects to the unlawful detainer action. This arises if there is some material facts tenants object to) or motion to dismiss (tenants file motions to dismiss when they've vacated the property or the unlawful detainer has no merits).
>
> Tenants may also have the right to request a trial as opposed to a hearing before a judge. If the tenant has filed for bankruptcy the court will suspend the hearing until the bankruptcy court takes action.

- The eviction process is on its way. The court will send a notice to your last known address indicating the hearing's date and time. If you chose not to have a trial, a judge will hear your case and decide the outcome. If your landlord violated any laws, the case can be dismissed or the judge can grant the landlord time to correct the error(s). Remember, service is important. You must be served according to your state laws. States may not require personal service, meaning service is good even if it's sent in the mail or posted on the door.

> Subsidized housing evictions strictly follow eviction laws to avoid further tenant lawsuits, while private owners may avoid adhering to laws, although this can seriously harm their case. In cases where there is rent

control and city-managed property, tenants typically have more attention paid to their rights.

## Common Tenant Responses To An Unlawful Detainer Action

Tenants have several options available for responding to an unlawful detainer action. The following are definitions of responses (typically motions filed on legal pleading format, see samples of pleadings at the end of the *Bankruptcy* chapter) commonly filed by tenants. With each response tenants must file a proof of service; this informs the court that all parties have been notified. Because each state's laws vary, it's wise for tenants to conform their motions to state laws.

### Demurrer

A type of motion where the defendant asserts that a response is unnecessary due to a legal defect in the complaint.

### Motion to Strike

This motion is similar to a demurrer but is used to request the court to strike (void) an answer due to a defect within it.

### Motion to Quash

A request for the court to quash (void) service of the summons and complaint. The motion is usually made on the grounds that the litigant is not under the jurisdiction of the court.

### Answer

A response from the defendant setting forth the grounds of the defense to the allegations contained within the complaint or the response from the plaintiff setting forth the grounds of the defense to the allegations contained within the cross-complaint.

### General Denial

A response from the defendant denying all allegations contained within the complaint or the response from the plaintiff denying all allegations within the cross-complaint.

In addition to responses to unlawful detainer actions, tenants can also file complaints against landlords for several reasons including forcible entry, harassment, and retaliation to name a few. Tenants wanting to pursue litigation against landlords, may find the local law library a useful source to locating sample motions.

## Filing Bankruptcy to Stop an Eviction

Bankruptcy will *temporarily* halt an eviction. This can buy a tenant more time to locate another home. Your landlord will either beg you to move or most likely, file a motion for relief from the automatic stay (*for more information see chapter one Bankruptcy*) to continue with the eviction. This is almost always granted to landlords who have already commenced with an eviction.

## Representing Yourself

As with any occasion you must appear before the courts, your appearance should be neat and professional. Eviction hearings are fairly brief, so outline your points and present documentation, which supports your statements. Remember to stay focused on your case and avoid succumbing to the emotional stress. Don't be swayed by exaggerations from opposing counsel, as this is designed to distract your attention. If you're prone to anxiety, inhale and exhale large breaths before you speak, to help remain calm. Plenty of books on representing yourself in court are available for those needing additional pointers.

## Hiring An Attorney

Hiring an attorney can be effective if your landlord has severely breached your lease agreement or has grossly violated the law. Be careful, some attorneys may need immediate cash, so they're not interested in the best outcome for their clients. Before making your selection carefully interview attorneys. Locate legal counsel whose focus is real estate law. You may also be able to utilize the services of a knowledgeable paralegal whose practice is dedicated to real estate law.

When you meet with your attorney bring all documentation that supports your claim and an outline of the events that led to the unlawful detainer action. A knowledgeable attorney will keep you informed of legal options, and can possibly reach an arrangement with your landlord to avoid further legal actions.

*The Best Lawyers In America* by Naifeh, Steven, & White. © 2003. Woodward/White Inc. $200.00 (USD).
*This is an expensive book, but it could be worth the costs if you desperately need to find reputable legal consul. I discovered this two volume set at a bookstore. Someone apparently ordered the guide and did not pick it up. The sales staff put them on the self. I've since purchased the books.*

The American Bar Association
www.abanet.org

## Resources for Tenants

The best resource for tenants is your local law library. You can find sample forms that comply with your state laws in addition to useful information.

*Every Tenant's Legal Guide.* By Janet Portman & Marcia Stewart. (c) 2003. Nolo Press. $29.95.
*This book has good ideas and information.*

www.law.cornell.edu/topics/landlord_tenant.html

www.illioniselegalaid.org

# Federal Statutes Protecting The Rights of Tenants

TITLE 42 > CHAPTER 45 > SUBCHAPTER II >TITLE 42 - THE PUBLIC HEALTH AND WELFARE, CHAPTER 45 - FAIR HOUSING

Sec. 1982. - Property rights of citizens

All citizens of the United States shall have the same right, in every State and Territory, as is enjoyed by white citizens thereof to inherit, purchase, lease, sell, hold, and convey real and personal property

Sec. 3604. - Discrimination in the sale or rental of housing and other prohibited practices

As made applicable by section 3603 of this title and except as exempted by sections 3603(b) and 3607 of this title, it shall be unlawful -

(a)

To refuse to sell or rent after the making of a bona fide offer, or to refuse to negotiate for the sale or rental of, or otherwise make unavailable or deny, a dwelling to any person because of race, color, religion, sex, familial status, or national origin.

(b)

To discriminate against any person in the terms, conditions, or privileges of sale or rental of a dwelling, or in the provision of services or facilities in connection therewith, because of race, color, religion, sex, familial status, or national origin.

(c)

To make, print, or publish, or cause to be made, printed, or published any notice, statement, or advertisement, with respect to the sale or rental of a dwelling that indicates any preference, limitation, or discrimination based on race, color, religion, sex, handicap, familial status, or national origin, or an intention to make any such preference, limitation, or discrimination.

(d)

To represent to any person because of race, color, religion, sex, handicap, familial status, or national origin that any dwelling is not available for inspection, sale, or rental when such dwelling is in fact so available.

(e)

For profit, to induce or attempt to induce any person to sell or rent any dwelling by representations regarding the entry or prospective entry into the neighborhood of a person or persons of a particular race, color, religion, sex, handicap, familial status, or national origin.

(f)

(1)

To discriminate in the sale or rental, or to otherwise make unavailable or deny, a dwelling to any buyer or renter because of a handicap of -

(A)

that buyer or renter, [1]

(B)

a person residing in or intending to reside in that dwelling after it is so sold, rented, or made available; or

(C)

any person associated with that buyer or renter.

(2)

To discriminate against any person in the terms, conditions, or privileges of sale or rental of a dwelling, or in the provision of services or facilities in connection with such dwelling, because of a handicap of -

(A)

that person; or

(B)

a person residing in or intending to reside in that dwelling after it is so sold, rented, or made available; or

(C)

any person associated with that person.

(3)

For purposes of this subsection, discrimination includes -

(A)

a refusal to permit, at the expense of the handicapped person, reasonable modifications of existing premises occupied or to be occupied by such person if such modifications maybe necessary to afford such person full enjoyment of the premises except that, in the case of a rental, the landlord may where it is reasonable to do so condition permission for a modification on the renter agreeing to restore the interior of the premises to the condition that existed before the modification, reasonable wear and tear excepted. [2]

(B)

a refusal to make reasonable accommodations in rules, policies, practices, or services, when such accommodations maybe necessary to afford such person equal opportunity to use and enjoy a dwelling; or

(C)

in connection with the design and construction of covered multifamily dwellings for first occupancy after the date that is 30 months after September 13, 1988, a failure to design and construct those dwellings in such a manner that -

(i)

the public use and common use portions of such dwellings are readily accessible to and usable by handicapped persons;

(ii)

all the doors designed to allow passage into and within all premises within such dwellings are sufficiently wide to allow passage by handicapped persons in wheelchairs; and

(iii)

all premises within such dwellings contain the following features of adaptive design:

(I)

an accessible route into and through the dwelling;

(II)

light switches, electrical outlets, thermostats, and other environmental controls in accessible locations;

(III)

reinforcements in bathroom walls to allow later installation of grab bars; and

(IV)

usable kitchens and bathrooms such that an individual in a wheelchair can maneuver about the space.

(4)

Compliance with the appropriate requirements of the American National Standard for buildings and facilities providing accessibility and usability for physically handicapped people (commonly cited as "ANSI A117.1") suffices to satisfy the requirements of paragraph (3)(C)(iii).

(5)

(A)

If a State or unit of general local government has incorporated into its laws the requirements set forth in paragraph (3)(C), compliance with such laws shall be deemed to satisfy the requirements of that paragraph.

(B)

A State or unit of general local government may review and approve newly constructed covered multifamily dwellings for the purpose of making determinations as to whether the design and construction requirements of paragraph (3)(C) are met.

(C)

The Secretary shall encourage, but may not require, States and units of local government to include in their existing procedures for the review and approval of newly constructed covered multifamily dwellings, determinations as to whether the design and construction of such dwellings are consistent with paragraph (3)(C), and shall provide technical assistance to States and units of local government and other persons to implement the requirements of paragraph (3)(C).

(D)

Nothing in this subchapter shall be construed to require the Secretary to review or approve the plans, designs or construction of all covered multifamily dwellings, to determine whether the design and construction of such dwellings are consistent with the requirements of paragraph 3(C).

(6)

(A)

Nothing in paragraph (5) shall be construed to affect the authority and responsibility of the Secretary or a State or local public agency certified pursuant to section 3610(f)(3) of this title to receive and process complaints or otherwise engage in enforcement activities under this subchapter.

(B)

Determinations by a State or a unit of general local government under paragraphs (5)(A) and (B) shall not be conclusive in enforcement proceedings under this subchapter.

(7)

As used in this subsection, the term "covered multifamily dwellings" means -

(A)

buildings consisting of 4 or more units if such buildings have one or more elevators; and

(B)

ground floor units in other buildings consisting of 4 or more units.

(8)

Nothing in this subchapter shall be construed to invalidate or limit any law of a State or political subdivision of a State, or other jurisdiction in which this subchapter shall be effective, that requires dwellings to be designed and constructed in a manner that affords handicapped persons greater access than is required by this subchapter.

(9)

Nothing in this subsection requires that a dwelling be made available to an individual whose tenancy would constitute a direct threat to the health or safety of other individuals or whose tenancy would result in substantial physical damage to the property of others

Sec. 3605. - Discrimination in residential real estate-related transactions

(a) In general

It shall be unlawful for any person or other entity whose business includes engaging in residential real estate-related transactions to discriminate against any person in making available such a transaction, or in the terms or conditions of such a transaction, because of race, color, religion, sex, handicap, familial status, or national origin.

(b) "Residential real estate-related transaction" defined

As used in this section, the term "residential real estate-related transaction" means any of the following:

(1)

The making or purchasing of loans or providing other financial assistance -

(A)

for purchasing, constructing, improving, repairing, or maintaining a dwelling; or

(B)

secured by residential real estate.

(2)

The selling, brokering, or appraising of residential real property.

(c) Appraisal exemption

Nothing in this subchapter prohibits a person engaged in the business of furnishing appraisals of real property to take into consideration factors other than race, color, religion, national origin, sex, handicap, or familial status

Sec. 3631. - Violations; penalties

Whoever, whether or not acting under color of law, by force or threat of force willfully injuries, intimidates or interferes with, or attempts to injure, intimidate or interfere with -

(a)

any person because of his race, color, religion, sex, handicap (as such term is defined in section 3602 of this title), familial status (as such term is defined in section 3602 of this title), or national origin and because he is or has been selling, purchasing, renting, financing, occupying, or contracting or negotiating for the sale, purchase, rental, financing or occupation of any dwelling, or applying for or participating in any service, organization, or facility relating to the business of selling or renting dwellings; or

(b)

any person because he is or has been, or in order to intimidate such person or any other person or any class of persons from -

(1)

participating, without discrimination on account of race, color, religion, sex, handicap (as such term is defined in section 3602 of this title), familial status (as such term is defined in section 3602 of this title), or national origin, in any of the activities, services, organizations or facilities described in subsection (a) of this section; or

(2)affording another person or class of persons opportunity or protection so to participate; or

(c) Carefully consider your options. If the lender has filed a *deed in lieu of foreclosure* you only have a short amount of time to act, less than 20 days.

any citizen because he is or has been, or in order to discourage such citizen or any other citizen from lawfully aiding or encouraging other persons to participate, without discrimination on account of race, color, religion, sex, handicap (as such term is defined in section 3602 of this title), familial status (as such term is defined in section 3602 of this title), or national origin, in any of the activities, services, organizations or facilities described in subsection (a) of this section, or participating lawfully in speech or peaceful assembly opposing any denial of the opportunity to so participate - shall be fined under title 18 or imprisoned not more than one year, or both; and if bodily injury results from the acts committed in violation of this section or if such acts include the use, attempted use, or threatened use of a dangerous weapon, explosives, or fire shall be fined under title 18 or imprisoned not more than ten years, or both; and if death results from the acts committed in violation of this section or if such acts include kidnapping or an attempt to kidnap, aggravated sexual abuse or an attempt to commit aggravated sexual abuse, or an attempt to kill, shall be fined under title 18 or imprisoned for any term of years or for life, or both.

| ATTORNEY OR PARTY WITHOUT ATTORNEY *(Name and Address)*: | TELEPHONE NO.: | FOR COURT USE ONLY |
|---|---|---|
| ATTORNEY FOR *(Name)*: | | |

NAME OF COURT:
STREET ADDRESS:
MAILING ADDRESS:
CITY AND ZIP CODE:
BRANCH NAME:

PLAINTIFF:

DEFENDANT:

| **ANSWER—Unlawful Detainer** | CASE NUMBER: |
|---|---|

1. Defendant *(names)*:

answers the complaint as follows:

2. *Check ONLY ONE of the next two boxes:*
   a. ☐ Defendant generally denies each statement of the complaint. *(Do not check this box if the complaint demands more than $1,000).*
   b. ☐ Defendant admits that all of the statements of the complaint are true EXCEPT
      (1) Defendant claims the following statements of the complaint are false *(use paragraph numbers from the complaint or explain)*:

      ☐ Continued on Attachment 2b(1).
      (2) Defendant has no information or belief that the following statements of the complaint are true, so defendant denies them *(use paragraph numbers from the complaint or explain)*:

      ☐ Continued on Attachment 2b(2).

3. AFFIRMATIVE DEFENSES   *(NOTE: For each box checked, you must state brief facts to support it in the space provided at the top of page two (item 3j).)*
   a. ☐ *(nonpayment of rent only)* Plaintiff has breached the warranty to provide habitable premises.
   b. ☐ *(nonpayment of rent only)* Defendant made needed repairs and properly deducted the cost from the rent, and plaintiff did not give proper credit.
   c. ☐ *(nonpayment of rent only)* On *(date)*:                           , before the notice to pay or quit expired, defendant offered the rent due but plaintiff would not accept it.
   d. ☐ Plaintiff waived, changed, or canceled the notice to quit.
   e. ☐ Plaintiff served defendant with the notice to quit or filed the complaint to retaliate against defendant.
   f. ☐ By serving defendant with the notice to quit or filing the complaint, plaintiff is arbitrarily discriminating against the defendant in violation of the Constitution or laws of the United States or California.
   g. ☐ Plaintiff's demand for possession violates the local rent control or eviction control ordinance of *(city or county, title of ordinance, and date of passage)*:

      *(Also, briefly state the facts showing violation of the ordinance in item 3j.)*
   h. ☐ Plaintiff accepted rent from defendant to cover a period of time after the date the notice to quit expired.
   i. ☐ Other affirmative defenses are stated in item 3j.

(Continued on reverse)

Form Approved by the
Judicial Council of California
982.1(95) [Rev. January 1, 1997]

**ANSWER—Unlawful Detainer**  

WEST GROUP
Official Publisher

Civil Code, § 1940 et seq.;
Code of Civil Procedure, § 425.12

PLAINTIFF (Name):

DEFENDANT (Name):

CASE NUMBER:

3. AFFIRMATIVE DEFENSES (cont'd)
j. Facts supporting affirmative defenses checked above (identify each item separately by its letter from page one):

(1) ☐ All the facts are stated in Attachment 3j.    (2) ☐ Facts are continued in Attachment 3j.

4. OTHER STATEMENTS
a. ☐ Defendant vacated the premises on (date):
b. ☐ The fair rental value of the premises alleged in the complaint is excessive (explain):

c. ☐ Other (specify):

5. DEFENDANT REQUESTS
a. that plaintiff take nothing requested in the complaint.
b. costs incurred in this proceeding.
c. ☐ reasonable attorney fees.
d. ☐ that plaintiff be ordered to (1) make repairs and correct the conditions that constitute a breach of the warranty to provide habitable premises and (2) reduce the monthly rent to a reasonable rental value until the conditions are corrected.
e. ☐ other (specify):

6. ☐ Number of pages attached (specify):

**UNLAWFUL DETAINER ASSISTANT (Business and Professions Code sections 6400-6415)**
7. (Must be completed in all cases) An unlawful detainer assistant ☐ did not ☐ did for compensation give advice or assistance with this form. (If defendant has received any help or advice for pay from an unlawful detainer assistant, state):
a. Assistant's name:                                     b. Telephone No.:
c. Street address, city, and ZIP:
d. County of registration:          e. Registration No.:          f. Expires on (date):

▶

_____          _____
(TYPE OR PRINT NAME)                                          (SIGNATURE OF DEFENDANT OR ATTORNEY)

▶

_____          _____
(TYPE OR PRINT NAME)                                          (SIGNATURE OF DEFENDANT OR ATTORNEY)

(Each defendant for whom this answer is filed must be named in item 1 and must sign this answer unless his or her attorney signs.)

**VERIFICATION**
(Use a different verification form if the verification is by an attorney or for a corporation or partnership.)
I am the defendant in this proceeding and have read this answer. I declare under penalty of perjury under the laws of the State of California that the foregoing is true and correct.
Date:

▶

_____          _____
(TYPE OR PRINT NAME)                                          (SIGNATURE OF DEFENDANT)

982.1(95) [Rev. January 1, 1997]
Martin Dean's Essential Forms ™                    **ANSWER - Unlawful Detainer**                    Page two

## Pick And Choose Your Battles

Don't go crazy fighting every issue and injustice, although you maybe right in each situation. Some insignificant battles can easily deter you from pursuing the big picture. Keep your objective in mind and fight to make that happen.

# Exessive Debts

*Call the roll in your memory of conspicuously successful
business giants and... you will be struck by the fact that
almost every one of them encountered inordinate difficulties
sufficient to crush all but the gamest spirits. Edison went
hungry many times before he became famous.*

B.C. Forbes

We all may have seen television programs that show famous stars lounging seaside at exclusive resorts in exotic places. When the announcer says the room cost $2,500 per night we balk at the excessive materialism yet we image ourselves jubilantly standing first in the buffet line. Even as a child I faithfully watched *Lifestyles of the Rich and Famous*, it's probably where I got my great sense of style. I think these types of shows contribute to our desire to accumulate debts; it's certainly easier to blame them. If we're not taking luxurious vacations, we're enjoying fine clothes, handbags and shoes; then we're certainly living in a well furnished home with all the latest electronics. There's one word that enables us to afford those luxuries and its credit.

Borrowing money is a necessity in today's economy. Whether the money is used to purchase a house, buy a car or pay college tuition chances are it's being done with someone else's money. Advantageous banks want to lend money to people who have a good track record with paying their bills. Those with large amounts of debts not being paid on time are headed straight for financial disaster. Before the storm erupts take control by eliminating credit cards and unnecessary debts. This chapter includes information on debt reduction, bill consolidation loans, as well as useful options for those overwhelmed with bills.

## I'm In Trouble Now, So What Should I Do?

You're probably feeling that you're 100 miles past frustration. If you must, file for chapter 7 bankruptcy. This can rid of you mounting credit card and medical bills. Those who have filed for bankruptcy in the past maybe eligible to reopen their case to include new charges; however first consult with a knowledgeable attorney or paralegal before attempting this on your own. This is also a good threat to creditors who refuse to make payment arrangements. When bankruptcy is not an option, make arrangements with creditors.

Take a deep breath. I know that most people have tried this step first, but read the information in this chapter and develop creative ways to make win/win situations for you and the creditor.

Consider solutions that make the creditor representative look good and eases your frustration. Take it one step at a time. Don't' attempt to call all your creditors on the same day, unless you have built yourself up for the challenge [without using stimulants]. Remember not to become excited; if the conversation is not going well speak with a manager, and their manager; if necessary ask for the name of the president of the company. Whatever you do, press forward. Should the conversations become hostile – hang up the telephone. They'll spend the next few minutes documenting how indifferent you are. Use this to your advantage. When you speak with the next person be short and to the point. Explain why you were upset and what they can do, within their power, to make it better. Always document the conversation should a lawsuit arise you'll have proof that you tried.

## Managing Debts

While we're focusing on finding money to pay our debts we often ignore bills as if the

creditor understands we're working hard to obtain the money to pay. The representatives at your creditor's office are interested in keeping their jobs. Finding viable solutions for you and creditors is easy with communication; he/she can keep their jobs and you can repay your debt.

You can do this! Don't be intimidated by their threatening letters, they're screaming to get your attention – and now they've gotten one hundred percent of it. Lists of hints below offer a starting point for negotiations with your creditors.

- Call the credit card company to request a reduction in finance charges and annual fees. In a recessed economy credit card companies are interested in keeping you as a customer.

- Explain problems that prevent you from making payments. Your lender may offer a lower monthly payment or even freeze payments if the problem is temporary.

- Call your creditors before they call you. This helps to keep you in charge. When you set dates and times to pay, work extra hard to keep your word. If your paycheck didn't arrive on time, call the lender and inform them of the new date and time they can expect payment.

## Hints for Financial Planning

We all want to know where the financial planners are when the air conditioning goes out in 120⁰ weather and the heating unit stops working during a blizzard. Always take necessary measures to ensure continual safety and comfort before disaster occurs. However, unforeseeable problems always arise at the worst times in our lives. It's key to move past the emergency and refocus on achieving financial stability after the immediate need has been satisfied. When we're rushed to take action we overspend and ignore potential options. Circumstances will always occur and you'll make it through those experiences as you have done so in the past: take time to breath and remember to trust yourself.

The hints below have been complied to assist those wanting to break free of debt cycles to ensure stability in the future. Personalize these options to suit your ability and needs.

- Professional financial planners insist that debtors create a budget to find out exactly where the money is being spent. It doesn't take months of record keeping within four weeks one can tell what expenses deplete the budget. For those with little motivation for creating a budget, try keeping your checkbook up to date for 3 months. Soon you'll be able to detect a spending pattern.

- Deposit at least 10% of your income into a savings account. In the event of an unforeseen emergency one can draw upon savings as a cushion.

- Create separate accounts for holiday spending, birthday gifts, and weddings. Plan ahead, even if your skip one year of gift giving to ensure you're on track for the following year.

- Avoid using credit cards. Keep one card and cut up the others. Call creditors immediately to close the extra accounts. If your credit is good, transfer the balances to a low interest credit card, *see Appendix B*.

- Withdraw a certain percentage of your income, in cash, for day to daily purchases.

- Impulsive shoppers should consider putting items on layaway or hold if the purchases exceed their weekly budget. Some stores will hold items if you pay a portion up front and promise to pay the remaining balance within 5 days. This

works if additional purchases that exceed the new weeks budget are not made.

- For those who purchase expensive items as therapy all the while living pay check to pay check, consider replacing your appetite for luxury with physical fitness or volunteering. Walking, bicycling, and jogging can be enjoyed at little expense, if any, and it's a great outlet to reliving stress.

## Robbing Peter to Pay Paul

Those of us who value shelter know the fear of losing a home or being evicted causes the green light of desperation to shine brightly in our eyes. This fright has birthed familiar phrases such as *desperate times call for desperate measures* and, a family favorite of mine, *robbing Peter to Pay Paul*. Before you embark on doing almost anything to keep your property take time to rationally think, research the long term effects of your options, and relax to generate new thoughts. Vehicle pawn shops, advance paycheck centers, and robbing quick marts should not be the solution to getting immediate cash, try building from the following ideas:

- Your creditors want money from you. They will work with you or lose their opportunity to receive the most return for their loan. **TALK** with your lender. If all else has failed, and you haven't been able to meet the deadlines then it's certainly desperate times.

- If you have an extra bedroom and bathroom, take on a roommate. Singles, typically of the same sex, can share a two bedroom place with one bathroom. Renters will pay a deposit plus first month's rent. The extra monthly cash can make save your home. This is ideal for those living near colleges.

- Create a job for yourself. Most people overwhelmed with work and caring for children desperately need day to day services done well at low costs. In a nut shell, offer to do a service that will ease another's life at inexpensive yet competitive rates. The following are a few ideas:

- **Mow neighbor's lawns** for an inexpensive rate (or offer more services than their current gardener).

- **Walk and clean up after neighbor's dogs.** A service dedicated to cleaning up after a dog is a fabulous idea – I will pay good money for this person.

- **Paint the trim around homes**. Most people can't afford new house paint; a fresh coat of paint around the trim improves a home's look. Realtors can be a good lead for those looking for these types of jobs as people selling their homes want to invest the least amount of money into their current property.

- **Have a garage sale**. *One person's trash is another person's treasure.* You'll be amazed at the amount of money garage sales generate especially if you encourage neighbors to participate, as neighborhood sales attract more buyers.

- **Create an employment agency**. You can be the first employee. Most business supply stores have ready made brochures that can be distributed to potential clients. You'll learn of job openings and can contract yourself to do the work or hire others to work on the jobs. It takes about one week to setup a home business and about one day to get a business license (provided you own all the necessary equipment).

- Those living in major cities can benefit from the high demanding lifestyles of others by becoming a **personal servant**. Create a business that delivers food, groceries, prescriptions as well as other special requests. Your client can call ahead to pay for the item and you'll deliver to them on time. Paste flyers around or hand them to bell man. This is an exceptional service for travelers staying at hotels who require certain items that are not supplied by the hotel.

- Inquire with utility and telephone companies about rate reduction programs that lower monthly payments. Utility and telephone companies have services for those considered low income to reduce monthly payments.

- Obtain groceries from churches or charitable organizations to save money for more significant bills.

- Typically when times are especially tough credit card payments are the last to be made. Those concerned with paying creditors can pay the balances off the lowest card first. Once that card is paid in full, begin paying additional money to the next card until all credit cards are paid in full. For example, if you owe $200 on one card and $3,000 on another card, pay the $200 card then close the account. Then apply the extra money previously used to pay the $200 card to the monthly payment of the $3,000 card.

- If you own a home with equity you may try obtaining a home equity loan to pay off debts or sale the home. It maybe difficult, but not impossible, to secure a home equity loan. After the loan is approved pay off your debts and rid yourself of credit cards. Home owners can find relief by eliminating the burden of maintaining a home and rooming with others who may need monthly rent.

## Controlling Creditors and Collection Agencies

When you're tired of pestering questions that have nothing to do with the fact that you can't pay, then it's time to take control of collection calls.

Everyone with credit should become familiar with the Fair Debt Collection Practices Act (*see chapter four*). This act protects debtors from creditor harassment. If problems have advanced to the point where collection agencies do the following:

- Call your office, if your employer objects (although your state's laws may protect your from collection calls that you do not agree to).
- Call your home before 8 a.m. or after 9 p.m.
- Address you in an abusive manner
- Embarrass you in front of others
- Call family or friends in an attempt to collect your debt
- Threaten criminal action without cause.
- Threaten to ruin your reputation if you don't pay
- Advertising that you owe a debt
- Inaccurately represent the amount you owe.

- Refuse to speak with your attorney. Creditor/collection agencies must speak with your attorney, and not you, if you have retained one.

Consumers can sue creditors and collection agencies for harassment and invasion of privacy as well as the physical and mental affects this causes. If collection calls have escalated beyond your ability to respond, contact a knowledgeable attorney whose practice is creditor-debtor rights.

Contact the Federal Trade Commission, the Better Business Bureau (*see Appendix E*), or your local attorney generals office.

## Wage Garnishments

Wage garnishments can prevent people from paying their debts. A garnishment occurs when a judgment has been entered for the defendant to pay a set amount of money. Creditors may attempt to collect funds by filing lawsuits against debtors. However, if garnishments are due to spousal and/or child support it is difficult to reverse. Debtors may have greater success combating wage garnishments from creditors.

Those awarded judgments can garnish bank accounts as well as income. To lift wage garnishments, debtors can file a form called *Notice of Motion for Wage Deduction Exemption Hearing* in the state and county where the judgment was awarded. The clerk's office can schedule a hearing for the motion. A proof of service must be filed showing that all parties have been served. If you have exempted wages, this proof must be presented before the court.

This maybe a difficult task if you earn a significant amount of money or the garnishments are due to spousal and/or child support as courts are more sympathetic to family support. For additional information on judgments, see *Judgments later in this chapter.* Garnishments are up to 15% of wages. Public benefits such as social security, welfare, and unemployment compensation are exempted from garnishment.

## Filing For Bankruptcy To Eliminate Debts

If your debts are mostly unsecured, such as credit cards and medical bills for example, then Chapter 7 bankruptcy maybe the best relief. For more information on Chapter 7 and 13 bankruptcies *see chapter one Bankruptcy.*

## Judgments

Judgments are court orders granting the plaintiff monetary relief. A judgment can only be entered after a lawsuit has been filed in court. If you are unemployed and have no assets, judgments are unenforceable. But for most working people unpaid judgments can cause a financial strain as the plaintiff is able to garnish wages and bank accounts. The courts will also accrue interest on unpaid judgments which will increase the size of the award.

Arrange to make payment arrangements over a period of time, if you have a judgment

against you. Wages cannot be garnished if payment arrangements are kept.

Those wanting to fight the validity of judgment should consult with a knowledgeable attorney for further information. A motion to vacate judgment can be filed, for some courts it must be filed within six months of the date the judgment was entered, and a new court date is set.

## Resources

*Your Rights When You Owe Too Much*, by Gudran Maria Nickel. (c) 2001. Sphinx Publishing. $16.95.

*You Don't Need A Layer*, by James M. Kramon, Esq. (c) 2002. Workman Publishing Co. Inc. $14.95.
*This book has good general information, samples, and forms. The author includes sample letters for collection companies and landlords.*

*Managing To Be Wealthy: Putting Your Financial Plan and Planner to Work For You*, by John E. Sestina © 2000. Dearborn Financial. $19.95.

# Let Go

Once upon a time in a far away place lived a young content bird. Surrounded by books, his favorite interest, this bird did not venture far outside of his home. Vital needs such as food and water were conveniently located next to him. Having all that he required the bird felt at peace. Rain or shine, he remained at home, which was an old comfortable abandoned cottage filled with all the books he thought he'll ever need. His joys, sadness, love affairs, and hates were all felt through reading.

One day a sick bird stumbled into his house. Studying his visitor closely he realized it was a young female who was sporadically breathing. The bird quickly researched treatments in medical books and practice different therapies. It took months to restore her health, but he patiently cared for his defenseless visitor. As she vulnerably lay in the bed, she watched the bird read books morning, noon, and night in between hours spent caring for her. One morning she spoke, *you have saved my life and now I want to free yours. Will you fly away with me?*

The studious bird didn't know how to reply. He looked around his home and noticed all the material he had yet to read. He thought to himself, how could I leave? – There are people I've yet to read about, experiences I've yet to know. Pacing in circles to sort out his turmoil he thought there's no way I can leave, but I find it hard to resist her kindness, could she truly be that compassionate?. At last he sighed. In a state of emotional exhaustion he replied, *I have yet to read about how to fly.*

# Chapter Six: Selling Possessions

*Whatever course you decide upon, there is always someone*
*to tell you that you are wrong. There are always difficulties*
*arising which tempt you to believe that your critics are right.*
*To map out a course of action and follow it to an end*
*requires…courage.*

Ralph Waldo Emerson

Selling your home, car, and possessions is an excellent decision to acquire cash and reduce debts. Items hiding in your garage could be of significant use to others. Share the wealth by selling unutilized belongings. The weeks my former home was in escrow, I held several garage sales; at first I reluctantly did so, but it worked out well. Items I thought would never sale, sold in a matter of minutes. By coupling with my neighbor I was able to sale much more.

Most of the information included in this chapter I experienced first hand, particularly selling residential property without using a real-estate agent. This is my favorite topic, as I have experienced the worst real-estate agents you can image. I found it hard to justify paying a 6 percent commission to a person I just met after spending my income to pay the mortgage note, insurance, and taxes over a period of years. Buyers typically locate an area they desire then attempt to purchase available property. You can save thousands of dollars by directing interested buyers to your home with a few signs.

## I'm In Trouble Now, So What Should I Do?

Depending on the asset's value, selling could be the best solution to rid yourself of financial debts. By letting go of objects, even those you once believed you could never part with; your life *somehow* becomes simpler. The burden of caring for extra things is released and you have passage to a new life.

It shouldn't take a lot of money to sell something. Simply place large print handmade signs around your neighborhood or at major intersections directing buyers to the sale.

Using Internet auction sites, such as eBay® is an excellent method for you to offload items. Follow the tips in this section and forge ahead.

Once you've committed to letting go, don't talk yourself out of it. Don't wait for the perfect day either, this is the best day to move forward.

## Selling Your Home

If you're considering selling your home to obtain cash and/or eliminate debts – Fantastic! It could be a significant amount of money waiting to finance your new life.

During my financial crises, I decided to sell many possessions, including my home to pay outstanding debts. I decided that I could reduce the price of my home to increase the chances of locating a buyer, since I ultimately sold the home without using a real-estate agent. I must confess that twice I enlisted the assistance of *ineffective* agents. Whether you choose to use an agent or not, your home could be your escape out of financial stress.

## Utilizing Real-Estate Agents

Clearly I advocate for home owners to sell their property without an agent. However, it doesn't mean that all real-estate agents are ineffective. If your lifestyle is busy and you need someone to run errands, schedule appointments, and remind you to deliver documents on time, then an agent can be the best solution.

In fact, some agents diligently work to locate the right buyer for your home, handle small tasks that can consume your day, refer you to specialists to make necessary repairs, and thoroughly review all documentation to ensure your interests are protected.

> An alternative to hiring an agent is paying a licensed agent/broker a consultation fee for preparing paperwork and negotiations with your buyer. Some real-estate attorney's will also perform this duty.

The following tips are useful if you have decided to enlist the assistance of a real-estate agent:

- Contact small realty companies first. Small firms may offer reduced rates on their commissions.

- Contact your state real-estate licensing board. Your state may have a web site where consumers can search if a real-estate license is valid (*see sample reports at the end of this section of a real-estate agent I researched who attempted to sell my home*).

- Locate an agent that you know and trust. This is one exception where referrals may not work. Another's experience with an agent may not be what you need. Find someone who can momentarily put their objectives aside to focus on effectively representing your best interest.

---

- Locate a licensed agent/broker who will act with the utmost respect of your needs.

- Your agreement with the realty company should be valid for no more than 30 days. Extend the contract if it takes longer to sell the property, provided that you are pleased with their service.

- The golden rule for consumers, **READ EVERYTHING YOU SIGN**. Avoid signing documents the moment their handed to you. Take, at least, 24 hours to read agreements. Consider paying an attorney to review agreements before you sign them, this could save you thousands of dollars later.

## Selling Your Home Without An Agent

Those residing in areas where existing homes are in demand will find it easier to sell your home. When potential buyers search the neighborhood, your *For Sale By Owner Signs* should be in sight at all major corners. I purchased the signs with arrows and had them point in the direction of my house.

Success in selling your home also depends on the neighborhood, accessibility of the home (homes not located in remote locations), and ability of the homeowner to accommodate potential buyers. A significant amount of a FSBO's (pronounced fizz-bo's – means For Sale By Owner) time is invested into selling the property. Instead of arguing with your agent to perform certain duties, you are solely responsible for completing tasks.

The most significant tip I can offer to sell your home without an agent is to try locating buyers who have purchased property in the past. An experienced buyer will offer less headache, and are not as time consuming as first time buyers who often want a used home in brand new condition for free, and who may refuse to understand why you will not make certain repairs. Stand your ground. If the repairs are reasonable, then meet the buyer half way on the costs or offer them a credit for the repairs. Experienced home buyers know what to expect and how hard to push.

> If you live away from the property, pay a responsible neighbor or family member to check on the property and escort potential buyers.

The following tips I offer to intelligent cost conscience courageous people who sell their homes themselves:

- Purchase several *For Sale By Owner* signs, especially those with the arrows, from a hardware store. Place them near other homes on the market listed by realty companies. Direct potential buyers to your home using the arrows. Don't miss the opportunity to post the signs during open houses. Beware, real-estate agents are treacherous, I had many of my signs confiscated when I posted them near their client's property. Make friends with your neighbors; should they identify the culprit demand your money for the signs. You may also choose to purchase large white cardboard and write For Sale By Owner with arrows directing potential buyers – it's certainly less expensive than purchasing signs.

- Reduce the price of your home by half the commission you would have paid a real-estate agent. Sellers can attract home buyers by offering a lower price than the current market. For example, if homes in your area sell for $300,000, a real-estate's commission will be $18,000 (this number does not include closing fees). Sellers can reduce their selling price by $9,000 (the new sales price will be $291,000) to attract more buyers.

- Have forms, such as offer agreements, ready in case your potential home buyer doesn't have any.

- Choose an escrow agency (also referred to as fiduciary agent) that doesn't discriminate against FSBOs. The escrow agent should provide necessary forms and keep you apprised of key dates (such as inspections, termite information, etc.). Don't be afraid, call around to locate the best escrow company for your needs.

- Don't waste your time showing your home to nosy neighbors and those wanting to buy your furniture. Take their names and numbers for contacting at the time of the moving sale.

- Conceal all of your valuables and other objects that can disappear.

- Bake cookies, pies, or other deserts that provide a soothing aroma. Avoid lighting incense, potpourri pots or pungent candles as this can cause allergies to erupt. You don't want perspective buyers to become ill while touring your home.

- Place fresh flowers in main rooms to add a feeling of warmth. Those concerned with allergies, can use artificial flowers.

- On sunny breezy days open windows, shades and curtains. If the home is being shown during winter months omit opening the windows, rather light the fireplace to add a cozy feeling.

- Arrange furniture so that it does not obstruct passage to an area. Moving it against the wall creates a spacious feeling.

- Clean your home. Having a spotless home isn't required, but moving papers and nick-knacks to boxes or closets allows the buyer to see the shape of the rooms. The bathrooms and kitchen should be the cleanest as most women inspect these areas.

- Be available to show your house, especially on the weekends.

- Don't deal with anyone who causes you to feel uncomfortable. Trust your instincts.

- Negotiate for your benefit. Know your lowest price, but start high. If the buyer can close the loan rapidly and you're ready to move, provide an incentive such as $1,500 toward closing costs if they close by a certain date.

- Don't become attached to the buyers [or the home]. You want out of the house and them inside. If it's doesn't work out, move on – don't waste any time trying to develop a personal relationship with them.

> Once your signs are out, real-estate agents will knock on your door in attempt to convince you to abandon your FSBO quest to list your home with their agency. Sellers should take this opportunity to offer the agent 2% commission of your highest selling price if the home is sold to their qualified buyer (although you will continue to represent yourself). Certainly if the home does not sell to their buyer, or the sale does not go through, they do not receive any commission.
>
> This brings me to another tip. Sellers can fax flyers to real-estate agencies offering a 2% commission (or whatever you desire) should the home sell to one of their buyers.

## Resources For Do-It Yourself Home Buyers and Sellers

*Buying and Selling A Home*, by Corey Sandler. (c) 2003 The Globe Pequot Press. $15.95 (USD).
*Examples of a purchase contract, disclosure documents and other forms are provided. This book contains detailed information about home buying and selling.*

*How To Buy or Sell Your Home Without A Broker,* by Milt Tanzer. (c) 2001 Prentice Hall Press. $20.00 (USD).
*The author includes several samples and a CD ROM with forms.*

## For Sale By Owner Web Resources

Some of these web sites may not be active, so I've listed several to choose.
www.netfsbo.com
www.sellyourhomeyourself.com
www.fsbo.com
www.usfsbo.com
www.easyhomeseller.com
www.thishouseforsale.com
www.fsbocentral.com
www.smartfsbo.com
www.fsboworld.net
http://fsbo.net
www.fisbo.com
www.realestatephotos.com
www.byownersales.com
www.fsbogroup.com
www.fsboweb.com
www.owners.com
www.americashomes.com
www.forsalebyowner.com
www.fsbo.net
www.fsboconnection.com
www.4salebyowner.com
www.nefsbo.com
www.privateowner.com
www.fsbohelp.com
www.fsbodirect.com
www.fsbo-home.com
www.forsalebyyou.com
www.usarealestate.net
www.homesforsale-us.com
www.ezbuy.com
http://fsbo-home.com
www.mis-fsbo.com
www.fsbocentral.com
www.realtyoptions.com
www.thishouseforsale.com
www.fsbogroup.com
www.privatelist.com
www.findahome.org

> In addition to the web sites listed above there are sites that offer specific information for a particular state. For instance, if your home is in the state of New York, try searching online for *For Sale By Owner New York.*

## The Home Selling Process

Once a buyer has been located it's time to commence with closing the deal. From the time you sign a contract with the buyer and the time your buyer takes possession can be as short as 7 days or as long as 60 days. The times vary depending on the capability of the buyer's lender to process the loan and the escrow company's ability to complete the paperwork. Each sale is different, as the buyer and seller needs are unique.

When selling your home while in bankruptcy, you may need additional time to obtain permission from the courts or obtain a release of the property. Also, sellers should inform their buyer of their bankruptcy status. For more information on selling property while in bankruptcy *see chapter one Bankruptcy.*

Those facing foreclosure should immediately contact their lender to stay the foreclosure if the home is in escrow. Fax a copy of the escrow documents to your lender's office to show you are committed to repaying your debt.

The sales contract is the script for the buyer, seller and escrow holder. It determines when the buyer and/or seller will perform. The escrow instructions are based on the terms of the contract. Always refer to your contract for deadlines and duties. The following steps to home closing were compiled during the sale of my home (these steps apply to the State of California. They are current as of the date of publication. The details vary depending on your state laws and the sales agreement):

- The buyer and seller agree on the contractual terms.

- Buyers deliver proof they are qualified for the loan, usually in the form of a pre approval letter from their lender.

- *Sellers in bankruptcy should provide a copy of the escrow front page and good faith estimate to the court and trustee's office. Courts may require a Motion to Sell Residential Property form.*

- Once both parties sign, the seller will deliver a copy to the escrow/fiduciary agent.

- The buyer takes the good faith deposit to the escrow company. Deposits are usually accepted in the form of money order or cashiers check.

- The escrow agent orders title information, pay off demand from the lender, and other mandatory documentation required by your state.

- Sellers provide copies of disclosure documents to the buyer, who signs each form. Either the buyer or seller can submit these forms to the escrow agency (*I delivered these forms to the escrow holder to prevent delays*).

- Buyers commence with inspections and requests repairs if any (depending on the price of the home and market demand, the seller should feel comfortable offering the property *as is*).

- Sellers order the termite report from a reputable termite company. Prior to committing to any one termite company, gather several estimates.

- The buyer's lender orders an appraisal of the property (the appraisal determines the current market value of the home, and it can be ordered anytime before the close of escrow). One important note, appraisal reports vary. When I attempted to sell my house a buyer presented an appraisal report with far less square footage than what I owned. This depreciated the value of the home, which he demanded that I reduce my selling price - I refused and found another buyer. The new buyer, using the same lender, appraised the square footage correctly. If there is a discrepancy the **buyer** should resolve this dispute.

- At some point the conditions set forth by the lender will be met and monies loaned to the borrower are sent to the escrow company – this is called loan funding. At this stage the seller is safe to commence with repairs and other work on the property. Should the buyer cancel the contract, all deposit monies could be awarded to the seller should litigation ensue.

- The buyer meets with the escrow holder to sign final loan documents, which are typically notarized by an authorized escrow agent.

- Sellers meet with the escrow agent to sign transfer of deed forms, federal tax documents, and state required documents.

- Buyers meet with the seller to perform their final inspection. The final inspection is to verify that, agreed upon, repairs have been made. Depending on the terms of your contract, the final walk through may or may not be a condition for the close of escrow. This, again depending on the sales contract, is solely performed to satisfy the buyer.

- Once the sale is completed the seller delivers keys to the buyer. Depending on the terms of your contract, the seller has a set amount of days to vacate the property. Proceeds from the sale are sent to the seller (or in cases of bankruptcy, the trustee's office if they have sent a demand notice to the escrow company).

## Obtaining Money While in Escrow

When experiencing a halt in cash flow you may find the buyer willing to release the escrow deposit once the loan reaches the funding stage. A simple statement can easily be added to your contract that permits the escrow holder to release funds once the buyer's lender has *funded* the loan. In most home sales, the buyer has a sincere desire to purchase the property and is willing to work with cash strapped sellers, especially if they've been given a fair deal on the home price. At loan funding the buyer is committed to the sale, unless something drastic happens. Consult with your escrow holder or attorney for further details.

## The Blow Out Yard Sale

*You never know how much stuff you own until you attempt to pack it in boxes.* This statement is so true. Those wanting to start a fresh new life should seriously consider letting go of old objects. I use to look down on yard sales until I had one of my own. Afterwards, I became the yard sale queen; throwing yard sales three weeks in a row. It was a good source for immediate cash, and I didn't have to pay movers to haul those items across country. Furthermore, selling some of my belongings caused me to better because I no longer had the responsibility of caring for them. It sort of freed me. Now those items belong to others who want to take care of them. Plus, when you start your new life, you'll want new things too, but be careful not to get into debt.

Rally your neighbors for the yard sale. This allows everyone to pitch in and each party can share in the preparation. Plus, the more stuff, the more people you'll attract. If you live alone, like I did, pay a teenager to help you haul heavy items out of the house. Post decorative signs along busy streets, and wait for your customers. During my yard sales, I offered reasonable deals, so I didn't bargain too much with people. Certainly, put aside your kind heart in order to deal squarely and fairly. If the items were expensive I would start high. For instance I was selling an oval shaped wood mirror for $60 dollars, although I only wanted $30. The right person came along and it was sold for $40.

## Selling Vehicles

During difficult financial times, try to eliminate all unnecessary debts. Should you reside in a state, such as California, where owning a car is a necessity you may choose to trade your vehicle in for a more economical automobile. Eliminating car notes can cure some financial stress. The more debt gone the happier you should feel. Check with family and friends for great deals on used vehicles.

If you plan on trading your car in for a less expensive vehicle, locate several trade in values. Web sites such as www.carsdirect.com and www.kbb.com *(web site for Kelly Blue Book)* used car prices.

Singles, particularly women, should enlist the assistance of neighbors to ride along for test drives. Take time to screen your buyers carefully, some individuals may not be serious.

Avoid becoming desperate to sell the car. Advantageous buyers can detect your desperation. Remain calm while negotiating. Car selling isn't difficult, either the buyer wants the deal or not.

Sellers are responsible for giving the buyer a *Bill of Sale*. This occurs once the buyer has paid, preferably in cash, for the vehicle. *The bill of sale* is a simple document that states the names the buyer and seller, the price for the vehicle, date of sale, current date, and description of the vehicle being sold (*if it's being sold AS IS ensure it's stated on the bill of sale to protect you against potential liabilities*).

Draft a *Bill Of Sale* if you sell the vehicle to a private party. The following list of tips I found online for creating a bill of sale:

- Include the essentials, including year, make, model and the Vehicle Identification Number (VIN). List the sale price, your name, the buyer's name and the date of sale. Be sure to record the mileage.

- Jot down a brief disclaimer stating that the vehicle is being sold "as is." Unless you knowingly misrepresent your car, an as-is disclaimer should protect you from any legal action. The best approach is to advise the buyer of any known problems.

- Keep the bill of sale for at least a year. You may need it for property tax purposes (to demonstrate, for example,

that you are no longer the owner and hence not liable for taxes beyond the date of sale).

- Notify your local Department of Motor Vehicles. Inform them that the car has been sold and cancel the registration. In some states you keep the plates, in others they go with the car. Check with your state authorities.

- In some states, the vehicle's title can serve as a ready-made bill of sale. There are boxes on the back where you fill in all of the above information. If not, you can draft a bill of sale by hand.

> Before placing your car on the market, obtain all necessary transfer forms from your local motor vehicle department. Having the documents ready can save time should your buyer fail to transfer the title. Log onto, www.dmv.org to locate the Department of Motor Vehicle office near you.

> Sellers in need of a tax right-off should seriously consider donating your vehicle. Many charitable agencies accept vehicles regardless if it's operational and you'll receive the highest value amount so that you can right if off on your taxes.

> Additional ideas can be found in the following book:
>
> *How To Buy and Sell Just About Everything.* By Jeff Wuorio. (c) 2003. The Free Press. $27.00 (USD).
> *An extensive book with great ideas. Includes career and business information.*

# STATE OF CALIFORNIA
# DEPARTMENT OF REAL ESTATE

The license information shown below represents public information taken from the Department of Real Estate's database at the time of your inquiry. It will not reflect pending changes which are being reviewed for subsequent database updating. Also, the license information provided includes formal administrative actions that have been taken against licensees pursuant to the Business and Professions Code and/or the Administrative Procedure Act. All of the information displayed is public information. Although the business and mailing addresses of real estate licensees are included, this information is not intended for mass mailing purposes.

License information taken from records of the Department of Real Estate on 5/26/03 11:10:16 AM

| | |
|---|---|
| **License Type:** | BROKER |
| **Name:** | Santos, Patricia |
| **Mailing Address:** | PO BOX 1413<br>CLAREMONT, CA 91711-<br>(Above address is marked unreliable in DRE database) |
| **License ID:** | 00758103 |
| **Expiration Date:** | 02/05/03 |
| **License Status:** | EXPIRED |
| **Original License Date:** | 01/23/90 (Unofficial -- taken from secondary records) |
| **Former Name(s):** | Geiger, Patricia<br><br>Salas, Patricia |
| **Main Office:** | NO CURRENT MAIN OFFICE ADDRESS ON FILE |
| **DBA** | Select Property<br>CANCELED<br><br>NO CURRENT DBAS |
| **Branches:** | NO CURRENT BRANCHES |
| **Affiliated Licensed Corporation(s):** | NO CURRENT AFFILIATED CORPORATIONS |
| **Comment:** | NO DISCIPLINARY ACTION<br><br>NO OTHER PUBLIC COMMENTS |

>>>> Public information request complete <<<<

http://www2.dre.ca.gov/PublicASP/pplinfo.asp?License_id=00758103

# Be Yourself

One summer's day, I was sitting at the beach in Tampa Florida. Above, the sun was blazing its rays on those of us enjoying the sound of the warm ocean. Many women wore scantly covered bikinis to display their redesigned bodies. Suddenly, a contrasting sight taking casual steady strides became my focus. She was a tall extremely heavy woman wearing a yellow bikini. As she glided above the sand her head swayed with the wind delivering their waves onto the beach. Her legs kept the pace of her soul and her thoughts were clearly not on those honored to observe this momentous wonder. My heart applauded her strength while my mouth dropped. *Where did she come from? Where does she live? Who is she?* This is what I pondered as she coasted through my life. The confidence it took for her to put on that bikini, then to walk out into the public, onto that beach was incomprehensible to me. I declared; I want her confidence!

Having endured various life crises and joys from the time I beheld this example I've graduated into the yellow bikini club. I remember each step I've taken to face fears, potential dangers and various unknowns. These confrontations have sharpened my confidence.

While writing the last sections for this book, I once again returned to the ocean. As I walked along the beach, heavy thoughts escaped to allow my head to sway; I was grateful that my body was once again united with the sand, wind and water. The woman with the yellow bikini glided through my thoughts each day I faced my fears, and this relaxing day I understood what processes makes up a composed state of total contentment where others opinions about me do not outweigh those of myself - confidence. My daily success is that I wouldn't want to be any other person than me.

*This is the art of courage: to see things as they are and still
believe that the victory lies not with those who avoid the
bad, but those who taste, in living awareness, every drop of
the good.*

Victoria Lincoln

Yᵒᵘ ou deserve an applause! Those who have survived bankruptcy, mounting debts, unemployment in addition to difficulties which arise as a result from these hardships, should feel proud of their perseverance. If you can undergo such bumpy financial paths then certainly you're made of courageous material. Recovering your savings after enduring financial disaster is your last battle, but it's certainly not uphill. Implementing budgeting tools/plans that fit your lifestyle is not difficult; however, it does require discipline. Reading financial planning books may help some, but it doesn't work for all of us. By simply reducing spending, increasing savings and, my challenge, practicing paying bills *on time* we can create a financially stable lifestyle. If anyone can do it, certainly you can.

I don't pride myself on financial management, so I attempt to put money in places where I can't withdraw it during Labor Day, after Christmas and just because sales. I've also had to abandon phrases like, *you only live once*, which sounds good until there isn't anymore money and I'm not dead. Facing my spending habits was an awakening from bankruptcy that has help shaped the way I financially plan my future. In addition, I've developed checkpoints that I consider before making purchases. For example, before I make a purchase I think about each dollar and ask myself, *what is so special about this item that it costs so much?* Before retaining someone's service I ask myself, *what is so valuable about their skills that I'm willing to part with so much money?* I've certainly become a conscientious consumer who attempts to avoid passion purchases; until I reach my favorite clothing store and then I often bypass the above questioning process.

The ideas presented in this chapter are designed for you to build upon for establishing a balanced financial lifestyle after surviving financial disasters.

## I'm Free of Financial Troubles, So What Should I Do?

Enjoy your freedom! Taste, bathe, shower and bask in the joys of living a debt free life; regardless of how you accomplished it, you did well. Remember that no matter if it's the *latest and greatest, newest edition, best look* you **will not** sacrifice your freedom. Find inexpensive creative ways to enjoy yourself. For those who are dating, prepare a home cooked meal with a special someone this is an excellent way to bond. It's cheaper and it could be healthier. Instead of movies each week, try having a celebration day for the ones you love. I've always wanted to be in a parade. A special day for me would be for everyone to wear boots and we march around the house to music. Coupons can make a potentially expensive night out financially reasonable. Many restaurants provide coupons offering discounted meals. I especially like the buy one get one free deals.

Be creative without going overboard. Soon you'll learn travel tips that can have you enjoying exclusive resorts for motel rates. By paying cash you'll often save additional costs on purchases too.

Like most people, I have to establish new credit and open another checking account. This is not the hardest part. Small banks offer checking accounts to those of us who are at the financial recovery stage. A list of secured credit card companies is provided in Appendix A for those needing credit. The hard part is over, take small steps and soon this will be a distant memory.

## Rebuilding Credit After Bankruptcy and Excessive Debts

Rebuilding credit isn't difficult. It will take time, typically two to seven years to achieve good credit. I interviewed a person familiar with credit repair who stated the fastest way to improving credit is to add positive credit to your report. He suggested recovering debtors should open secured credit card accounts every six months to one year. Once they obtain the card, perform only one transaction per month. Immediately pay off the debt, but keep the card up to one year. After the year has past close the account and open another. This can go on for years with multiple cards. I haven't tried his recommendation [by the time of printing this book], but the main idea is to add positive credit to your report without adding exorbitant amounts debts.

The main battle consumers will face is finding an honest source for credit repair, if time is too slow of an approach. While you're searching for the right credit repair company, continue to pay your bills on time and, of course, attempt to add positive credit to your records. Remember that you can repair your own credit for free. Certainly you will not fall victim to fraud by using this approach. To begin, get a copy of you credit reports from all three bureaus (*see Credit Bureau's Address, Telephone Numbers, and Web sites in this chapter*). Should you notice incorrect or erroneous information, dispute those items. Additional information is provided in the *Correcting Credit Report Errors* section in this chapter.

Those with a good payment history after bankruptcy will find home lenders willing to finance loans after two years of positive credit.

Whichever path you pursue, the worst should be over and now you're starting with solid experience. Be selective and carefully consider your options.

## Secured Credit Cards

Secured credit cards can be of value to those wanting to add credit history to credit reports. Each card company has a set amount they require deposited into a secured savings account before dispensing a card. The annual percentage rate is typically outrageous, and some require a processing fee, application fee, and/or yearly use fee. Some card companies will transfer your card from secured to unsecured if a consistent payment history is made and the card is held for a set period of time.

Those who have *impaired credit* will often find offers for secured credit cards in your mail. These are typically low initial deposit cards; however they usually require additional investment for activation. Carefully **READ** the fine print, as secured cards have expensive late penalty fees, and costly yearly fees. Certainly pay your monthly balances on time for this to be a viable credit rebuilding source if you open a secured credit card. Borrower's monthly payments and delinquencies are reported to credit bureaus. I've used a secured credit card in the past, and it worked well until I noticed unauthorized charges on my bill. I found that it was difficult working with the agents to correct the discrepancy (Don't worry I didn't list that secured credit card company in this book). To resolve the problem, I sent letters quoting sections of the Fair Credit Reporting Act, and threatened a small claims suit. In addition, I attempted to communicate with a person, such as a supervisor, who could correct the error. It's fair to mention that these types of problems are not limited to secured credit card companies, I've certainly have had problems with traditional banks as well – it's also fair to mention that on rare occasions I've been wrong. Refer to Appendix A for the names, telephone numbers and addresses of secured credit card companies.

## Prepaid Debit/Credit Cards

Lately, I've seen signs at gas stations offering prepaid credit cards. These cards operate similarly to a debit card with a national credit agency insignia that processes charges. Payments are not reported to credit agencies, as credit is not extended rather the card dispenses money from pre-deposits. Those wanting to establish new credit should avoid these cards. However, for those needing the use of a credit card, such as those who frequently travel, can circumvent excessive fees by obtaining a prepaid card. There is a fee to obtain this card. If you're able to open a checking or savings account, you're far better off using your debit card or simply paying with cash. Some banks and credit unions will open a <u>savings account</u> to anyone regardless of their check writing past. These banks may also offer debit cards to savings account depositors.

## Purchasing Property After Financial Disaster

Undesirable credit should not deter anyone from purchasing a home. Many lending sources will finance a potential buyer's home regardless of their past credit (however it's done at a higher price). In addition, many states have buyer assistance programs to help those with less than perfect credit, single buyers, and first time home purchasers. It's ideal to obtain the best interest rate for your home, but it's not mandated that those with impaired credit should wait. Web sites such as: <u>www.bankrate.com</u> and <u>www.mortgagemag.com</u> provide lender information for nearly any type of loan. Many lenders offer comparable rates to those whose bankruptcies have been discharged for two years or more from the loan application date. Those with previous foreclosures, usually within seven years, may find obtaining another mortgage extremely difficult.

*Subprime* loans are typically offered to those with less than perfect credit. These loans may impose extra payment points (percentage of the loan amount charged to the borrower for taking the loan), a higher interest rate, and prepayment penalty clauses. Each lender's terms vary, so it's wise to research several lenders before committing yourself to a loan. If you're determined, visit the web sites listed above. Search for less than perfect credit loans, and read the lenders requirements. Your new home can be waiting a click away.

Ravenous banks have developed several strategies to entice *subprime* borrowers. Loan packages offering balloon payment for several months can be detrimental to those needing time to acclimate to a mortgage payment. Consider staying with traditional loan programs to avoid future financial disaster.

> Those who have negative information on their credit reports that prevent them from making purchases, such as a home, should speak with a supervisor to expedite the corrections of the erroneous information. It takes persistence, but don't give up!
>
> Also, some homeowners offer lease to own programs for persons who need more time to buy.

## Buying a Car with Less Than Perfect Credit

Before you consider obtaining a high interest loan for an automobile read the *Auto Repossession* chapter in this book. Should you pursue obtaining an auto loan then you're in luck. Car loans are easily obtained despite what information is contained on your credit report. With lenders offering annual percentage rates (APR) as high as 23%, you'll be financing the car of your forthcoming nightmare. Consumers with past credit problems needing a vehicle should seriously consider paying cash or take an aggressive negotiator along with you to the dealership.

Most car dealerships have several loan packages that range from perfect to horrific credit. Believe it or not, dealerships usually have more sources for those with impaired credit than those with perfect credit. This is so for several reasons; one being, loan applications from borrower's with less than perfect credit are typically denied. Certainly, that's what the dealership will tell you. Many financiers offer *kickbacks* to dealerships who secure high risk loans. These are attractive to salesmen who receive commissions. What this means for consumers is you can be offered the worst possible loan first, but the best for the dealerships pockets. Consumers have the right to refuse these offers. Check online for competitive car loan rates before you visit the dealership. Don't feel intimated because of negative information on your credit report, salesmen remind you of this to break your spirit. Acknowledge the credit problems and the fact they have lenders ready to give them money as soon as they lower the price and present you with a feasible deal. Encourage them to stop wasting your time.

> I've found most banks will offer low rates despite credit history if the borrower is able to pay 20% down on the purchase price. This maybe a lofty investment, but it could save thousands of dollars in costs and interest.

## Correcting Credit Report Errors

Should you notice errors reported by any one credit bureau you have the right to dispute the item(s). Appendix C contains a form for disputing erroneous items on credit reports. The credit reporting agency will also provide dispute forms to those who obtain their credit reports directly from their agency. After this form is fully completed, attach supporting documentation that proves your position. The form provided in Appendix D should be used to inform the agency, who denied you credit, that there has been a mistake. This form should be sent to the credit bureau reporting the error and the agency denying your credit.

Completely fill in both forms and retain copies for your records. The Fair Credit Reporting Act entitles consumers to have incomplete or inaccurate information corrected without charge. From personal experience, while I was attempting to purchase my first home, I was able to fax over my dispute forms with supporting documentation. The correction times varied. Some bureaus corrected the information while I was on hold, and others took several follow up telephone calls. When I spoke with a representative I explained the urgency due to the negative information was impeding me from making a home purchase.

Once consumers dispute items the credit bureaus will investigate. The time frame varies on the bureau, the Fair Credit Report Act says *within a reasonable time*. The credit bureau will contact the creditor and search public records to verify the reporting accuracy. If the disputed item(s) are not verified, the credit bureau must delete the information and/or correct the error(s). In addition to correcting inaccuracies the credit bureau is responsible for sending notifications to parities that have checked your credit record within the past 6 months.

> Some credit repair agencies charge fees for disputing items regardless of the accuracy. They count on creditor's lack of response to help consumers repair their credit. It can take months for the service to be of benefit, if at all.
>
> Credit repair companies charge fees for correcting credit errors. There are a significant number of fraudulent credit repair companies who offer to perform services that consumers can accomplish on their own for far less costs.

## Credit Bureau's Addresses, Telephone Numbers, and Web sites

CBI/Equifax
Equifax Credit Information Services, Inc.
P.O. Box 740241
Atlanta, GA 30374
800-685-1111
800-562-4437
www.equifax.com

Experian
P.O Box 2104
Allen, TX 75013-2104
888-397-3742
www.experian.com/consumer

Trans Union
Consumer Disclosure Center
P.O. Box 1000
Chester, PA 19022
800-916-8800
800-888-4213
www.tuc.com

> Those needing immediate access to your credit report should visit the bureaus web sites to obtain copies.
>
> Free copies of your credit report can be obtained for the following reasons:
>
> - If you have been turned down, within 60 days, for credit for employment, insurance or a rental unit because of information on your credit report.
> - Each year consumers who are unemployed, (those intending to file for unemployment within the next 60 days), receiving public assistance such as welfare, and those who believe they are a victim of fraud or identity theft are entitled to one free copy.
>
> Furthermore, the credit bureaus must provide someone to help you interpret the information contained on your credit report.

## Adding Information to Your Credit File

Consumers can add information pertaining to your credit and history to your report. For example, you can add credit that wasn't reported to the bureaus and include additional details to items reported to the credit bureaus. Credit supplied by gasoline companies aren't always reported to the credit bureaus.

Consumers who have been unsuccessful removing disputed information can add a statement, up to 100 words, that communicates your position. Each time your credit report is sent out, this statement must be included.

Credit bureaus may allow, although they're not required, consumers to add accounts that have not been reported to their agency. A fee maybe charged for this service. Once the credit is verified, it will be added to your credit file.

> **How Long Information Stays On Your Credit:**
> With some exceptions credit bureaus report most negative information for seven years beginning from the date prior to the delinquency. Payments made in between this time and additional actions taken by the creditor extends the reporting date.

## Resources

*The Complete Guide to Credit Repair*, Bill Kelly Jr. © 2001. Adams Media Corporation. ($9.95)

*Repair Your Own Credit and Deal With Debt*, Brette McWhorter Sember. ©2003. Sphinx Publishing. ($18.95)

*The Budget Kit 3rd Edition*. Judy Lawrence © 2000. Dearborn Trade. $16.95.

*Managing To Be Wealthy: Putting Your Financial Plan and Planner to Work For You*, by John E. Sestina © 2000. Dearborn Financial. $19.95.

www.quicken.com
www.ivilliage.com/money
http://creditscoring.com
www.debtworkout.com
www.consumer-action.org
www.ftc.gov

**Federal Deposit Insurance Corporation**
(*Banking Complaints*)
25 Ecker Street, Suite 1600
San Francisco, CA 94105

**Frugal Living Resources**

www.livingfrugal.com
www.miserlymoms.com
www.sheapskatemontly.com
www.stretcher.com
www.esmarts.com
www.finaid.org/loans/forgiveness.phtml

# Appendix A

List of Secured Credit Card Companies

Amalgamated Bank of Chicago
800-723-0303

Plains Commerce Bank
605-948-2344

Wells Fargo Bank
800-642-4720

TrustCo Bank
518-377-3311

American Pacific Bank
800-610-1201

HSBC Bank USA
800-975-4722

Bank of America, NA
800-678-2632

First National Bank of Marin
702-269-1100

Union Plus/Household Bank
800-651-5108

Washington Mutual Bank
800-382-3334

First PREMIER Bank
800-987-5521

Sovereign Bank
877-SOV-BANK

Evans National Bank
716-549-1000

Bank of Smithtown
631-360-9300

# Appendix B

Low/No Fee Credit Cards

Wachovia Bank
800-922-4684

Pulaski Bank & Trust Co.
800-980-2265

M& T Bank
800-362-6299

Adirondack Trust Co.
518-584-5844

Fidelity National Bank
404-639-6700

Union Planters Bank
800-847-7378

Astoria Federal Savings &
Loan
800-ASTORIA

Stissing National Bank of
Pine Plains
518-398-5711

Ohio Savings Bank
800-696-2222

Fleet National Bank
800-225-5353

M&I Marshall & Ilsley Bank
608-240-7328

MBNA America Bank
800-441-7048

United Trust Bank
732-448-4075

USAA Savings Bank
800-365-8722

Troy Savings Bank
518-270-3200

North Fork Bank
212-764-1001

Roslyn Savings Bank
516-942-6000

Firstrust Savings Bank
800-545-7899

Merrick Bank
801-545-6600

First Niagara Bank
800-421-0004

Associated Card Services Bank
800-472-7708

State Farm Bank, FSB
877-SF4-BANK

Tompkins Trust Company
607-273-3210

First National Bank of Chester
County
610-692-3000

Ballston Spa National Bank
518-885-6781

Chase Manhattan Bank USA
800-412-5661

Simmons First National Bank
800-883-5151

Metropolitan National Bank
800-883-2511

Household Bank, FSB
800-685-9080

First North American
National Bank
770-423-7900

First Union National Bank
800-377-3404

Emigrant Savings Bank
800-688-2265

Blue from American Express
800-641-2400

Washington Mutual Bank
800-382-3334

Warwick Savings Bank
845-986-2206

Union Planters Bank
800-847-7378

# Appendix C

# Form A – Correction of Credit Report Errors

**(NOTICE OF DISPUTED INFORMATION AND STATEMENT CORRECTING ADVERSE INFORMATION)**

**CONSUMER'S COMBINED NOTICE DISPUTING THE ACCURACY AND COMPLETENESS OF INFORMATION IN CREDIT FILE AND STATEMENT SETTING FORTH NATURE OF DISPUTE PURSUANT TO U.S. FAIR CREDIT REPORTING ACT.**

RE:    Consumer's Name:   _____

        Credit File No.:     _____

        Creditor:           _____

I hereby give notice that I am disputing the accuracy or completeness of the information in my credit file, reported by the above named creditor for the following reasons:_____

_____

_____

_____

_____

_____

_____

_____

_____

_____

Consumer's Signature

_____

Street Address

_____

City, State, Zip Code

# Appendix D

# Correction of Credit Report Errors

### (REQUEST TO DISSEMINATE CORRECTED INFORMATION)

### CONSUMER'S REQUEST TO CONSUMER REPORTING AGENCY TO FURNISH CORRECTED CREDIT INFORMATION TO THIRD PARTIES PURSUANT TO U.S. FAIR CREDIT REPORTING ACT.

RE:    Consumer's Name: _____

         Credit File No.: _____

         Creditor: _____

Person Received Credit Report:

_____

Street Address: _____

City, State, Zip Code: _____

I hereby request that you furnish to the above named person: (1) notification that the item reported by the above named creditor has been deleted from my credit file of (2) that my "statement" setting forth the nature of the dispute.

_____

(Consumer's signature)

_____

Street Address

_____

City, State, Zip Code

# Appendix E

## State, County and City Government Consumer Protection Offices (and Web Sites)*

*Toll free numbers may only operate within the state the agency is listed

## Alabama

### County Offices

Office of the Attorney General
Consumer Affairs Section
11 South Union Street
Montgomery, AL 36130
334-242-7335
Toll free in AL: 800-392-5658
Web site: www.ago.state.al.us

## Alaska

### State Offices

Consumer Protection Unit
Office of the Attorney General
1031 West 4th Avenue
Suite 200
Anchorage, AK 99501-5903
907-276-8554
Web site: www.law.state.ak.us

## Arizona

### State Offices

Consumer Protection and Advocacy Section
Office of the Attorney General
1275 West Washington Street
Phoenix, AZ 85007
602-542-3702
602-542-5763 (consumer information and complaints)
Toll free in AZ: 800-352-8431
TDD: 602-542-5002
Fax: 602-542-4579
Web site: www.ag.state.az.us

Office of the Attorney General
Consumer Protection
400 West Congress South Bldg., Suite 315
Tucson, AZ 85701
520-628-6504
Toll free in AZ: 800-352-8431
Fax: 520-628-6532
Web site: www.ag.state.az.us

## New Jersey

### State Offices

Department of Law and Public Safety
Division of Consumer Affairs
PO Box 45025
Newark, NJ 07101
972-504-6200
Toll free: 800-242-5846
E-mail: askconsumeraffairs@smtp.lps.state.nj.us
Web site: www.state.nj.us/lps/ca/home.htm

### County Offices

William Ross III, Director
Atlantic County Division of Consumer Affairs
1333 Atlantic Avenue
8th Floor
Atlantic City, NJ 08401
609-343-2376
609-345-6700
Fax: 609-343-2322
Web site:
www.aclink.org/law/mainpages/conshome.htm

Camden County Office of Consumer
Protection/Weights and Measures
Jefferson House
Lakeland Road
Blackwood, NJ 08012
609-374-6161
609-374-6001
Toll free in NJ: 800-999-9045
Fax: 609-232-0784
E-mail: consumer@co.camden.nj.us
Web site: www.co.camden.nj.us

Department of Consumer Affairs and Weights
and Measures
4 Moore Road
Cape may Court House, NJ 08210
609-463-6475
Fax: 609-465-4639
E-mail: mbrogan@co.cape-may.nj.us

**County Offices**

Cochise County Attorney's Office
Post Office Drawer CA
Bisbee, AZ 85603
520-432-9377
Fax: 520-432-4280

Greenlee County Attorney's Office
P.O. Box 1717
Clifton, AZ 85533
928-865-4108
Fax: 928-865-4665

Coconino County Attorney's Office
110 East Cherry Avenue
Flagstaff, AZ 86001
928-779-6518
Fax: 928-779-5618

Pinal County Attorney's Office
P.O. Box 887
Florence, AZ 85232
520-8686-6271
Fax: 520-868-6521

Gila County Attorney's Office
1400 East Ash Street
Globe, AZ 85501
928-425-3231 ext. 298
Fax: 928-425-3720

Navajo County Attorney's Office
P.O. Box 668
Holbrook, AZ 86025
928-524-4026
Fax: 928-524-4244

Mohave County Attorney's Office
315 North 4th Street
P.O. Box 7000

Essex County Division of Consumer
Action/Consumer Services
50 South Clinton Street
Suite 3201
Ease Orange, NJ 07018
973-395-8350
Fax: 973-395-8433

Office of Consumer Affairs
County of Hunterdon
P.O. Box 2900
Flemington, NJ 08822
908-806-5174
Fax: 908-806-4286
E-mail: jferrari@hclibr.eclipse.net

Monmouth County Department of Consumer
Affairs
50 East Main Street
P.O. Box 1255
Freehold, NJ 07728-1255
732-431-7900
Fax: 732-845-2037

Hudson County Division of Consumer Affairs
595 Newark Avenue
Jersey City, NJ 07306
201-795-6295
201-795-6163
Fax: 201-795-6462
Burlington County Office of Consumer
Affairs/Weights and Measures
49 Rancocas Road
P.O. Box 6000
Mount Holly, NJ 08060
609-265-5098 Weights and Measures
609-265-5054 Consumer Affairs
Fax: 609-265-5065

Division of Consumer Affairs
Somerset County
P.O. Box 3000
Somerville, NJ 08876-1262
908-231-7000 ext. 7400
E-mail: consumeraffairs@co.somerset.nj.us
Web site: www.co.somerset.nj.us

Ocean County Department of Consumer
Affairs/Weights and Measures
1027 Hooper Avenue

Kingman, AZ 86402-7000
928-753-0719
Fax: 928-753-2669


Santa Cruz County Attorney's Office
2150 North Congress Drive, Suite 201
Nogales, AZ 85621
520-375-7780
Fax: 520-761-7859


La Paz County Attorney
County Attorney
1320 Kofa Avenue
Parker, AZ 85344
928-669-6118
Fax: 928-669-2019


Yavapai County Attorney's Office
Yavapai County Courthouse
255 East Gurley
Prescott, AZ 86301
928-771-3344
Fax: 928-771-3110


Graham County Attorney's Office
Graham County Courthouse
800 West Main
Safford, AZ 85546
928-428-3620
Fax: 928-428-7200


Apache County Attorney's Office
P.O. Box 637
St. Johns, AZ 85936
928-337-7560
Fax: 928-337-2427


Yuma County Attorney's Office

P.O. Box 2191
Toms River, NJ 08754-2191
732-929-2105
Toll free in NJ: 800-722-0291 ex. 2105
Fax: 732-506-5330


Mecer County Consumer Affairs
640 South Broad Street Room 404
P.O. Box 8068
Trenton, NJ 08650-0068
609-989-6671
Fax: 609-989-6670


Passaic County Department of Consumer
Affairs
1310 Route 23 North
Wayne, NJ 07470
973-305-5881
Fax: 973-628-1796


County of Passaic
Department of Law and Public Safety
Div of Weights and Measures – CS
1310 Route 23 North
Wayne, NJ 07470
973-605-5750 Weights and Measures
973-305-5881 Consumer Protection
Fax: 973-628-1796
E-mail: pcca@advanix.net


Union County Division of Consumer Affairs
300 North Avenue East
P.O. Box 186
Westfield, NJ 07091
908-654-9840
Fax: 908-654-3082
E-mail: fpeterson@unioncountynj.org
Web site: www.unioncountynj.org


Gloucester County Department of Consumer
Protection/Weights and Measures
152 North Broad Street
P.O. Box 337
Woodbury, NJ 08096
856-853-3349
856-853-3350
TDD: 856-848-6616
Fax: 609-853-6813
E-mail: jsilvest@co.golucester.nj.us


**City Offices**

---

168 South Second Avenue
Yuma, AZ 85364
928-329-2270
Fax: 928-329-2284

### City Offices

Consumer Affairs Division
Tucson City Attorney's Office
1501 N. Oracle Annex
P.O. Box 27210
Tucson, AZ 85726-7210
520-791-4886
Fax: 520-791-4991

### Arkansas

### State Offices

Consumer Protection Division
Office of the Attorney General
323 Center Street
Suite 200
Little Rock, AR 72201
501-682-2007
501-682-2341 Consumer Hotline
800-4448-3014 Crime Victims Hotline
501-682-1334 Local Do Not Call Program
Toll free: 800-482-8982
TDD: 501-682-6073
Fax: 501-682-8118
E-mail: consumer@ag.state.ar.us
Web site: www.ag.state.ar.us

### California

### State Offices

Bureau of Automotive Repair
California Department of Consumer Affairs
10240 Systems Parkway
Sacramento, CA 95827
916-255-4300
Toll free in CA: 800-952-5210
TDD: 916-255-1369
Web site: www.autorepair.ca.gov

California Department of Consumer Affairs
400 R Street
Suite 300
Sacramento, CA 95814

Maywood Consumer Affairs
Bourough of Maywood
459 Maywood Avenue
Maywood, NJ 07607
201-845-5749

Mountainside Consumer Affairs
1455 Coles Avenue
Mountainside, NJ 07092
908-232-6600

Director Consumer Affairs
Township of North Bergen
Municipal Building
4233 Kennedy Blvd.
North Bergen, NJ 07047
201-392-2137 (community service)
201-330-7291 (consumer protection)
Fax: 201-392-8551

Plainfield Action Services
City Hall Annex
510 Watchung Avenue
Plainfield, NJ 07060
908-753-3519
Fax: 908-753-3540

Secaucus Department of Consumer Affairs
Municipal Government Center
1203 Patterson Plank Road
Secaucus, NJ 07094

916-445-4465
916-445-2643 (Correspondence and Complaint Review Unit)
Toll free in CA: 800-952-5210
TDD/TYY: 916-322-1700 or 800-326-2297
Web Site: www.dca.ca.gov

Office of the Attorney General
Public Inquiry Unit
P.O. Box 944255
Sacramento, CA 94244-2550
916-322-3360
Toll free in CA: 800-952-5225
TDD: 916-324-5564
Web site: www.caag.state.ca.us

**County Offices**

Kern County District Attorney's Office
Criminal Division
1215 Truxtun Avenue
4th Floor
Bakersfield, CA 93301
6661-868-2350
Fax: 661-868-2135
E-mail: ymichael@co.kern.co.us

Consumer Affairs Unit
Solano County District Attorney's Office
600 Union Avenue
Fairfield, CA 94533
707-421-6859
707-421-6800
Fax: 707-421-7986

Fresno County District Attorney's Office1250
Business Affairs Unit
Van Ness Avenue
2nd Floor
Fresno, CA 93721
559-488-3836
559-488-3156
Fax: 559-485-1315

Los Angeles County Department of Consumer Affairs
500 West Temple Street
Room B-96
Los Angeles, CA 90012-2706
213-974-1452
Fax: 213-687-0233

201-330-2008

Consumer Affairs Office
1976 Morris Avanue
Union, NJ 07083
908-851-5458
908-851-8501

Wayne Township Consumer Affairs
475 Valley Road
Wayne, NJ 07470
201-694-1800 ext. 3290

Weehawken Consumer Affairs
400 Park Avenue
Weehawken, NJ 09087
201-319-6005
Fax: 201-319-0112

Woodbridge Consumer Affairs
Woodbridge Township
Municipal Building
One Main Street
Woodbridge, NJ 07095
732-602-6058
Fax: 732-602-6016

**New Mexico**

**State Offices**

Consumer Protection Division
Office of the Attorney General
P.O. Drawer 1508

Web site: www.consumer-affiars.co.la.ca.us

407 Galisteo
Santa Fe, NM 87504-1508
505-827-6060
Toll free in NM: 800-678-1508
Fax: 505-827-6685
Web site: www.ago.state.nm.us

Contra Costa County District Attorney's Office
627 Ferry Street
Martinez, CA 94553
925-646-4620
Fax: 925-646-4683

**New York**

**State Offices**

Bureau of Consumer Frauds and Protection
Office of the Attorney General
State Capitol
Albany, NY 12224
518-474-5481
Toll free in NY: 800-771-7755 (hotline)
Fax: 518-474-3618
Web site: www.oag.state.ny.us

Consumer Affairs Division
Napa County District Attorney's Office
931 Parkway Mall
P.O. Box 720
Napa, CA 94559
707-253-4211
707-253-4059
Fax: 707-253-4041

New York State Consumer Protection Board
5 Empire State Plaza
Suite 2101
Albany, NY 12223-1556
518-474-3514
518-474-8583 (capital region)
Toll free: 800-697-1220
Fax: 518-474-2474
E-mail: donna.net@consumer.state.ny.us
Web site: www.consumer.state.ny.us

Consumer & Environmental Unit
San Mateo County District Attorney's Office
400 County Center
4th Floor
Redwood City, CA 94063
650-363-4651

Consumer Frauds and Protection Bureau
Office of the Attorney General
120 Broadway 3rd Floor
New York, NY 10271
212-416-8300
Toll free: 800-771-7755
Fax: 212-416-6003

Consumer and Environmental Protection
Division
Sacramento County District Attorney's Office
P.O. Box 749
906 G Street, Suite 700
Sacramento, CA 95812-0749
916-874-6174
Fax: 916-874-7660
Consumer Protection Division
P.O. Box 1131
Salinas, CA 93902
831-755-5073

Consumer Fraud and Protection Bureau
New York state Office of the Attorney general
Harlem Regional Office
163 West 125th Street
New York, NY 10027-8201
212-961-4475
Fax: 212-961-4003

Fax: 831-755-5608

San Diego County District Attorney's Office
330 W. Broadway, Suite 700
San Diego, CA 92101
619-531-4070
Fax: 619-531-4481
Web site: www.sandiegoda.com

San Francisco County District Attorney's Office
732 Brannan Street
San Francisco, CA 94103
415-551-9595 (public inquiries)
Fax: 415-551-9504
Web site: www.ci.sf.ca.us/casf/

Santa Clara County District Attorney's Consumer
Protection Unit
70 West Hedding Street
West Wing, 4th Floor
San Jose, CA 95110
408-792-2880 (consumer protection)
408-792-2881 (small claims advisory)
Fax: 408-279-8742
Web site: www.santaclara-da.org/consumer.html

Economic Crime Division
Consumer Fraud Department
County Government Center
1050 Monterey Street, Room 235
San Luis Obispo, CA 93408
805-781-5856
Fax: 805-781-1173
Web site: www.sloda.com

Marin County Mediation Services
4 Jeannette Prandi Way
San Rafeal, CA 94903
415-499-7454
Fax: 415-499-3673

Marin County District Attorney's Office
Hall of Justice, Room 130
3501 Civic Center Drive
San Rafeal, CA 94903

Plattsburgh Regional Office
Office of Attorney General
70 Clinton Street
Plattsburgh, NY 12901
518-562-3282
Fax: 518-562-3294

Consumer Fraud and Protection Bureau
New York State Office of the Attorney General
Westchester Regional Office
101 East Post Road
White Plains, NY 10601-5008
914-422-8155
Fax: 914-422-8706

**Regional Offices**

Binghamton Regional Office
New York State Office of the Attorney General
State Office Building – 17th Floor
44 Hawley Street
Binghamton, NY 13901-4433
607-721-8771
Toll free: 800-771-7755
Fax: 607-721-8789
Web site: www.oag.state.ny.us

Brooklyn Regional Office
New York State Office of the Attorney General
Consumer Fraud Bureau
55 Hanson Place, Room 732
Brooklyn, NY 11217
718-722-3949
Fax: 718-722-3951

Buffalo Regional Office
New York State Office of the Attorney General
Statler Towers
107 Delaware Avenue, 4th Floor
Buffalo, NY 14202
716-853-8400
Toll free: 800-771-7755
Fax: 853-8414

Suffolk Regional Office
Office of the Attorney General
300 Motor Parkway, Suite 205
Hauppauge, NY 11788

415-499-6495
Fax: 415-499-3719
E-mail: consumer@co.marin.ca.us
Web site:
www.co.marin.ca.us/depts/DA/main/index.cfm

Consumer Protection Unit
Santa Barbara County District Attorney's
Office1105 Santa Barbara Street
Santa Barbara, CA 93101
805-568-2300
Fax: 805-568-2398

Division of Consumer Affairs
Santa Cruz County District Attorney's Office
701 Ocean Street
Room 200
Santa Cruz, CA 95060
831-454-2050
TDD/TYY: 831-454-2123
Fax: 831-454-2920
E-mail: dat155@co.santa-cruz.ca.us
Web site: www.CO.Santa-Cruz.CA/US

San Joaquin County District Attorney's Office
Consumer Affairs Prosecution Unit
222 East Weber, Room 412
P.O. Box 990
Stockton, CA 95202
209-468-9321
Fax: 209-468-0314

Consumer Fraud and Environmental Prosecution
Unit
Tulare County District Attorney's Office
221 S. Mooney Blvd. Room 224
Visalia, CA 93291
559-733-6411
Fax: 559-730-2658

Consumer/Environmental Protection Unit
Orange County District Attorney's Office
401 Civic Center Drive
West Santa Ana, CA 92701
714-347-8706
Fax: 714-568-1250

516-231-2401
Fax: 516-435-4757

Poughkeepsie Regional Office
New York State Office of the Attorney General
235 Main Street
Poughkeepsie, NY 12601
914-485-3920
Toll free: 800-771-7755
TDD/TYY Toll free: 800-788-9898
Fax: 914-452-3303
Web site: www.oag.state.ny.us

Rochester Regional Office
Office of the Attorney General
144 Exchange Blvd., 2nd Floor
Rochester, NY 14614
716-546-7430
Toll free: 800-771-7755
TDD: 716-327-3249
Fax: 716-546-7514
Web site: www.oag.state.ny.us

Syracuse Regional Office
Office of the Attorney General
615 Erie Blvd. West, Suite 102
Syracuse, NY 13204-2465
315-448-4848
Fax: 315-448-4851

Utica Regional Office
Office of the Attorney General
207 Genesee Street, Room 504
Utica, NY 13501
315-793-2225
Toll free: 800-771-7755
Fax: 315-793-2228
Web site: www.oag.state.ny.us

Officer of the Attorney General
Watertown Regional Office
Dulles State Office Building
317 Washington Street
Watertown, NY 13601
315-785-2444
Toll free: 800-771-7755

## City Offices

Consumer Protection Division
Los Angeles City Attorney's Office
200 North Main Street
1600 City Hall East
Los Angeles, CA 90012
213-485-4515
Fax: 213-847-0402

Consumer and Environmental Protection Unit
San Diego City Attorney's Office
1200 Third Avenue
Suite 700
San Diego, CA 92101-4106
619-533-5600
Web site: www.sannet.gove/city-attorney

Consumer Protection and Fair Housing
1685 Main Street
Room 310
Santa Monica, CA 90401
310-458-8336
Fax: 310-395-6727
E-mail: consumers@ci.santa-monica.ca.us
Web site: www.pen.ci.santa-monica.ca.us/atty/consumer_protection/

## Colorado

### State Offices

Colorado Attorney General's Office
1525 Sherman Street
Denver, CO 80203-1760
303-866-5079
Toll free: 800-222-4444
Fax: 303-866-5443

Fax: 315-785-2294
Web site: www.oag.state.ny.us

## County Offices

Department of Consumer Affairs
Albany County Courthouse
#40
Albany, NY 12207
518-487-5048
Web site: www.albanycounty.com

Consumer Fraud Bureau
Erie County District Attorney's Office
Statler Towers
107 Delaware Avenue 4th Floor
Buffalo, Ny 14202
716-853-8404
Toll free in NY: 800-771-7755
Fax: 716-853-8414

Orange County Department of Consumer
Affairs
99 Main Street
Goshen, NY 10924
845-291-2400
Fax: 845-291-2385

Suffolk County Executive's Office of Consumer
Affairs
North County Complex, Building 340
Veterans Memorial Highway
Hauppauge, NY 11788
516-853-4600
Fax: 516-853-4825

**County Offices**

Economic Crime Division
El Paso and Teller Counties District Attorney's Office
105 East Vermijo, Suite 205
Colorado Springs, CO 80903-2083
719-520-6002
Fax: 719-520-6006
Web site: www.co.el-paso.co.us/DistrictAttorney/default.asp

Denver District Attorney's Economic Crimes Unit
303 West Colfax Avenue, Suite 1300
Denver, CO 80204
720-913-9179
TDD/TTY: 720-913-9182
Fax: 720-913-9177
Web site: www.denverda.org

Archuleta, LaPlata and San Juan Counties District Attorney's Office
P.O. Drawer 3455
Durango, CO 81302
970-247-8850
Fax: 970-259-0200

Weld County District Attorney's Office
P.O. Box 1167
Greeley, CO 80632
970-356-4010
Fax: 970-352-8023

Pueblo County District Attorney's Office
201 West 8th Street, Suite 801
Pueblo, CO 81003
719-583-6030
Fax: 719-583-6666

Ulster County District Attorney's Consumer Fraud Bureau
20 Lucas Avenue
Kingston, NY 12404
845-340-3260

Nassau County Office of Consumer Affairs
160 Old Country Road
Mineloa, NY 11501
516-571-2600

Sullivan County Department of Consumer Affairs
Sullivan County Government Center
100 North Street, P.O. Box 5012
Monticello, NY 12701-5012
845-794-3000
Fax: 845-794-0230

Rockland County Office of Consumer Protection
50 Sanatorium Road
Building P
Pomona, NY 10970
914-364-2681
Fax: 914-364-2694

Dutchess County Department of Consumer Affairs
94-A Peach Road
Poughkeepsie, NY 12601
914-486-2949
Fax: 845-486-2947

**Connecticut**

**State Offices**

Department of Consumer Protection
165 Capitol Avenue
Hartford, CT 06106
860-713-6300
Toll free in CT: 800-842-2649
Fax: 860-713-7239
Web site: www.state.ct.us/dcp

**City Offices**

City of Middletown
245 DeKoven Drive
P.O. Box 1300
Middletown, CT 06457-1300
860-344-3491
TDD: 860-344-3521
Fax: 860-344-3561

**Delaware**

**State Offices**

Consumer Protection Unit
Office of Attorney General
820 North French Street
5th Floor
Wilmington, DE 19801
302-577-8600
Toll free in DE: 800-220-5424
Fax: 302-577-3090
Web site: www.state.de.us/attgen/consumer.htm

**District of Columbia**

**District of Columbia Offices**
Office of the Corporate Counsel
441 4th Street NW
Suite 450-N
Washington, DC 20001
202-442-9828 (consumer hotline)
Fax: 202-727-6546

**Florida**

**State Offices**

Economic Crimes Division

Schenectady County Consumer Affairs
64 Kellar Avenue
Schenectady, NY 12307
518-356-6795
518-356-7473
Fax: 518-357-0319

Frauds Bureau
Westchester County District Attorney's Office
111 Grove Street
White Plains, NY 10601
914-285-3414
Fax: 914-285-3594

Westchester County District Attorney's Office
111 Martin Luther King Jr. Boulevard
County Courthouse
White Plains, NY 10601
914-285-3303
Fax: 914-285-3594

Westchester County
Department of Consumer Protection
112 East Post Road
4th Floor
White Plains, NY 10601
914-285-2162
Fax: 914-825-3115

**City Offices**

Queens Neighborhood Office
New York City Department of Consumer
Affairs

Office of the Attorney General
110 SE 6th Street, 10 Floor
For Lauderdale, FL 333301
954-712-4600
Fax: 954-712-4700
Web site: www.legal.firn.edu

Consumer Litigation Section
110 SE 6th Street
 Fort Lauderdale, FL 33301
954-712-4600
Fax: 954-7124706

Economic Crimes Division
Office of the Attorney General
135 West Central Blvd., 10th Floor
Century Plaza, Suite 1000
Orlando, FL 32801
407-999-5588
Fax: 407-245-0365

Economic Crimes Division
Office of the Attorney General
The Capitol, Suite PL01
Tallahassee, FL 32399-1050
850-414-3300
Fax: 850-488-4483

Department of Agriculture & Consumer Services
Terry L. Rhoads Building
2005 Apalachee
Tallahassee, FL 32399
850-922-2966
Toll free in FL: 800-432-7352
Fax: 850-410-3839
Web site: www.800helpfla.com

120-55 Queens Blvd.
Room 301
Kew Gardens, NY 11424
718-286-2990
Fax: 718-286-2997

Mt. Vernon Office of Consumer Protection
City Hall
11th Floor
Mount Vernon, NY 10550
914-665-2433
Fax: 914-665-2496

New York City Department of Consumer
Affairs
42 Broadway
New York, NY 10004
212-487-4444
212-487-4481 (Spanish)
212-487-4488 (Chinese)
TDD: 212-487-4465
Fax: 212-487-4197
Web site:
www.ci.nyc.ny.us/html/dca/home.html

Town of Colonial Consumer Protection
Memorial Town Hall
Newtonville, NY 12128
518-783-2790

Schenectady Bureau of Consumer Protection
City Hall, room 204
Jay StreetSchenectady, NY 12305
518-382-5061
Fax: 518-382-5074

**County Offices**

Pinellas County Office of Consumer Protection
15251 Roosevelt Blvd
Suite 209
Clearwater, FL 33760
727-464-6200
TDD/TTY: 727-464-6088
Fax: 727-464-6129
Web site: www.pinellascounty.org

Broward County Consumer Affairs Division
115 South Andrews Avenue
A460
Fort Lauderdale, FL 33301
954-765-5350, ext. 232
Fax: 954-765-5309
Web site: www.broward.org/consumer

Dade County Economic Crime Unit
Office of the State Attorney
1350 NW 12th Avenue
5th Floor, Graham Building
Miami, FL 33135-2111
305-547-0671
Fax: 305-547-0717

Consumer Services Department
Miami-Dade County
140 West Flagler Street
Suite 903
Miami, FL 33130
305-375-3677 (Consumer Hotline)
TDD/TYY: 305-375-4177
Fax: 305-375-4120
E-mail: consumer@miamidade.gov
Web site: www.co.miami-dade.fl.us/csd

Pasco County Consumer Affairs Division
7530 Little Road
New Port Richey, FL 34654
727-847-8106

New Justice Conflict Resolution Services, Inc.
1153 West Fayette Street, Suite 301
Syracuse, NY 13204
315-471-4676
Fax: 315-475-0769

Office of Consumer Protection
City of Yonkers
87 Nepperhan Avenue
Yonkers, NY 10701
914-377-6808
Fax: 914-377-6811

**North Carolina**

**State Offices**

Consumer Protection Division
Office of the Attorney General
P.O. Box 629
Raleigh, NC 27602
919-716-6000
Fax: 919-716-6050
Web site: www.jus.state.nc.us/cpframe.htm

**North Dakota**

**State Offices**

Consumer Protection and Antitrust Division
Office of the Attorney General
600 East Boulevard Avenue
Department 125
Bismarck, ND 58505-0040
701-328-3404
Toll free in ND: 800-472-2600
TTY 800-366-6888
Fax: 701-328-3535
Web site:
www.ag.state.nd.us/ndag/cpat/cpat.html

Office of the Attorney General
600 East Boulevard Avenue
Department 125
Bismarck, ND 58505-0040

352-521-5179
Fax: 727-847-8191

Orange County Consumer Fraud Unit
415 North Orange Avenue
P.O. Box 1673
Orlando, FL 32802
407-836-2490
Fax: 407-836-2376
E-mail: fraudhelp@sao9.org
Web site: www.orangecountyfl.net

Hillsborough County Consumer Protection
Agency
8900 N. Armenia Avenue, Suite 222
Tampa, FL 33604-1067
813-903-3432
Fax: 813-903-3432
Web site: www.hillsboroughcounty.org

Palm Beach County Division of Consumer
Affairs
50 South Military Trail, Suite 201
West Palm Beach, FL 33415
561-233-4820
Toll free: 800-930-5124 (Palm Beach County)
Fax: 561-233-4838
E-mail: consumer@co.palm-beach.fl.us

701-328-2210
TTY: 800-366-6888
Fax: 701-328-2226
Web site: www.ag.state.nd.us

## Ohio

### State Offices

Ohio Consumers' Counsel
77 South High Street
15th Floor
Columbus, OH 43266-0550
614-466-8574 (outside OH)
Toll free in OH: 877-PICK-OCC (877-742-5622)
E-mail: occ@occ.state.oh.us
Web site: www.state.oh.us/cons/

Ohio Attorney General's Office
30 East Broad Street
25th Floor
Columbus, OH 800-282-0515
TDD: 614-466-1393
Fax: 614-728-7583
E-mail: consumer@ag.state.oh.us
Web site: www.ag.state.oh.us

### County Offices

Summit County Office of Prosecuting Attorney
53 University Avenue
Akron, OH 44308-1680
330-643-2800
TDD/TYY: 330-643-8277 (criminal)
Fax: 330-643-2137 (civil)

## City Offices

City of Jacksonville Division of Consumer Affairs
St. James Building
117 West Duval Street, Suite M-100
Jacksonville, FL 32202
904-630-3467
Fax: 904-630-3458
Web site:
www.coj.net/pub/consumer/consumer.htm

## Offices

Economic Crimes Division
Office of the Attorney General
Westwood Center
2002 North Lois Avenue, Suite 520
Tampa, FL 33607
813-801-0600
Fax: 813-871-7262

## Georgia

### State Offices

Governor's Office of Consumer Affairs
2 Martin Luther King, Jr. Drive
Suite 356
Atlanta, GA 30334
404-656-3790
Toll free in GA (outside Atlanta area): 800-869-1123
Fax: 404-651-9018
Web site: www2.state.ga.us/gaoca

## Hawaii

### State Offices

Office of Consumer Protection
Department of Commerce and Consumer Affairs345 Kekuanaoa Street Room 12
Hilo, HI 96720
808-933-0910
Fax: 808-933-8845

Office of Consumer Protection
Department of Commerce and Consumer Affairs
235 South Beretania Street
Room 801

Economic Crime
Franklin County Office of Prosecuting Attorney
369 South High Street
Columbus, OH 43215
614-462-3555
Fax: 614-462-6103

Portage County Office of Prosecuting Attorney
466 South Chestnut Street
Ravenna, OH 44266-3000
330-269-4593
Fax: 330-297-3856

## City Offices

Department of Community Development
Cincinnati Office of Consumer Services
City Hall Room 126
801 Plum Street
Cincinnati, OH 45202
513-352-6146
Fax: 513-352-5241

## Oklahoma

### State Offices

Department of Consumer Credit
4545 North Lincoln Blvd., #104
Oklahoma City, OK 73105
405-521-3653
Fax: 405-521-6740

Oklahoma Attorney General
Consumer Protection Unit
4545 N. Lincoln Avenue
Suite 260

Honolulu, HI 96813
808-586-2636
Fax: 808-586-2640

Office of Consumer Protection
Department of Commerce and Consumer Affairs
1063 L Main Street, Suite C216
Wailuku, HI 96793
808-984-2844
Fax: 808-243-5807
Web site: www.state.hi.us/dcca/

## Idaho

### State Offices

Consumer Protection Unit
Idaho Attorney General's Office
650 West State Street
Boise, ID 83720-0010
208-334-2424
Toll free in ID: 800-432-3545
Fax: 208-334-2830
Web site: www.state.id.us/ag

## Illinois

### State Offices

Office of the Attorney General
1001 East Main Street
Carbondale, IL 62901
618-529-6400
Toll free in IL: 800-243-0607 (consumer hotline
serving southern Illinois)
TDD: 618-529-0607
Fax: 618-529-6416

Consumer Fraud Bureau
100 West Randolph
12th Floor
Chicago, IL 60601
312-814-3580
Toll free in IL: 800-386-5438
Fax: 618-529-6416

Oklahoma City, OK 73105
405-521-2029
Toll free: 800-448-4904
Fax: 405-528-1867
Web site: www.oag.state.ok.us

Consumer Protection Division
Office of the Attorney General
440 South Houston, Suite 505
Tulsa, OK 74127-8913
918-581-2885
Fax: 9178-581-2917
Web site: www.oag.state.ok.us

## Oregon

### State Offices

Financial Fraud/Consumer Protection Section
Department of Justice
1162 Court Street, NE
Salem, OR 97310
503-378-4732
503-378-4320 (hotline Salem only)
503-229-5576 (hotline Portland only)
Toll free in OR: 811-811-9392
Fax: 503-378-5017
Web site: www.doj.state.or.us

Bureau of Consumer Protection
Office of the Attorney General
14th Floor, Strawberry Square
Harrisburg, PA 17120
717-787-9707
Toll free in PA: 800-441-2555
Fax: 717-787-1190
Web site: www.attorneygeneral.gov

Health Care Unit
Office of the Attorney General
14th Floor, Strawberry Square
Harrisburg, PA 17120
717-705-6938
Toll free in PA: 877-888-4877
Fax: 717-787-1190

Consumer Fraud Bureau
100 West Randolph
12th Floor
Chicago, IL 60601
312-814-3580
Toll free in IL: 800-386-5438
TDD: 312-814-3374
Fax: 312-814-2549 or 312-814-3806
Web site: www.ag.state.il.us

Consumer Protection Division of the Attorney
General Office
100 West Randolph
12th Floor
Chicago, IL 60601
312-814-3000
TDD: 312-793-2852
Fax: 312-814-2593

Governor's Office of Citizens assistance
222 South College Room 106
Springfield, IL 62706
217-782-0244
Toll free in IL: 800-642-3112
Fax: 217-524-4049
E-mail: governor@state.il.us

**County Offices**

Cook County State Attorney's Office
Consumer Fraud Division
69 West Washington
Suite 700
Chicago, IL 60091
312-603-8700

Madison County Office of State's Attorney
157 North Main Street, Suite 402
Edwardsville, IL 62025
618-692-6280
Fax: 618-656-7312

Department of Consumer Affairs Service Central
Illinois
Office of the Attorney General
500 South Second Street

Office of the Consumer Advocate
Office of the Attorney General
Forum Place, 5th Floor
Harrisburg, PA 17101-1921
717-783-5045 (utilities only)
Toll free in PA: 800-684-6560
Fax: 717-783-7152
E-mail: pacoca@ptd.net
Web site: www.oca.state.pa.us

**Regional Offices**

Bureau of Consumer Protection
Allentown Regional Office
Office of Attorney General
810 Hamilton Street
Fourth Floor
Allentown, PA 18101
610-821-6690
Fax: 610-821-6529

Bureau of Consumer Protection
Ebensburg Regional Office
Office of the Attorney General
171 Lovell Avenue
Suite 202
Ebensburg, PA 15931
814-471-1831
Fax: 814-471-1840

Bureau of Consumer Protection
Erie Regional Office
Office of the Attorney General
1001 State Street
Suite 1009
Erie, PA 16501
814-871-4371
Fax: 814-871-4848

Bureau of Consumer Protection
Harrisburg Regional Office
Office of the Attorney General
301 Chestnut Street, Suite 105
Harrisburg, PA 17101
717-787-7109
Fax: 717-772-3560

Bureau of Consumer Protection
Philadelphia Regional Office
Office of the Attorney General
21 South 12th Street

Springfield, IL 62706
217-782-1090
Toll fee in IL: 800-243-0618
217-785-2771
Fax: 217-782-1097
E-mail: agconsmr@mail.state.il.us
Web site: www.ag.state.il.us

**City Offices**

Chicago Department of Consumer Service
121 North LaSalle Street
Room 808
Chicago, IL 60602
312-744-4006
TDD: 312-744-9385
Fax: 312-744-9089
Web site: www.ci.chi.il.us/ConsumerServices/

City of Des Plaines Consumer Protection Office
City of Des Plaines
1420 Miner Street Des Plaines, IL 60016
847-391-5006
Fax: 847-391-5378
E-mail: admin@desplians.org

Second Floor
Philadelphia, PA 19107
215-560-2414
Fax: 215-560-2494

Bureau of Consumer Protection
Pittsburgh Regional Office
Office of the Attorney General
564 Forbes Avenue
6th Floor Manor Building
Pittsburgh, PA 15219
415-565-5135

Bureau of Consumer Protection
Scranton Regional Office
Office of the Attorney General
214 Samter Building
101 Penn Avenue
Scranton, PA 18503
570-963-4913
Fax: 570-963-3418

**Indiana**

**State Offices**

Consumer Protection Division
Office of the Attorney General
Indiana Government Center South
402 West Washington Street, 5th Floor
Indianapolis, IN 46204
319-232-6201
Toll free IN: 800-382-5516 Consumer Hotline
Fax: 317-232-7979
Web site: www.in.gov/attorneygeneral

**County Offices**

Marrion County Prosecuting Attorney's Office
560 City-County Building
200 East Washington Street
Indianapolis, IN 46204-3363
317-327-3892
TDD/TTY: 317-327-5186
Fax: 317-327-5409
Web site: www.indygov.org

**Iowa**

**State Offices**

Consumer Protection Division
Office of the Attorney General
Director of Consumer Protection Division
1300 East Walnut, Street, 2nd Floor
Des Moines, IA 50319
515-281-5926
Fax: 515-281-6771
E-mail: consumer@ag.state.ia.us
Web site: www.IowaAttorneyGeneral.org

Kansas

State Offices

Consumer Protection Division
Office of the Attorney General
120 SW 10th
4th floor
Topeka, KS 66612-1597
785-296-3751
Toll free in KS: 800-432-2310
TDD/TTY: 785-291-3767

**County Offices**

Beaver County Alliance for Consumer
Protection
699 Fifth Street
Beaver, PA 15009-1997
721-728-7267
Fax: 724-728-6762

Bucks County Consumer Protection, Weights
and Measures
50 North Main Street
Doylestown, PA 18901
215-348-7442
Fax: 215-348-4570

Montgomery County Human services Center
1430 DeKalb Street
Norristown, PA 19404-0311
610-278-3565
Fax: 610-278-5228

Economic Crime Unit
Philadelphia District Attorney's Office
1421 Arch Street
Philadelphia, PA 19102
215-686-8750
Fax: 215-686-8765

Fax: 785-291-3699
E-mail: cprotect@ksag.org
Web site: www.ink.org/public/ksag

**County Offices**

Consumer Protection Division
Johnson County Courthouse
100 North Kansas Avenue
Olathe, KS 66061
913-715-3003
Fax: 913-715-3040

Office of the District Attorney
Consumer Fraud & Economic Crime Division
535 North Main Street 1st Floor
Wichita, KS 67206-3747
316-383-7921
Toll free in KS: 800-432-2310
Fax: 316-383-4669
E-mail: consumer@sedgwick.gov

**Kentucky**

**State Offices**

Consumer Protection Division
Office of the Attorney General
1024 Capital Center Drive
Frankfort, KY 40601
502-636-5389
Toll free in KY: 888-432-9257
Fax: 502-573-8317
E-mail: consumerprotection@law.state.ky.us
Web site: www.kyattorneygenerl.com/cp

Consumer Protection Division
Office of the Attorney General
9001 Shelbyville Road
Suite 3
Louisville, KY 40222
502-425-4825
Fax: 502-573-8317

**Louisiana**

Chester Consumer Affairs
601 Westtown Road, Suite 295
West Chester, PA 19382-4991
610-344-6150

**Rhode Island**

**State Offices**

Vivian Spencer, Director
Consumer Unit
Consumer Protection Unit
Department of Attorney General
150 South Main Street
Providence, RI 02903
401-274-4400
Senior Line: 888-621-1112
TDD: 401-453-0410
Fax: 401-222-5110

Consumer Credit Counseling Services
535 Centerville Road
Suite 103
Warwick, RI 02886
Toll free: 800-208-2227
Fax: 401-732-0250
Web site: www.creditcounseling.org

**South Carolina**

**State Offices**

Office of the Attorney General
P.O. Box 11549
Columbia, SC 29211
803-734-3970
Fax: 803-734-4323
Web site: www.scattorneygeneral.org

SC Department Consumer Affairs

**State Offices**

Consumer Protection Section
Office of the Attorney General
301 Main Street Suite 1250
Baton Rouge, LA 70801
Toll free nationwide: 800-351-4889
Fax: 225-342-9637
Web site: www.ag.state.la.us

**County Offices**

Consumer Protection Section
Jefferson Parish District Attorney
200 Derbigny Street
5th Floor Courthouse Annex
Gretna, LA 70053
504-368-1020
Fax: 504-368-4562

**Maine**

**State Offices**

Office of Consumer Credit Regulation
35 State House Station
Augusta, ME 04333-0035
207-624-8527
Toll free in ME: 800-332-8529
TDD/TYY: 207-624-8563
Fax: 207-582-7699
Web site: www.mainecreditreg.org

Public Conti, Division Chief
Public Protection Division
Office of the Attorney General
6 State House Station
Augusta, ME 04333
207-626-8800

**Maryland**

**State Offices**

Consumer Protection Division
Office of the Attorney General
200 Saint Paul Place
16th Floor

2801 Devine Street
P.O. Box 5757
Columbia, SC 29205-5757
803-734-4200
Columbia, SC 29205-5757
803-734-4200
Toll Free in SC: 800-922-1594
Fax: 803-734-4286
E-mail: scdca@infoave.net
Web site: www.state.sc.us/consumer

Office of Executive Policy and Program
1205 Pendleton Street
Room 308
Columbia, SC 29201
803-734-0457
Toll free in SC only: 866-300-9333
Fax: 803-734-0799
Web site: www.myscgov.com

**South Dakota**

**State Offices**

Office of the Attorney General
500 East Capitol
State Capitol Building
Pierre, SD 57501-5070
605-773-4400
Toll free in SD: 800-300-1986
TDD: 605-773-6585
Fax: 605-773-7163

**Tennessee**

**State Offices**

Division of Consumer Affairs
5th Floor
500 James Robertson Parkway
Nashville, TN 37243-0600
615-741-4737
Toll free in TN: 800-342-8385
Fax: 615-532-4994
Web site: www.state.tn.us/consumer

Division of Consumer Protection
Consumer Advocate and Protection
Tennessee Attorney General's Office
P.O. Box 20207

Baltimore, MD 21202-2021
401-528-8662 (consumer complaint hotline)
410-576-6550 (consumer information)
TDD: 410-576-6372 (Maryland only)
Fax: 410-576-7040
E-mail: consumer@oag.state.md.us
Web site: www.oag.state.md.us/consumer

Business Licensing & Consumer Service
Motor Vehicle Administration
6601 Ritchie Highway, NE
Glenn Burnie, MD 21062
410-768-7248
Fax: 410-768-7602

**Regional Offices**

Maryland Attorney General's Office
Consumer Protection Division
138 East Antietam Street, Suite 210
Hagerstown, MD 21740-5684
301-791-4780
410-576-6372
Fax: 301-791-7178

Easter Shore Branch Office
Consumer Protection Division
Office of the Attorney General
201 Baptist Street
Suite 30
Salisbury, MD 21801-4976
410-543-6620
Fax: 410-543-6642
Web site: www.oag.state.md.us

**County Offices**

Howard County Office of Consumer Affairs
6751 Columbia Gateway Drive
Columbia, MD 21046
410-313-6420
Fax: 410-313-6453

Montgomery County Division of Consumer
Affairs
100 Maryland Avenue
Suite 330
Rockville, MD 20850
240-777-3636

Nashville, TN 37243-0491
615-741-1671
Fax: 615-532-2910

**Texas**

**State Offices**

Consumer Protection/Austin Regional Office
P.O. Box 12548
Austin, TX 78711-2548
512-463-2185
Fax: 512-463-8301
Web site: www.oag.state.tx.us

Consumer Protection Division
Office of the Attorney General
P.O. Box 12548
Austin, TX 78711-2548
512-463-2070
Fax: 512-463-8301

Office of Public Insurance Counsel
333 Guadalupe
Suite 3-120
Austin, TX 78701
512-322-4143
Fax: 512-322-4148
Web site: www.opic.state.tx.us

Consumer Protection/Houston Regional Office
Office of the Attorney General
808 Travis, Suite 812
Houston, TX 77002
713-223-5886, ext. 118
Fax: 713-223-5821

**Regional Offices**

Consumer Protection Division/Dallas Regional
Office
Office of the Attorney General
1600 Pacific Avenue, Suite 1700

TDD: 240-777-3679
Fax: 240-777-3768
Web site: www.co.mo.md.us/hca

**Massachusetts**

**State Offices**

Executive Office of Consumer Affairs and
Business Regulation
10 Park Plaza Room 5170
Boston, MA 02116
617-973-8700 general information
617-973-8787 consumer hotline
Toll free in MA: 888-283-3757
TDD/TTY: 617-973-8790
Fax: 617-973-8798
E-mail: consumer@state.ma.us
Web site: www.state.ma.us/consumer

Consumer Protection and Antitrust Division
Office of the Attorney General
200 Portland Street
Boston, MA 02114
617-727-8400 The consumer Hotline –
information and referral to local county and city
government consumer offices (listed below) that
work in conjunction with the Department of the
Attorney General
Fax: 617-727-3265
Web site: www.ago.state.ma.us

Consumer Protection and Antitrust Division
Office of the Attorney General – Springfield
436 Dwight Street
Springfield, MA 01103
413-784-1240
Fax: 413-784-1244

**County Offices**

Mayor's Office of Consumer Affairs and
Licensing
Boston City Hall
Room 817
Boston, MA 02201
617-635-3834
617-635-4165
Fax: 617-635-4174

Dallas, TX 75201-3513
214-969-5310
Fax: 214-969-7615

Consumer Protection/El Paso Regional Office
Office of the Attorney General
401 East Franklin Street, Suite 530
El Paso, TX 79901
915-834-5800

Consumer Protection/Lubbock Regional Office
916 Main Street, Suite 806
Lubbock, TX 79401-3410
806-747-6307
Web site: www.oag.state.tx.us

Consumer Protection/McAllen Regional Office
Office of the Attorney General
3201 North McColl Road, Suite B
956-682-4547
Fax: 956-682-1957
Web site: www.oag.state.tx.us

Consumer Protection/San Antonio Regional
Office
Office of the Attorney General
115 East Travis Street, Suite 925
San Antonio, TX 78205-1615
210-224-1007
Fax: 210-225-1075
**County Offices**

Department of Environmental and Health
Services
City Hall
1500 Marilla, Room 7A-North
Dallas, TX 75201
214-670-5216
Fax: 214-670-3863

Cambridge Consumer's Council
831 Massachusetts Avenue
Cambridge, MA 02139
617-349-6150
Fax: 617-349-6148
Web site: www.ci.cambridge.ma.us/~Consumer

Fall River Consumer Program
One Government Center
Fall River, MA 02722
508-324-2672
Fax: 508-324-2626

Consumer Protection Division
North Western District Attorney's Office
238 Main Street
Greenfield, MA 01301
413-774-5102
Fax: 413-773-3278

Consumer Protection Program
Haverhall Community Action, Inc.
149 Main Street
Hyannis, MA 02601
508-771-0700
Toll free: 800-867-0701
Fax: 508-771-3011
Web site: www.consumercouncil.com

Greater Lawrence Community Action Council,
Inc.
Consumer Protection Program
350 Essex Street
Lawrence, MA 08410
978-681-4990
Fax: 978-681-4949
Web site: www.glcac.org

Middlesex Community College Law Center
Local Consumer Program
33 Kearney Square Room 117
Lowell, MA 01852
978-656-3342

City of Dallas Economic Development
Department
City Hall
500 Marilla, Room 5C-South
Dallas, TX 75201
241-670-1685
Fax: 214-670-0158

Harris County Consumer Fraud Division
Harris County District Attorney's Office
1201 Franklin
Suite 600
Houston, TX 77002-1901
713-755-5836
713-755-5840
Fax: 713-755-5262

**Utah**

**State Office**

Division of Consumer Protection
Department of Commerce
160 East 300 South
Box 146704
Salt Lake City, UT 841114-6704
801-530-6601
Fax: 801-530-6001
Web site: www.commerce.state.ut.us

**Vermont**

**State Offices**

Office of the Attorney General
Antitrust and Consumer Litigation Section
900 East Main Street
Richmond, VA 23219
804-786-21116
Toll free: 800-451-1525
Fax: 804-786-0122
Web site: www.oag.state.va.us

Office of Consumer Affairs
Department of Agriculture and Consumer
Services
Washington Building, Suite 100
P.O. Box 1163

Fax: 978-656-3339
E-mail: dunnk@middlesex.cc.ma.us

Consumer Assistance Office – Metro West, Inc.
209 West Central Street
Natick, MA 01760
508-8812
Fax: 508-647-0661

Newton-Brookline Consumer Office
Newton City Hall
1000 Commonwealth Avenue
Newton, MA 02465
617-552-7205
Fax: 617-552-7027

Mass PIRG Consumer Action Center
182 Green Street
North Weymouth, MA 02191
781-335-0280
Fax: 781-340-3991
E-mail: jfoyconsumeraction2@juno.com

Berkshire County Consumer Advocates, Inc.
150 North Street
Pittsfield, MA 01201
413-443-9128
Toll free: 800-540-9128
Fax: 413-496-9225

South Shore Community Action Council, Inc.
265 South Meadow Road
Plymouth, MA 02360
508-747-7575 ext. 226
Fax: 508-746-5140

Mayor's Office of Consumer Information
City of Springfield
1243 Main Street
Springfield, MA 01103
413-787-6437

Consumer Council of Worcester County
484 Main Street
2nd Floor
Worcester, MA 01608-1690

Richmond, VA 23219
804-786-2042
Toll free in VA: 800-552-9963
TDD: 800-828-1120
Fax: 804-371-7479
Web site: www.vdacs.state.va.us

**County Offices**

Office of Citizen and Consumer Affairs
#1 Court House Plaza, Suite 310
2100 Clarendon Blvd.
Arlington, VA 22201
703-228-3260
Fax: 703-228-3295
Web site: www.co.arlington.va.us

Fairfax County Department of
Telecommunications and Consumer Services
12000 Government Center Parkway, Suite 433
Fairfax, VA 22035
703-222-8435
Fax: 703-322-9542

**City Offices**

City of Alexandria
City Hall
P.O. Box 178
Alexandria, VA 223313
703-838-4350
Fax: 703-838-6426
Web site: www.ci.alexandria.va.us

Consumer Affairs Division
Office of the Commonwealth's Attorney
2425 Nimmo Parkway
Virginia Beach, VA 23456-9060
757-426-5836
Fax: 757-427-8779
Web site: www.vbgov.com/dept/oca/

**Washington**

**State Offices**

508-754-1176
Fax: 508-754-0203

## Michigan

### State Offices

Bureau of Automotive Regulation
Michigan Department of State
Lansing, MI 48918-1200
517-373-4777
Toll free in MI: 800-292-4204
Fax: 517-373-0964

Consumer Protection Division
Office of the Attorney General
P.O. Box 30213
Lansing, MI 48909
517-373-1140 (complaint information)
517-373-1110
Fax: 517-241-3771

### County Offices

Bay County Consumer Protection Unit
1230 Washington – Courthouse
Bay City, MI 48707-5994
517-895-4139
Fax: 517-895-4167

Consumer Protection Department
Macomb County
Office of the Prosecuting Attorney
Macomb County Administration Building
One South Main Street 3rd Floor
Mt. Clemens, MI 48043
810-469-5600
810-469-5350
Fax: 810-469-5609

Consumer Resource Center
Office of the Attorney General
103 East Holly Street, Suite 308
Bellingham, WA 98225-4728
360-738-6185

Consumer Resource Center
Office of the Attorney General
500 N. Morain Street, Suite 1250
Kennewick, WA 99336-2607
509-734-2967

Consumer Resource Center
Office of the Attorney General
905 Plum Street Building 3
P.O. Box 40118
Olympia, WA 98504-0118
360-753-6210

Consumer Reosurce Center
Office of the Attorney General
900 Fourth Avenue, Suite 2000
Seattle, WA 98164-1012
206-464-6684
Toll free in WA: 800-551-4636 (consumer resource centers)
Toll free TDD in WA: 800-276-9883
Fax: 206-464-6451
Web site: www.wa.gov/ago

Consumer Resource Center
Office of the Attorney General
1116 West Riverside Avenue
Spokane, WA 99201-1194
509-456-3123

Consumer Resource Center
Office of the Attorney General
Consumer Protection Division
1019 Pacific Avenue, 3rd Floor
Tacoma, WA 98402-4411
253-2904
Toll free: 800-551-4636
Toll free: /800-276-9883 in state only
Fax: 253-593-2449
Web site: www. wa.gov/ago
Consumer Resource Center
Office of the Attorney General

1220 Main Street, Suite 510
Vancouver, WA 98660
360-759-2150

**City Offices**

City of Detroit Consumer Affairs Department
65 Cadillac Square
Suite 1600
Detroit, MI 48226
313-224-3508
313-224-6995 (complaints)
Fax: 313-224-2796
Web site: www.ci.detroit.mi.us

**Minnesota**

**State Offices**

Consumer Services Division
Minnesota Attorney General's Office
1400 NCL Tower
445 Minnesota Street
St. Paul, MN 55101
612-296-3353
Toll free: 800-657-3787
E-mail: consumer.ag@state.mn.us
Web site: www.ag.state.mn.us/consumer

**City Offices**

Fraud Division
900 4th Avenue, #1002
Seattle, WA 98164
206-296-9010
Fax: 206-296-9009
Web site: www.metrokc.gov/proatty/

Revenue and Consumer Affairs
Seattle Department of Finance
805 South Dearborn Street
Seattle, WA 98134
206-386-1298
Fax: 206-386-1129
E-mail: seattle.consumer-affairs@ci.seattle.wa.us
Web site:
www.pan.ci.seattle.wa.us/esd/consumer

**County Offices**

Hennepin County Citizen Information Hotline
Office of Hennepin County Attorney
C-2000 County Government Center
Minneapolis, MN 55487
612-348-4528
TDD/TTY: 612-348-6015
Fax: 612-348-9712
E-mail: citizeninfo@hennipin.mn.us
Web site:
www.co.hennepin.mn.us/coatty/hcatty.htm

**City Offices**

Division of Licenses & Consumer Services
Minneapolis Department of Regulatory Services
City Hall, Room 1C
350 South 5th Street
Minneapolis, MN 55415
612-673-2080
TDD?TTY: 612-373-3300-3360
Fax: 612-673-3399
W-mail: opa@ci.minneapolis.mn.us
Web site: www.ci.minneapolis.mn.us

**Mississippi**

**State Offices**

Consumer Protection Division of the Mississippi
Attorney General's Office
P.O. Box 22947
Jackson MS 39225-2947
601-359-4230
Toll free in MS: 800-281-4418
Fax: 601-359-4231
Web site: www.ago.state.ms.us

Bureau of Regulatory Services
Department of Agriculture and Commerce
121 North Jefferson Street
P.O. Box 1609
Jackson, MS 39201
601-359-1111
Fax: 601-354-6502
Web site: www.mdac.state.ms.us

**Missouri**

**State Offices**

Revenue and Consumer Affairs Section
Executive Services Department
Division of Finance
600 4th Avenue, #103
Seattle, WA 98104-1891
206-233-7837
Fax: 206-684-5170

**West Virginia**

**State Offices**

Consumer Protection Division
Office of the Attorney General
812 Quarrier Street, 6th Floor
P.O. Box 1789
Charleston, WV 25326-1789
304-558-8986
Toll free in WV: 800-368-8808
Fax: 304-558-0184
E-mail: consumer@wvnet.edu
Web site: www.state.wv.us/wvag

Division of Weights and Measures Section
570 MacCorkle Avenue
St. Albans, WV 24177
304-722-0605

**Wisconsin**

**State Offices**

Division of Trade and Consumer Protection
Department of Agriculture
Trade and Consumer Protection
3610 Oakwood Hills Parkway
Eau Claire, WI 54701-7754
715-839-3848
Toll free in WI: 800-422-7128
Fax: 715-839-1645

Consumer Protection and Trade Offense
Division
P.O. Box 899
1530 Rax Court
Jefferson City, MO 65102
573-751-6887
573-751-3321
Toll free in MO: 800-392-8222
TDD/TTY toll free in MO: 800-729-8668
Fax: 573-751-7948
E-mail: attgenmail@moago.org
Web site: www.ago.state.mo.us

**Montana**

**State Offices**

Consumer Affairs Unit
Department of Administration
1424 Ninth Avenue
Box 200501
Helena, MT 59620-0201
406-444-4312 (Miscellaneous)
406-444-9405 (Telemarketing)
406-444-1588 (Automotive)
Fax: 406-444-2903

Nebraska

State Offices

Department of Justice
2115 State Capitol
P.O. Box 98920
Lincoln, NE 68509
402-471-2682
Toll free in state: 800-727-6432
Fax: 402-471-0006
Web site: www.nol.org/home/ago

Nevada

State Offices

Nevada Conumer Affairs Division
1850 East Sahara

Department of Agriculture Trade & Consumer
Protection
Division of Trade and Consumer Protection
200 North Jefferson Street
Suite 146A
Green Bay, WI 54301
920-448-5110
Fax: 920-448-5118
Web site: www.datcp.state.wi.us
Division of Trade and Consumer Protection
Department of Agriculture
2811 Agriculture Drive
P.O. Box 8911
Madison, WI 53708
608-224-4953
Toll free in WI: 800-422-7128
TDD?TTY: 608-224-5058
E-mail: Datephotline@wheel.datep.state.wi.us
Web site: www.datcp.state.wi.us

**County Offices**

Consumer Fraud Unit
Milwaukee County District Attorney's Office
821 West State Street, Room 405
Milwaukee, WI 53233-2485
414-278-4585
Fax: 2231955

Racine County Sheriff's Department
717 Wisconsin Avenue
Racine, WI 53403
262-363-3126
Fax: 262-367-5279

**Wyoming**

**State Offices**

Office of the Attorney General
Consumer Protection Unit

Suite 101
Las Vegas, NV 89104
702-486-7355
Toll free: 800-326-5205
TDD: 702-486-7901
Fax: 702-486-7371
E-mail: ncad@fyiconsumer.org
Web site: www.fyiconsumer.org

Bureau of Consumer Protection
555 E. Washington Avenue, Suit 3900
Las Vegas, NV 89101
702-486-3420

Consumer Affairs Division
Departmetn of Business and Industry
4600 Keitzke Lane, Building B, Suite 113
Reno, NV 86502
775-688-1800
Toll free in NV: 800-326-5202
TDD: 775-486-7901
Fax: 702-688-1803

**New Hampshire**

**State Office**

Consumer Protection and Antitrust Bureau
New Hampshire Attorney General's Office
33 Capitol Street
Concord, NH 03301
603-271-3641
TDD toll free: 800-735-2964
Fax: 603-271-2110
Web site:
www.state.nh.us/nhdoj/consumer/cpb.html

123 State Capitol Building
Cheyenne, WY 82002
307-777-7874
Toll free in WY only: 800-438-5799
E-mail: agwebmaster@state.wy.us
Web site: www.attorneygeneral.state.wy.us

# Appendix F

United States Bankruptcy Court Addresses, Telephone Numbers, and Web Sites

**Alabama (Northern)**

Northern Division at Decatur Alabama
400 Well Street
(P.O. Box 2748)
**Decatur**, AL 35602-1289
Telephone: 256-353-2817
Web site: www.alnb.uscourts.gov

**Alabama (Southern)**

Southern District of Alabama
201 St. Louis Street
**Mobile**, AL 36602

251-441-5391
Southern Division at Birmingham Alabama
1800 5th Avenue North, Room 120
**Birmingham**, AL 35203-2111
205-714-4000
Fax: 205-714-3913

Web site: www.alsb.uscourts.gov

**Alabama (Eastern)**

Eastern Division at Anniston Alabama
1129 Noble Street
(P.O. Box 2008)
**Anniston**, AL 36202-2008
256-741-1500
Fax: 256-741-1503

Web site: www.alnb.uscourts.gov

**Nebraska**

Omaha Office
US Bankruptcy Court
111 South 18th Plaza, Suite 1125
**Omaha**, NE 68102
402-661-7444
Fax: 402-661-7492

**Lincoln Office**
US Bankruptcy Court
460 Federal Building
100 Centennial Mall North
**Lincoln**, NE 68508
402-437-5100
Fax: 402-437-5454

Web site: www.neb.uscourts.gov

**Nevada**

Las Vegas Court
US Bankruptcy Court
Lloyd D. George Federal Building
333 Las Vegas Boulevard South
**Las Vegas**, NV 89101
702-388-6257

Reno Court
US Bankruptcy Court
300 Booth Street
Room 1109
**Reno**, NV 89509
775-784-5559

Web site: www.nvb.uscourts.gov

**New Hampshire**

District of New Hampshire
US Bankruptcy Courts
275 Chestnut Street, Room 404
**Manchester**, NH 03101
603-222-2600
Fax: 5603-666-7408

Web site: www.nhb.uscourts.gov

**Alabama (Middle)**

Middle District of Alabama
One Church Street
Ground Floor
P.O. Box 1248
**Montgomery**, AL 36102
334-954-3800
Fax: 334-954-3819

Web site: www.almb.uscourts.gov

**Alabama (Western)**

Western Division at Tuscaloosa Alabama
1118 Greensboro Avenue
(P.O. Box 3226)
**Tuscaloosa**, AL 354-3226
205-752-0426
Fax: 205-752-6468
www.alnb.uscourts.gov

**New Jersey**

Camden
US Bankruptcy Court – **Street Address**
District of New Jersey
401 Market Street
**Camden**, NJ 08101
856-757-5486

US Bankruptcy Court – **Mailing Address**
District of New Jersey
P.O. Box 2067
Camden, NJ 08101

Newark
US Bankruptcy Court – **Street Address**
District of New Jersey
Martin Luther King, Jr. Federal Building
50 Walnut Street
**Newark**, NJ 07102
973-645-4764

US Bankruptcy Court – **Mailing Address**
District of New Jersey
P.O. Box 1352
Newark, NJ 07101-1352

Clarkson S. Fisher Courthouse
402 East state Street
**Trenton**, NJ 08608
609-989-2129

Web site: www.njb.uscourts.gov

**New Mexico**

US Bankruptcy Court - Clerk's Office
Federal Building and US Courthouse
421 Gold Avenue SW, Room 316 (POB 546)
**Albuquerque**, NM 87102 (POB zip: 87103-0546)

Web site: www.nmcourt.fed.us/bkdocs

**Alaska**

Historical Courthouse
605 West Fourth Avenue, Suiye 138
**Anchorage**, AK 99501
907-271-2655

US Courthouse
101 12th Avenue, Room 370
**Fairbanks**, AK 99701
907-456-0349

US District Court
709 W. 9th Avenue, Room 979
**Juneau**, AK 99802
907-586-7458
This US District Court accepts Bankruptcy Pleadings and forwards them to Anchorage for processing.

US Bankruptcy Court
648 Mission Street, Room 507
**Ketchikan**, AK 99901
907-247-7576

www.akb.uscourts.gov

**Arizona**

**Phoenix**
US Bankruptcy Court
2929 N. Central Avenue, 9th Floor
**Phoenix**, AZ 85012
602-640-5800

**Tucson**
US Bankruptcy Court
110 S. Church Avenue, Suite 8112
**Tucson**, AZ 85701
520-620-7500

**Yuma**
US Bankruptcy Court
325 W. 19th Street, Suite D
**Yuma**, AZ 85364
928-783-2288

Web site: www.azb.uscourts.gov

**New York (Eastern)**

Brooklyn Office (Headquarters)
US Bankruptcy Court, EDNY
75 Clinton Street
**Brooklyn**, NY 11201
718-330-2188

Central Islip Office (Divisional)
US Bankruptcy Court, EDNY
Long Island Federal Courthouse
290 Federal Plaza
**Central Islip**, NY 11722
631-712-6200

Web site: www.nyeb.uscourts.gov

**New York (Northern)**

Albany Office
US Bankruptcy Court
James T. Foley US Courthouse
445 Broadway, Suite 330
**Albany**, NY 12207
518-247-1661

Utica Office
US Bankruptcy Court
Alexander Pirnie US Courthouse
10 Broad Street, Room 230
**Utica**, NY 13502
315-793-8101

Web site: www.nynb.uscourts.gov

**Arkansas**

**US Bankruptcy Courthouse**
300 West 2nd Street
P.O. Box 3777
**Little Rock**, AR 72203-3777
501-918-5500
Web site: www.arb.uscourts.gov

**California (Central)**

**Los Angeles**
**US Bankruptcy Court**
Edward R. Roybal
Federal Building and Courthouse
255 East Temple Street
**Los Angeles**, CA 90012

**US Bankruptcy Court**
Federal Building (for filing petitions)
300 North Los Angeles Street
**Los Angeles**, CA 90012
213-894-3118

**Northern Division**
1415 State Street
**Santa Barbara**, CA 93101-2511
805-884-4800

**Riverside**
3420 Twelfth Street
**Riverside**, CA 92501
909-774-1000

**San Fernando Valley**
21041 Burbank Boulevard
**Woodland Hills**, CA 91367
818-587-2900

**Santa Ana**
Ronald Reagan Federal Building and United
States Courthouse
411 West Fourth Street
**Santa Ana**, CA 92704-4593
714-338-5300

Web site: www.cacb.uscourts.gov

**New York (Southern)**

Alexander Hamilton Custom House
One Bowling Green
**New York**, NY 1004-1408
212-668-2870

Poughkeepsi Court
176 Church Street
**Poughkeepsie**, NY 12601
845-452-4200

White Plains Court
300 Quarropas Street
**White Plains**, NY 10601
914-390-4060

Web site: www.nysb.uscourts.gov

**New York (Western)**

Buffalo
Olympic Towers
300 Pearl Street, Suite 250
**Buffalo**, NY 14202-2501
716-551-4130

Rochester
1220 US Courthouse
100 State Street
**Rochester**, NY 14614
585-263-3148

Web site: www.nywb.uscourts.gov

**California Eastern**

**Sacramento Division**
501 I Street, Suite 3-200
**Sacramento**, CA 95814
916-930-4400

**Fresno Division**
1130 O Street, Suite 2656
**Fresno**, CA 93721
559-498-7217

**Madesto Division**
1130 12th Street Suite C
**Modesto**, CA 95354
209-521-5160

Web site: www.caeb.uscourts.gov

**California Northern**

**Santa Rosa Division**
99 South "E" Street
**Santa Rosa**, CA 95404
707-525-8539

**San Francisco Division**
US Bankruptcy Court
Post Office Box 7341
**San Francisco**, CA 94120-7341

US Bankruptcy Court
235 Pine street, 19th Floor
**San Francisco**, CA 94104
415-268-2300, extension 0

**Oakland Division**
US Bankruptcy Court
1300 Clay Street
**Oakland**, CA 94612
510-879-3600

**San Jose Division**
United States Courthouse, Room 3035
280 South First Street
**San Jose,** CA 95113-3099
408-535-5118

Web site: www.canb.uscourts.gov

**North Carolina (Western)**

Charlotte Office
US Bankruptcy Court – **Street Address**
401 West Trade Street
**Charlotte**, NC 28202

US Bankruptcy Court – **Mailing Address**
P.O. Box 34189
Charlotte, NC 28234-4189
704-350-7500

Asheville Division
100 Otis Street
Room 112
**Asheville**, NC 28801
828-771-7300

Web site: www.ncwb.uscourts.gov

**California (Southern)**

**US Bankruptcy Court**
Jacob Weinberger US Courthouse
325 West F Street
**San Diego**, CA 92101-6998
626-557-5620

Web site: www.casb.uscourts.gov

**Colorado**

**US Bankruptcy Court for the District of Colorado**
US Custom House, 721 19th Street
**Denver**, CO 80220-2508
303-844-4045

www.cob.uscourts.gov/bindex.htm

**Connecticut**

**Bridgeport Office**
915 Lafayette Boulevard
**Bridgeport**, CT 06604
203-579-5808

**Hartford Main Office**
450 Main Street
**Hartford**, CT 06103
860-240-3675

**New Haven Office**
157 Church Street
**New Haven**, CT 06510
203-773-2009

Web site: www.ctb.uscourts.gov

**North Carolina (Middle)**

Greensboro Court
US Bankruptcy Court – **Street Address**
101 S. Edgeworth Street
**Greensboro**, NC 27401

Greensboro Court
US Bankruptcy Court – **Mailing Address**
P.O. Box 23100
Greensboro, NC 27420-6100
336-333-5647

Winston – Salem Court
US Bankruptcy Court
226 S. Liberty Street
**Winston – Salem**, NC 27101
336-631-5340

Web site: www.ncmb.uscourts.gov

**North Carolina (Eastern)**

Wilson Division
US Bankruptcy Court
P.O. Drawer 2807
1760 Parkwood Blvd
**Wilson**, NC 27894-2807
252-237-0248

Raleigh Division
US Bankruptcy Court
P.O. Box 1441
300 Fayetteville Street Mall
Second Floor
**Raleigh**, NC 27602-1441
919-856-4752

**Delaware**

United States Bankruptcy Court
District of Delaware
824 North Market Street, 5th Floor
**Wilmington**, DE 19801
302-252-2900

Web site: www.deb.uscourts.gov

**Florida (Middle)**

Tampa
801 N. Florida Avenue
Suite 727
**Tampa**, FL 33602-3899
813-301-5162

Orlando
135 W. Central Boulevard
Suite 950
**Orlando**, FL 32801
407-648-6365

Jacksonville
P.O. Box 559
Jacksonville, FL 33201
311 W. Monroe Street
Room 206
**Jacksonville**, FL 32202
904-232-2852
Web site: www.flmb.uscourts.gov

**North Dakota**

Fargo Bankruptcy Court
Courtroom Number Three
Second Floor
Quentin N. Burdick US Courthouse
655 First Avenue North
**Fargo**, ND 701-297-1000

Bismark Bankruptcy Court
US Courthouse and Federal Building
220 East Rosser Avenue
**Bismarck**, ND

Web site: www.ndb.uscourts.gov

**Ohio (Northern)**

Akron
US Federal Building
455 US Courthouse
2 South Main Street
**Akron**, OH 44308
330-375-5840

Canton
Frank T. Bow Federal Building
201 Cleveland Avenue, S.W'
**Canton**, OH 44702-1929
330-489-4426

Cleveland
Key Tower, Room 3103
127 Public Square
**Cleveland**, OH 44114-1309
216-522-4373

Toledo
411 US Courthouse and Custom House
1716 Spielbusch Avenue
**Toledo**, OH 43624
419-259-6440

Youngstown
Nathaniel R. Jones Federal Building & US
Courthouse
10 East Commerce Street
**Younstown**, OH 44503-1621
330-746-7027

Web site: www.ohnb.uscourts.gov

**Florida (Southern)**

Claude D. Pepper Federal Building
51 S.W. 1st Avenue, Room 1517
**Miami**, FL 33130
305-714-1800

US Courthouse
299 E. Broward Blvd., room 112
**Fourth Lauderdale**, FL 33301
954-769-5700

Paul G. Rogers Federal Building
701 Clematis Street, Room 202
**West Palm Beach**, FL 33401
561-514-4100

Web site: www.flsb.uscourts.gov


**Georgia (Northern)**

Atlanta Division
Richard B. Russell Federal Building an US
Courthouse
75 Springs Street, SW
**Atlanta**, GA 30303
404-215-1000

Gainesville Division
121 Spring Street SE
Room 120
**Gainesville**, GA 30501
678-450-2700

Newnan Division
18 Greenville Street
**Newnan**, GA 30264
678-423-3000

Rome Division
600 East First Street
**Rome**, GA 30161-3187
Clerk's office: Room 339 Federal Building
706-378-4000

Web site: www.ganb.uscourts.gov


**Oregon**

Portland Office
US Bankruptcy Court
1001 SW 5th Avenue #700
**Portland**, OR 97204
503-326-2231

Eugene Office
US Bankruptcy Court
151 W 7th Avenue, #300
P.O. Box 1335
**Eugene**, OR 37440
541-465-6448

Web site: www.paeb.uscourts.gov


**Pennsylvania (Western)**

Main Office
US Bankruptcy court
5414 U.S. Steel Tower
600 Grant Street
**Pittsburgh**, PA 15219
412-644-2700

Johnstown Office
US Bankruptcy Court
Penn Traffic Building
319 Washington Street
**Johnstown**, PA 15901

Erie Office
US Bankruptcy Court
Suite 501
717 State Street
**Erie**, PA 16501
814-453-7580
Fax: 814-453-3795

Web site: www.pawb.uscourts.gov

**Georgia (Middle)**

US Bankruptcy Court
Middle District
433 Cherry Street
P.O. Box 1957
**Macon**, GA 31202
478-752-3506
Fax: 478-752-8157

Albany Courthouse
CB King US Courthouse
Second Floor
233 Broad Street
**Albany**, GA 31701

Athens Courthouse
US Courthouse and Post Office
115 East Hancock Avenue
**Athens**, GA 30601

Columbus Courthouse
One Arsenal Place
901 Front Avenue
**Columbus**, GA 31902

Thomasville Courthouse
US Courthouse and Post Office
404 North Broad Street
**Thomasville**, GA 31792

Valdosta Courthouse
US Courthouse and Post Office
401 North Patterson Street
**Valdosta**, GA 31601

Web site: www.gamb.uscourts.gov

**Rhode Island**

380 Westminster Street
6th Floor, Suite 615
**Providence**, RI 02903
401-528-4477
Fax: 401-528-4470

Web site: www.rib.uscourts.gov

**South Carolina**

South District of Carolina
US Bankruptcy Court – **Street Address**
1100 Laurel Street
**Columbia**, SC 29201

US Bankruptcy Court – **Mailing Address**
P.O. Box 1448
Columbia, SC 29202
803-765-5636

Web site: www.scb.uscourts.gov

**Georgia (Southern)**

Savannah
125 Bull Street, Room 304
**Savannah**, GA 31401
912-650-4020

Augusta
500 East Ford Street
**Augusta**, GA 30901
706-849-4400

Brunswick
801 Gloucester Street, Suite 220
**Brunswick**, GA 31520
912-280-1330

Web site: www.gasd.uscourts.gov

**Idaho**

Northern Division – Coeur d'Alene Office
205 N. 4th Street, Room 202
**Coeur d'Alene**, ID 83814
208-664-4925
Fax: 208-765-0270

Central Division –Moscow Office
220 E. 5th Street, Room 304
**Moscow**, ID 83843
208-882-7612
Fax: 208-883-1576

James A McClure Federal Building and United States Courthouse
US Courts – District of Idaho
550 W. Fort Street
**Boise**, ID 83724
208-334-1074
Fax: 208-334-1361

United States Courts – District of Idaho
Eastern Division
801 E. Sherman Street
**Pocatello**, ID 83201
208-478-4123
Fax: 208-478-4106

**South Dakota**

Central Division
Bankruptcy Courthouse
Federal Building and US Courthouse
Room 210
225 S. Pierre Street
**Pierre**, SD
605-224-0560
Fax: 605-224-9020

Western Division
Third Floor Magistrate's
Courtroom
Federal Building and US Courthouse
515 9th Street
**Rapid City**, SD
605-343-6335
Fax: 605-343-4367

Northern Division
Fourth Floor Federal District Courtroom
US Post Office and Courthouse
102 4th Avenue, SE
**Aberdeen**, SD
605-226-7281
Fax: 605-226-7478

Western Division
Third Floor Magistrate's Courtroom
Federal Building and US Courthouse
515 9th Street

**Illinois (Northern)**

Eastern Division
219 S. Dearborn
**Chicago**, IL 60604
312-435-5694
Fax: 312-408-7750

Western Division
211 S. Court Street
**Rockford**, IL 61101
815-987-4350
Fax: 815-987-4205

Web site: www.ilnb.uscourts.gov

**Illinois (Southern)**

United States Bankruptcy Court
Melvin Price Federal Courthouse
750 Missouri Avenue
**East St. Louis**, IL 62201
618-482-9400

United States Bankruptcy Court
Federal Courthouse
301 West Main Street
**Benton**, IL 62812
618-435-2200

Web site: www.ilsb.uscourts.gov

**Indiana (Northern)**

US Bankruptcy Court - **Mailing Address**
Northern District of Indiana

**Rapid City**, SD
605-343-6335
Fax: 605-343-4367

Southern Division
Bankruptcy Courtroom
400 S. Phillips Avenue
**Sioux Falls**, SD
605-330-4544
Fax: 605-330-4560

Web site: www.sdb.uscourts.gov

**Tennessee (Middle)**

Middle District of Tennessee
US Bankruptcy Court
701 Broadway
**Nashville**, TN 37203
615-736-5590

Web site: www.tnmb.uscourts.gov

**Tennessee (Eastern)**

Eastern Division
*Temporary location. Call the courthouse for current location*
US Bankruptcy Court
Clerk's Office
6 Stonebridge Blvd.
Suite HJ
**Jackson**, TN 38305
731-668-4354

Web site: www.tneb.uscourts.gov

**Tennessee (Western)**

Western Division
200 Jefferson Avenue
Suite 413
**Memphis**, TN 38103
901-328-3500

Web site: www.tnwb.uscourts.gov

**Texas (Western)**

Old Post Office Building
615 East Houston Street
P.O. Box 1439

P.O. Box 2547
**Fort Wayne**, IN 46801-2547

US Bankruptcy Court - **Street Address**
Northern District of Indiana
E.Ross Adair Federal Building and United States
Courthouse
1300 South Harrison Street
Fort Wayne, IN 46802
260-420-5100

US Bankruptcy Court – **Mailing Address**
Northern District of Indiana
5400 Federal Plaza
**Hammond**, IN 46320

US Bankruptcy Court – **Street Address**
Northern District of Indiana
5400 Federal Plaza
Hammond, IN 46320
219-852-3480

US Bankruptcy Court - **Mailing Address**
Northern District of Indiana
P.O. Box 890
Lafayette, IN 47902-0890

US Bankruptcy Court – **Street Address**
Northern District of Indiana
Charles A. Halleck Federal Building
230 North Fourth Street
**Lafayette,** IN 47901
765-420-6300

US Bankruptcy Court – **Mailing Address**
Northern District of Indiana
P.O. Box 7003
**South Bend**, IN 46634-7003

US Bankruptcy Court – **Street Address**
Northern District of Indiana
Robert K. Rodibaugh United States
Bankruptcy Courthouse
401 South Michigan Street
**South Bend**, IN 46601
574-968-2100

Web site: www.innb.uscourts.gov

**San Antonio**, TX 78295-1439
210-472-6720
Fax: 210-472-5196

Homer J. Thornberry Federal Judicial Building
903 San Jacinto Blvd., Suite 322
**Austin**, TX 78701
512-916-5237
Fax: 512-916-5278

**Indiana (Southern)**

**Indianapolis**
US Bankruptcy Court
116 US Courthouse
46 E. Ohio Street
**Indianapolis**, IN 46204

Send mail to:
P.O. Box 44978
**Indianapolis**, IN 46244
317-229-3800
Fax: 317-229-3801

**New Albany**
US Bankruptcy Court
110 US Courthouse
121 West Spring Street
**New Albany**, IN 47150
812-542-4540
Fax: 812-542-4541

**Evansville Division**
US Bankruptcy Court
352 Federal Building
101 Northwest Martin L. King Boulevard
**Evansville**, IN 47708
812-434-6470
Fax: 812-434-6471

**Terre Haute**
US Bankruptcy Court
Federal Building
30 N. 7th Street
**Terre Haute**, IN 47808
812-238-1550
Fax: 812-238-1831

Web site: www.insb.uscourts.gov

**Iowa (Northern)**

US Bankruptcy Court – **Address for hearings**
8th Floor
425 Second Street SE
**Cedar Rapids**, IA 54207

US Bankruptcy Court – **Address for filings**
P.O. Box 74890
**Cedar Rapids**, IA 52407-4890

United States Bankruptcy Courthouse
8515 Lockheed
**El Paso**, TX 79925
915-779-7362
Fax: 915-779-5693

US Post Office Annex
Room P-163
100 East Wall Street
**Midland**, TX 79701
432-683-1650
Fax: 432-683-1643

US Bankruptcy Court
800 Franklin Avenue
Suite 140
**Waco**, TX 76701
254-750-1513
Fax: 254-750-1529

Web site: www.txwb.uscourts.gov

US Bankruptcy Court – **Address for hearings**
US Courthouse
380 6th Street
**Sioux City**, IA 51102

US Bankruptcy Court – **Address for Filings**
P.O. Box 3857
**Sioux City**, IA 51102-3857

Web site: www.ianb.uscourts.gov

**Kansas**

US Bankruptcy Court
167 U.S. Courthouse
401 N. Market
**Wichita**, KS 67202
316-269-6486

US Bankruptcy Court
240 US Courthouse
444 S.E. Quincy
**Topeka**, KS 66683
785-295-2750

US Bankruptcy Court
500 State Avenue
**Kansas City**, KS 66101
913-551-6732

Web site: www.ksb.uscourts.gov

**Kentucky (Eastern)**

US Bankruptcy Court – **Mailing Address**
Box 1111
Lexington, KY 40588-1111

US Bankruptcy Court – **Street Address**
100 E. Vine Street
Suite 200
**Lexington**, KY 40507
859-233-2608

Web site: www.kyeb.uscourts.gov

**Texas (Eastern)**

**Tyler**
US Bankruptcy Court
2nd Floor
200 E. Ferguson Street
**Tyler**, TX 75702
903-590-1212

**Plano**
US Bankruptcy Court
Suite 300 B
660 North Central Expressway
**Plano**, TX 75074
972-509-1240

**Beaumont**
US Bankruptcy Court
Suite 100
300 Willow Street
**Beaumont**, TX 77701
409-839-2617

Web site: www.txeb.uscourts.gov

**Texas (Northern)**

Amarillo Court Location – **Mailing Address**
US Bankruptcy Court
P.O. Box 15960
**Amarillo**, TX 79105-0969

Amarillo Court Location – **Street Address**
624 S. Polk
Suite 100
**Amarillo**, TX 79101-2389

Forth Worth Court Location
Eldon B. Mahon US Courthouse
501- W. Tenth Street

**Fort Worth**, TX 76102-3643

Dallas Court Location
US Bankruptcy Court and US Courthouse
Earl Cabell Building
1100 Commerce Street, Room 1254
**Dallas**, TX 75242
214-753-2000

Lubbock Court Location
US Bankruptcy Court
306 Federal Building
1205 Texas Avenue
**Lubbock**, TX 7904-4002

Web site: www.txnb.uscourts.gov

## Texas (Southern)

US District and Bankruptcy Clerk
5401 Bob Casey United States Courthouse
515 Rusk Avenue
**Houston**, TX 77002
713-250-5500

US District/Bankruptcy Clerk
P.O. Box 2300
**Galveston**, TX 77553
409-766-3530

US District Clerk – Street Address
312 S. Main Street, Room 406
**Victoria**, TX 77901
361-788-5000

US District Clerk – Mailing Address
P.O. Box 1638
Victoria, TX 77902

US District Clerk
1133 N. Shoreline Blvd.
**Corpus Christi**, TX 78401
361-888-3142

US District Clerk
600 E. Harrison, 1st Floor
**Brownsville**, TX 78520
956-548-2500

US District Clerk

## Kentucky (Western)

US Bankruptcy Court
**Western District of Kentucky**
601 West Broadway, Suite 450
**Lousiville**, KY 40202
502-627-5800

Web site: www.kywb.uscourts.gov

## Louisiana (Eastern)

US Bankruptcy Court
**Eastern District of Louisiana**
501 Magazine Street, Suite 601
**New Orleans**, LA 70130
504-589-7878

Web site: www.laeb.uscourts.gov

1701 W. Bus. Hwy 83, Suite 1011
**McAllen**, TX 78501
956-618-8065

US District Clerk
P.O. Box 597
Laredo, TX 78042
956-723-3542

Web site: www.txsb.uscourts.gov

**Utah**

Frank E. Moss, US Courthouse
350 South Main Street, #301
**Salt Lake City**, UT 84101
801-524-6687

Web site: www.utb.uscourts.gov

**Vermont**

**US Bankruptcy Court District of Vermont**
67 Merchants Row
P.O. Box 6648
**Rutland**, Vermont 05702-6648
802-776-2000
Fax: 802-776-2020

Web site: www.vtb.uscourts.gov

**Virginia (Eastern)**

**Alexandria Office**
US Bankruptcy Court – **Street Address**
200 S. Washington Street
**Alexandria**, VA 22314

US Bankruptcy Court – **Mailing Address**
P.O. Box 19247
Alexandria, VA 22320-0247
703-258-1200

**Norfolk Office**
US Bankruptcy Court – **Street Address**
600 Granby Street

**Louisiana (Western)**

US Bankruptcy Court
300 Jackson Street
Suite 116
**Alexandria**, LA 71301
318-445-1890

US Bankruptcy Court
231 South Union Street
Second Floor
**Opelousas**, LA 70570
337-948-3451

US Bankruptcy Court
300 Fannin Street
Suite 2201
**Shreveport**, LA 71101
318-676-4267

Web site: www.lawb.uscourts.gov

**Maine**

**Portland Office**
US Bankruptcy Court – Street Address
537 Congress Street
2nd Floor
**Portland**, ME 04101
207-780-3482
Fax: 207-780-3679

US Bankruptcy Court – Mailing Address
P.O. Box 17575
Portland, ME 04112-8575

**Bangor Office**

US Bankruptcy Court – Street Address
202 Harlow Street
3rd Floor
**Bangor**, ME 04401
207-945-0348
Fax: 207-945-0304

US Bankruptcy Court – Mailing Address
P.O. Box 1109
Bangor, ME 04402

**Maryland**

**Baltimore Division**
US Bankruptcy Court
Garmatz Federal Courthouse
101 West Lombard Street
Suite 8308
**Baltimore**, MD 21201
410-962-2688

**Greenbelt Division**
Federal Courthouse
6500 Cherrywood Lane
Suite 300
**Greenbelt**, MD 20770
301-344-8018

Web site: www.mdb.uscourts.gov

4th Floor
**Norfolk**, VA 23510

US Bankruptcy Court – **Mailing Address**
P.O. Box 1938
**Norfolk**, VA 23501-1938
757-222-7500

**Richmond Office**
US Bankruptcy Court – Street Address
1100 E. Main Street
Room 301
**Richmond**, VA 23219

US Bankruptcy Court – Mailing Address
1100 E. Main Street
Room 310
**Richmond**, VA 23219
804-916-2400

Web site: www.vaeb.uscourts.gov

**Virginia (Western)**

**Roanoke Office**
US Bankruptcy Court
210 Church Avenue SW, Room 200
Roanoke, VA 24011
540-857-2391
Fax: 540-857-2873

**Lynchburg Office**
US Bankruptcy Court
1100 Main Street, Room 226
**Lynchburg**, VA 24504
434-845-0317
Fax: 434-845-1801

**Harrisonburg Office**
US Bankruptcy Court
116 N. Main Street, Room 223
P.O. Box 1407
**Harrisonburg**, VA 22802
540-434-8327
Fax: 540-434-9715

Web site: www.vawb.uscourts.gov

## Massachusetts

**Boston**
US Bankruptcy Court
1101 Thomas P. O'Neill, Jr. Federal Building
10 Causeway Street
**Boston**, MA 02222-1074
617-565-8950
Fax: 565-6650

**Worcester**
US Bankruptcy Court
Donahue Federal Building
595 Main Street, Room 211
**Worcester**, MA 01608-2076
508-770-8900
Fax: 508-793-0189

Web site: www.mab.uscourts.gov

## Michigan (Western)

**Bay City Court**
US Bankruptcy Court
111 First Street
**Bay City**, MI 48707
989-894-8840

**Detroit Court**
US Bankruptcy Court
211 West Fort Street
**Detroit**, MI 48226
313-234-0065

**Flint Court**
US Bankruptcy Court
226 West Second Street
**Flint**, MI 48502
810-325-4126

Web site: www.mieb.uscourts.gov

## Washington (Eastern)

**Yakima Office Location**
US Bankruptcy Court
402 E. Yakima Avenue, Suite 200
**Yakima**, WA 98901
509-454-5660
Fax: 509-454-5778

**Spokane Office**
US Bankruptcy Court – Street Address
904 W. Riverside Suite 304
**Spokane**, WA 99201

US Bankruptcy Court – Mailing Address
P.O. Box 2164
**Spokane**, WA 99210-2164
509-353-2404
Fax: 509-353-2404

Web site: www.waeb.uscourts.gov

## Washington (Western)

**Seattle**
US Bankruptcy Court
Park Place Building
1200 Sixth Avenue
Room 315
**Seattle**, WA 89101
206-553-7545

**Tacoma**
US Bankruptcy Court
1717 Pacific Avenue
Suite 2100
**Tacoma**, WA 98402-3233
253-593-6310

Web site: www.wawb.uscourts.gov

## Wisconsin (Western)

**Minnesota**

**Duluth Office**
US Bankruptcy Court
416 US Courthouse
515 West First Street
**Duluth**, MN 55802
218-529-3600

**Fergus Falls Office**
US Bankruptcy Court
204 US Courthouse
**Fergus Falls**, MN 56537
218-739-4671

**Minneapolis Office**
US Bankruptcy Court
301 US Courthouse
300 South Fourth Street
**Minneapoli**s, MN 55416
612-644-5200

St. Paul Office
US Bankruptcy Court
200 US Courthouse
316 N. Robert Street
**St. Paul**, MN 55101
651-848-1000

Web site: www.mnb.uscourts.gov

**Missouri (Eastern)**

St. Louis
Eastern Division District of Missouri
Thomas F. Eagleton
US Courthouse
111 South Tenth Street
Fourth Floor
**St. Louis**, MO 63102
314-244-4500
Fax: 314-244-4990

Hannibal
Northern Division Eastern District of Missouri
801 Broadway
**Hannibal**, MO 63401
314-221-0757

**Madison Division**
US Bankruptcy Court
120 North Henry Street, Room 340
(53703)
P.O. Box 548
**Madison**, WI 53701-0548
608-264-5178

**Eau Claire Division**
US Bankruptcy Court
500 South Barstow Street
(54701)
P.O. Box 5009
**Eau Claire**, WI 54702-5009
715-839-2980

Web site: www.wiw.uscourts.gov

**Wyoming**

Cheyenne Office
US Bankruptcy Court
2120 Capitol Avenue, Suite 6004
**Cheyenne, WY** 82001
307-433-2200

Casper Office
US Bankruptcy Court
111 South Wolcott
**Casper, WY** 82601
307-261-5444
Web site: www.wyb.uscourts.gov

Fax: 314-221-9027

Cape Giradeau
Southeastern Division
Eastern District of Missouri
339 Broadway
**Cape Girardeau**, MO 63701
573-334-6391
Fax: 573-334-6429

Southern District of Illinois
P.O. Box 309
**East St. Louis**, IL 62202
618-482-9400

**Missouri Western**

Western Division at Kansas City
Charles Evans Whittaker Courthouse
400 E. 9th Street
**Kansas City**, MO 64106

Central Division at Jefferson City
US State Courts
US Courthouse
131 W. High Street
**Jefferson City**, MO 65101
573-636-4015

Southern Division at Springfield
US Courts
US Courthouse
222 N. John Q. Hammons Parkway
**Springfield**, MO 65808

Web site: www.mow.uscourts.gov

**Montana**

US Bankruptcy Court District of Montana
400 North Main Street
**Butte**, MT 59701
406-782-3338

Web site: www.mieb.uscourts.gov

Surviving Financial Disasters

# Appendix G

## Official Federal Bankruptcy Forms

Some states have modified petition forms, prior to completing the petition forms interested persons should locate state conforming forms at their local bankruptcy clerk's office or online. The forms provided are current Federal Bankruptcy Forms as of the date of publishing this book.

| United States Bankruptcy Court<br>District of | VOLUNTARY PETITION |
|---|---|

| IN RE (Name of debtor-if individual, enter Last, First, Middle) | NAME OF JOINT DEBTOR (Spouse) (Last, First, Middle) |
|---|---|
| ALL OTHER NAMES used by the debtor in the last 6 years<br>(include married, maiden and trade names) | ALL OTHER NAMES used by the joint debtor in the last 6 years<br>(include married, maiden and trade names) |
| SOC. SEC./TAX I.D. NO. (If more than one, state all) | SOC. SEC./TAX I.D. NO. (If more than one, state all) |
| STREET ADDRESS OF DEBTOR (No. and street, city, state, zip) | STREET ADDRESS OF JOINT DEBTOR (No. and street, city, state, zip) |
| COUNTY OF RESIDENCE OR OF THE<br>PRINCIPAL PLACE OF BUSINESS: | COUNTY OF RESIDENCE OR OF THE<br>PRINCIPAL PLACE OF BUSINESS: |
| MAILING ADDRESS OF DEBTOR (It different from street address) | MAILING ADDRESS OF JOINT DEBTOR (If different from street address) |

LOCATION OF PRINCIPAL ASSETS OF BUSINESS DEBTOR
(It different from address above)

## INFORMATION REGARDING DEBTOR (Check the Applicable Boxes)

VENUE (Check any applicable box)

☐ Debtor has been domiciled or has had a residence, principal place of business or principal assets in this District for 180 days immediately preceding the date of this petition or for a longer part of such 180 days than in any other District.

☐ There is a bankruptcy case concerning debtor's affiliate, general partner or partnership pending in this District.

| TYPE OF DEBTOR (Check one box) | CHAPTER OR SECTION OF BANKRUPTCY CODE UNDER WHICH THE PETITION IS FILED<br>(Check one box) |
|---|---|
| ☐ Individual(s) ☐ Railroad<br>☐ Corporation ☐ Stockbroker<br>☐ Partnership ☐ Commodity Broker<br>☐ Other _____ | ☐ Chapter 7　　☐ Chapter 11　　☐ Chapter 13<br>☐ Chapter 9　　☐ Chapter 12<br>☐ §304-Case Ancillary to Foreign proceeding |

| NATURE OF DEBTS (Check one box)<br>☐ Consumer/Non-business　　☐ Business<br>　　　Chapter 11 Small Business (Check all boxes that apply)<br>☐ Debtor is a small business as defined in 11 U.S.C. § 101.<br>☐ Debtor is and elects to be considered a small business under 11 U.S.C. §1121 (e). (Optional) | FILING FEE (Check one box)<br>☐ Filing fee attached<br>☐ Filing fee to be paid in installments. (Applicable to individuals only) Must attach signed application for the court's consideration certifying that the debtor is unable to pay fee except in installments.<br>Rule 1006(b). See Official Form No. 3. |
|---|---|

| STATISTICAL/ADMINISTRATIVE INFORMATION (Estimates only)<br>☐ Debtor estimates that funds will be available for distribution to unsecured creditors.<br>☐ Debtor estimates that, after any exempt property is excluded and administrative expenses paid, there will be no funds available for distribution to unsecured creditors. | THIS SPACE FOR COURT USE ONLY |
|---|---|

ESTIMATED NUMBER OF CREDITORS

☐ 1 -15　☐ 16-49　☐ 50-99　☐ 100-199　☐ 200-999　☐ 1000-over

ESTIMATED ASSETS

| $0 to<br>$50,000 | $50,001 to<br>$100,000 | $100,001 to<br>$500,000 | $500,001 to<br>$1 million | $1,000,001 to<br>$10 million | $10,000,001 to<br>$50 million | $50,000,001 to<br>$100 million | More than<br>$100 million |
|---|---|---|---|---|---|---|---|
| ☐ | ☐ | ☐ | ☐ | ☐ | ☐ | ☐ | ☐ |

ESTIMATED DEBTS

| $0 to<br>$50,000 | $50,001 to<br>$100,000 | $100,001 to<br>$500,000 | $500,001 to<br>$1 million | $1,000,001 to<br>$10 million | $10,000,001 to<br>$50 million | $50,000,001 to<br>$100 million | More than<br>$100 million |
|---|---|---|---|---|---|---|---|
| ☐ | ☐ | ☐ | ☐ | ☐ | ☐ | ☐ | ☐ |

# Voluntary Petition
*(This page must be completed and filed in every case)*

| Name of Debtor(s) | FORM B1, Page |
|---|---|

| PRIOR BANKRUPTCY WITHIN LAST 6 YEARS (If more than one, attach additional sheet) | | |
|---|---|---|
| Location<br>Where Filed: | Case Number: | Date Filed: |

| PENDING BANKRUPTCY CASE FILED BY ANY SPOUSE PARTNER, OR AFFILIATE OF THIS DEBTOR (If more than one, attach additional sheet) | | |
|---|---|---|
| Name of Debtor: | Case Number: | Date Filed: |
| District: | Relationship: | Judge: |

## SIGNATURES

### Signature(s) of Debtor(s) (Individual/Joint)

I declare under penalty of perjury that the information provided in this petition is true and correct.
[If petitioner is an individual whose debts are primarily consumer debts and has chosen to file under Chapter 7] I am aware that I may proceed under chapter 7, 11, 12 or 13 of title 11, United States Code, understand the relief available under each such chapter, and choose to proceed under chapter 7.

I request relief in accordance with the chapter of title 11, United States Code, specified in this petition.

X _____
Signature of Debtor

X _____
Signature of Joint Debtor

_____
Telephone and FAX Number (If not represented by attorney)

_____
Date

### Signature of Debtor (Corporation/Partnership)

I declare under penalty of perjury that the information provided in this petition is true and correct and that I have been authorized to file this petition on behalf of the debtor.

The debtor requests relief in accordance with the chapter of title 11, United States Code, specified in this petition.

X _____
Signature of Authorized Individual

_____
Print or Type Name of Authorized Individual

_____
Title of Individual Authorized by Debtor to File this Petition

_____
Date

### Signature of Attorney

X _____
Signature of Attorney for Debtor(s)

_____
Printed Name of Attorney for Debtor(s)

_____
Firm Name

_____
Address

_____
Telephone and FAX Number

_____
Date

### Exhibit A

(To be completed if debtor is required to file periodic reports (e.g., forms 10K and 10Q) with the Securities and Exchange Commission pursuant to section 13 or 15(d) of the Securities Exchange Act of 1934 and is requesting relief under chapter 11.)

☐ Exhibit A is attached and made a part of this petition.

### Exhibit B

(To be completed if debtor is an individual whose debts are primarily consumer debts) I, the attorney for the petitioner named in the foregoing petition, declare that I have informed the petitioner that [he or she] may proceed under chapter 7, 11, 12, or 13 of title 11, United States Code, and have explained the relief available under each such chapter.

X _____
Signature of Attorney for Debtor(s)          Date

### Signature of Non-Attorney Petition Preparer

I certify that I am a Bankruptcy Petition Preparer as defined in 11 U.S.C. § 110, that I prepared this document for compensation, and that I have provided the debtor with a copy of this document.

_____
Printed or Typed Name of Bankruptcy Petition Preparer

_____
Social Security Number

_____
Address

Names and Social Security Numbers of all other individuals who prepared or assisted in preparing this document.

If more than one person prepared this document, attach additional signed sheets conforming to the appropriate Official Form for each person.

X _____
Signature of Bankruptcy Petition Preparer

_____
Date

A Bankruptcy Petition Preparer's failure to comply with the provisions of Title 11 and the Federal Rules of Bankruptcy Procedure may result in fines or imprisonment or both. 11 U.S.C. § 110, 16 U.S.C. § 156.

# UNITED STATES BANKRUPTCY COURT
## DISTRICT OF

In re _____     Case No. _____

                          Debtor                          (If known)

                                          Chapter _____

# Exhibit "A" to Voluntary Petition

1. Debtor's employer identification number is _____

2. If any of debtor's securities are registered under section 12 of the Securities and Exchange Act of 1934, the SEC file number is _____ .

3. The following financial data is the latest available information and refers to debtor's condition on

_____ .

                             a. Total assets                _____

                             b. Total liabilities           _____

|  | AMOUNT | Approximate number of holders |
|---|---|---|
| Fixed, liquidated secured debt |  | _____ |
| Contingent secured debt |  | _____ |
| Disputed secured claims |  | _____ |
| Unliquidated secured debt |  | _____ |

|  | AMOUNT | Approximate number of holders |
|---|---|---|
| Fixed, liquidated unsecured debt |  | _____ |
| Contingent unsecured debt |  | _____ |
| Disputed unsecured claims |  | _____ |
| Unliquidated unsecured debt |  | _____ |
| Number of shares of preferred stock | _____ | _____ |
| Number of shares of common stock | _____ | _____ |

Comments, if any:

4. Brief description of debtor's business:

5. List the name of any person who directly or indirectly owns, controls, or holds, with power to vote, 20% or more of the voting securities of debtor:

6. List the names of all corporations of which 20% or more of the outstanding voting securities are directly or indirectly owned, controlled, or held, with power to vote, by debtor:

## DECLARATION UNDER PENALTY OF PERJURY
## ON BEHALF OF A CORPORATION OR PARTNERSHIP

I [the president *or* other officer *or* an authorized agent of the corporation] [*or* a member *or* an authorized agent of the partnership] named as the debtor in this case, declare under penalty of perjury that I have read the foregoing Exhibit "A" and that it is true and correct to the best of my information and belief.

Date _____

✗ _____
Signature

# UNITED STATES BANKRUPTCY COURT
## District of

**In re**

CASE NUMBER: _____

CHAPTER _____

Debtor(s).

### APPLICATION TO PAY FILING FEES
### IN INSTALLMENTS

In accordance with Federal Rules of Bankruptcy Procedure, Rule 1006, application is made for permission to pay the filing fee on the following terms:

_____  with the filing of the petition, and the balance of

_____  in _____ installments, as follows:

_____  on or before _____

_____  on or before _____

I (We) certify that I (we) am (are) unable to pay the filing fee except in installments. I (We) further certify that I (we) have not paid any money or transferred any property to an attorney or any other person for services in connection with this case or with any other pending bankruptcy case and that I will not make any payment or transfer any property for services in connection with the case until the filing fee is paid in full.

Date: _____

**X**_____
Applicant

**X**_____
Co-applicant

_____
Address

_____
City/State/ZIP Code

### CERTIFICATION AND SIGNATURE OF NON-ATTORNEY BANKRUPTCY PETITION PREPARER (11 U.S.C. § 110)

I certify that I am a Bankruptcy Petition Preparer as defined in 11 U.S.C. § 110, that I prepared this document for compensation, and that I have provided the debtor with a copy of this document.

_____
Printed or Typed Name of Bankruptcy Petition Preparer

_____
Social Security Number

_____
Address

_____
City/State/ZIP Code

Name and Social Security Numbers of all other individuals who prepared or assisted in preparing this document. If more than one person prepared this document, attach additional signed sheets conforming to the appropriate Official Form for each person.

**X**_____
Signature of Bankruptcy Petition Preparer

Date: _____

**A Bankruptcy Petition Preparer's failure to comply with the provisions of Title 11 and the Federal Rules of Bankruptcy Procedure may result in fines or imprisonment or both. 11 U.S.C. § 110; 18 U.S.C. § 156.**

# ORDER APPROVING APPLICATION TO PAY FILING FEE IN INSTALLMENTS

The foregoing Application to Pay Filing Fee in Installments is hereby approved.

IT IS FURTHER ORDERED that until the filing fee is paid in full the debtor shall not pay, and no person shall accept, any money for services in connection with this case, and the debtor shall not relinquish, and no person shall accept, any property as payment for services in connection with this case.

**Clerk of the Court**

Date: _____     By:_____

**Deputy Clerk**

COPY OF ORDER HANDED/MAILED TO DEBTOR(S), ATTORNEY FOR DEBTOR(S), TRUSTEE AND US TRUSTEE:

_____          _____
Date                                                              Deputy Clerk

**NOTICE OF JUDGMENT OR ORDER
ENTERED ON DOCKET**

_____

**UNITED STATES BANKRUPTCY COURT**
**DISTRICT OF**

Case No. _____

In re _____

Debtor                                    Chapter _____

## LIST OF CREDITORS HOLDING 20 LARGEST UNSECURED CLAIMS

Following is the list of the debtor's creditors holding the 20 largest unsecured claims. The list is prepared in accordance with Fed. R. Bankr. P. 1007(d) for filing in this chapter 11 [or chapter 9] case. The list does not include (1 ) persons who come within the definition of "insider" set forth in 11 U.S.C. § 101(30), or (2) secured creditors unless the value of the collateral is such that the unsecured deficiency places the creditor among the holders of the 20 largest unsecured claims.

| (1) Name of creditor and complete mailing address including zip code | (2) Name, telephone number and complete mailing address, including zip code, of employee, agent, or department of creditor familiar with claim who maybe contacted | (3) Nature of claim (trade debt, bank loan, government contract, etc.) | (4) Indicate if claim is contingent, unliquidated, disputed or subject to setoff | (5) Amount of claim [if secured also state value of security] |
|---|---|---|---|---|

In re _____          Case No. _____

Debtor

# LIST OF CREDITORS HOLDING 20 LARGEST UNSECURED CLAIMS
## (CONTINUED)

| (1) Name of creditor and complete mailing address including zip code | (2) Name, telephone number and complete mailing address, including zip code, of employee, agent, or department of creditor familiar with claim who maybe contacted | (3) Nature of claim (trade debt, bank loan, government contract, etc.) | (4) Indicate if claim is contingent, unliquidated, disputed or subject to setoff | (5) Amount of claim [if secured also state value of security] |
|---|---|---|---|---|
| | | | | |

In re _____     Case No. _____
Debtor

| (1) Name of creditor and complete mailing address including zip code | (2) Name, telephone number and complete mailing address, including zip code, of employee, agent, or department of creditor familiar with claim who maybe contacted | (3) Nature of claim (trade debt, bank loan, government contract, etc.) | (4) Indicate if claim is contingent, unliquidated, disputed or subject to setoff | (5) Amount of claim [if secured also state value of security] |
| --- | --- | --- | --- | --- |
|  |  |  |  |  |

## DECLARATION UNDER PENALTY OF PERJURY
## ON BEHALF OF A CORPORATION OR PARTNERSHIP

I, [the president *or* other officer *or* an authorized agent of the corporation] [or a member *or* an authorized agent of the partnership] named as the debtor in this case, declare under penalty of perjury that I have read the foregoing "List of Creditors Holding 20 Largest Unsecured Claims" and that it is true and correct to the best of my information and belief.

Date _____

✗ _____

Signature

_____

(Print Name and Title)

# INSTRUCTIONS REGARDING SCHEDULES

These schedules shall be used to comply with § 521(1) of the Code and Rule 1007(b). Schedules A,B,D,E, and F constitute the schedule of assets and liabilities. Schedules I and J constitute a schedule of current income and current expenditures for individual and joint debtors.

The order of the schedules has been arranged with the summary sheet in front and with the schedules of assets appearing first, followed by the schedule of liabilities. this structure corresponds to the customary pattern by which trustees and creditors review these documents and to the format of the accounting profession for balance sheets.

*Review the specific instructions for each schedule before completing the schedule.*

Leasehold interests in both real and personal property are to be reported in schedule G - Executory Contracts and Unexpired Leases. This information should not be repeated in the schedule of assets.

Generally in these schedules, a creditor's claim will be listed only once, even if the claim is secured only in part, or is entitled only in part to priority under §507(a) of the Code, with the remainder of the claim to be treated as a general unsecured claim. For example, a partially secured creditor whose claim is reported in Schedule D - Creditors Holding Secured Claims will be listed together with the value of the property securing the claim and a notation of the amount of any unsecured portion of the claim. Information concerning the unsecured portion should not be repeated in Schedule F - Creditors Holding Nonpriority Unsecured Claims. Any resulting overstatement of the amounts owed on secured and priority claims as reported on the summary sheet is offset by a corresponding understatement of the amount owed on unsecured claims.

If a debtor has no property or no creditors in a particular category, an affirmative statement to that effect is required. Married debtors should indicate whether spouses are filing jointly or separately liable for debts, using the columns provided in the schedules.

## Schedule A - Real Property.

Instructions at the top of the form indicate the scope of the interests in property to be reported on the schedule. Leasehold interests of the debtor are not reported here but on the Schedule of Executory Contracts and Unexpired Leases. The trustee will request copies of deeds or other instruments necessary for the administration of the estate.

## Schedule B - Personal Property.

This schedule is to be used for reporting all of the debtor's interests in personal property except leases and executory contracts, which are to be listed on the Schedule of Executory Contracts and Unexpired Leases. Several new categories of property have been added to the schedule, i.e., aircraft, and interests in IRA, ERISA, Keogh, or other pension or profit-sharing plans. To minimize the potential for concealment of assets, the debtor must declare whether the debtor has any property in each category on the schedule. The trustee can request copies **of any documents concerning the debtor's property necessary to the administration of the estate.**

## Schedule C - Property Claimed as Exempt.

The form of the schedules eliminates duplication of information provided elsewhere. The location of property, for example, is disclosed in the schedules of real and personal property. The requirement that the debtor state the present use of the property is best left to inquiry by the trustee. Exemptions in some states are granted by constitutional provisions; accordingly, the requirement that the debtor state the "statute" creating an exemption has been changed to request a statement of the relevant "law".

This schedule requires that the debtor state the market value of the property in addition to the amount claimed as exempt.

## Schedule D - Creditors Holding Secured Claims.

Schedules, D, E, and F have been designed with address boxes to match the number of characters which can be accommodated on the computerized noticing systems used by the courts. The size also closely approximates that of standard mailing labels. Space is designated at the top of the box for the debtor's account number with the creditor. The design of the form is intended to reduce the volume of misdirected creditor mail.

The form requires the debtor to state affirmatively that a claim is disputed, unliquidated, or contingent. The existence of any type of codebtor is to be disclosed, but details are to be provided in Schedule H, as they are not needed here. Duplication of information has been kept to a minimum. Requests for details concerning negotiable instruments and the consideration of a claim, are let to the trustee's inquiries.

## Schedule E - Creditors Holding Unsecured Priority Claims.

.The schedule lists all of the types of claims entitled to priority and requires the debtor to indicate the existence of claims in each category. Continuation sheets are provided. The type of priority claim is to be noted at the top of the continuation sheet, and each type must be reported on a separate sheet. This schedule also requires the debtor to indicate the existence of any codebtors. As in Schedule D -

Creditors Holding Secured Claims, requests for information concerning judgments and negotiable instruments have been deleted.

### Schedule F - Creditors Holding Unsecured Nonpriority Claims.
This schedule is generally in conformity with the other schedules of creditors. If a claim is subject to setoff, the debtor is required to so state.

### Schedule G - Executory Contracts and Unexpired Leases.
Rule 1007(b) required the debtor to file a schedule of executory contracts and unexpired leases, unless the court orders otherwise. All unexpired leases of either real or personal property are to be reported on this schedule. The schedule also requires the debtor to disclose specific information to assist the trustee in identifying leases which must be assumed within 60 days are the order for relief or be deemed rejected under § 365(d) of the Code.

### Schedule H - Schedule of Codebtors.
This schedule is designed to provide the trustee and creditors with information about codebtors of all types other than spouses in joint cases. the completed schedule provides information concerning non-debtor parties, such as guarantors and non-debtor spouses having an interest in property as tenants by the entirety. In chapter 12 and chapter 13 cases, the completed schedule also indicates those persons who maybe entitled to certain protections from creditor action under §§ 1201 and 1301 of the Code.

### Schedule I - Schedule of Current Income of Individual Debtor(s) and Schedule J - Schedule of Current Expenditures of Individual Debtor(s).
Chapter 13 statement style changes have been made so that these schedules can be used by individual and joint debtors in all chapters.

| In re | | Case No. | |
|---|---|---|---|
| | Debtor(s) | | (If known) |

# SCHEDULE A - REAL PROPERTY

Except as directed below, list all real property in which the debtor has any legal, equitable, or future interest, including all property owned as a co-tenant, community property, or in which the debtor has a life estate.   Include any property in which the debtor holds rights and powers exercisable for the debtor's own benefit. If the debtor is married, state whether husband, wife, or both own the property by placing an "H," "W," "J," or "C" in the column labeled "Husband, Wife, Joint, Or Community."   If the debtor holds no interest in real property, write "None" under "Description and Location of Property."

Do not list interests in executory contracts and unexpired leases on this schedule. List them in Schedule G - Executory Contracts and Unexpired Leases.

If an entity claims to have a lien or hold a secured interest in any property, state the amount of the secured claim. See Schedule D. If no entity claims to hold a secured interest in the property, write "None" in the column labeled "Amount of Secured Claim."

If the debtor is an individual or if a joint petition is filed, state the amount of any exemption claimed in the property only in Schedule C - Property Claimed as Exempt.

| DESCRIPTION AND LOCATION OF PROPERTY | NATURE OF DEBTOR'S INTEREST IN PROPERTY | HUSBAND, WIFE, JOINT OR COMMUNITY | CURRENT MARKET VALUE OF DEBTOR'S INTEREST IN PROPERTY, WITHOUT DEDUCTING ANY SECURED CLAIM OR EXEMPTION | AMOUNT OF SECURED CLAIM |
|---|---|---|---|---|
| | | | | |
| | | TOTAL → | $ | |

(Report also on Summary of Schedules)

| In re | | Case No. | |
|---|---|---|---|
| | Debtor(s) | | (If known) |

## SCHEDULE B - PERSONAL PROPERTY

Except as directed below, list all personal property of the debtor of whatever kind. If the debtor has no property in one or more of the categories, place an "X" in the appropriate position in the column labeled "None". If additional space is needed in any category, attach a separate sheet properly identified with the case name, and the number of the category. If the debtor is married, state whether husband, wife, or both own the property by placing an "H," "W," "J," or "C" in the column labeled "Husband, Wife, Joint, or Community." If the debtor is an individual or a joint petition is filed, state the amount of any exemptions claimed only in Schedule C - Property Claimed as Exempt.

Do not list interests in executory contracts and unexpired leases on this schedule. List them in Schedule G - Executory Contracts and Unexpired Leases.

If the property is being held for the debtor by someone else, state that person's name and address under "Description and Location of Property."

| TYPE OF PROPERTY | NONE | DESCRIPTION AND LOCATION OF PROPERTY | HUSBAND, WIFE, JOINT OR COMMUNITY | CURRENT MARKET VALUE OF DEBTOR'S INTEREST IN PROPERTY, WITHOUT DEDUCTING ANY SECURED CLAIM OR EXEMPTION |
|---|---|---|---|---|
| 1. Cash on hand. | ☐ | | | |
| 2. Checking, savings or other financial accounts, certificates of deposit or shares in banks, savings and loan thrift, building and loan, and homestead associations, or credit unions, brokerage houses, or cooperatives. | ☐ | | | |
| 3. Security deposits with public utilities, telephone companies, landlords, and others. | ☐ | | | |
| 4. Household goods and furnishings, including audio, video, and computer equipment. | ☐ | | | |
| 5. Books; pictures and other art objects; antiques; stamp, coin, record tape, compact disc, and other collections or collectibles. | ☐ | | | |
| 6. Wearing apparel. | ☐ | | | |
| 7. Furs and jewelry. | ☐ | | | |
| 8. Firearms and sports, photographic, and other hobby equipment. | ☐ | | | |
| 9. Interests in insurance policies. Name insurance company of each policy and itemize surrender or refund value of each. | ☐ | | | |
| 10. Annuities. Itemize and name each issuer. | ☐ | | | |

| In re | | | Case No. | |
|-------|--|--|----------|--|
| | | Debtor(s) | | (If known) |

## SCHEDULE B - PERSONAL PROPERTY
### (Continuation Sheet)

| TYPE OF PROPERTY | NONE | DESCRIPTION AND LOCATION OF PROPERTY | HUSBAND, WIFE, JOINT OR COMMUNITY | CURRENT MARKET VALUE OF DEBTOR'S INTEREST IN PROPERTY, WITHOUT DEDUCTING ANY SECURED CLAIM OR EXEMPTION |
|---|---|---|---|---|
| 11. Interests in IRA, ERISA, Keogh, or other pension or profit sharing Plans. Itemize. | ☐ | | | |
| 12. Stock and interests in incorporated and unincorporated businesses. Itemize. | ☐ | | | |
| 13. Interests in partnerships or joint ventures. Itemize. | ☐ | | | |
| 14. Government and corporate bonds and other negotiable and nonnegotiable instruments. | ☐ | | | |
| 15. Accounts Receivable. | ☐ | | | |
| 16. Alimony, maintenance, support, and property settlements to which the debtor is or maybe entitled. Give particulars. | ☐ | | | |
| 17. Other liquidated debts owing debtor including tax refunds. Give particulars. | ☐ | | | |
| 18. Equitable or future interests, life estates, and rights or powers exercisable for the benefit of the debtor other than those listed in Schedule of Real Property. | ☐ | | | |
| 19. Contingent and non-contingent interests in estate of a decedent, death benefit plan, life insurance policy, or trust. | ☐ | | | |
| 20. Other contingent and unliquidated claims of every nature, including tax refunds, counterclaims of the debtor, and rights to setoff claims. Give estimated value of each. | ☐ | | | |
| 21. Patents. copyrights, and other intellectual property. Give particulars. | ☐ | | | |
| 22. Licenses, franchises, and other general intangibles. Give particulars. | ☐ | | | |

## SCHEDULE B - PERSONAL PROPERTY
### (Continuation Sheet)

| TYPE OF PROPERTY | NONE | DESCRIPTION AND LOCATION OF PROPERTY | HUSBAND, WIFE, JOINT OR COMMUNITY | CURRENT MARKET VALUE OF DEBTOR'S INTEREST IN PROPERTY, WITHOUT DEDUCTING ANY SECURED CLAIM OR EXEMPTION |
|---|---|---|---|---|
| 23. Automobiles, trucks, trailers, and other vehicles and accessories. | ☐ | | | |
| 24. Boats, motors, and accessories. | ☐ | | | |
| 25. Aircraft and accessories. | ☐ | | | |
| 26. Office equipment, furnishings, and supplies. | ☐ | | | |
| 27. Machinery, fixtures, equipment, and supplies used in business. | ☐ | | | |
| 28. Inventory. | ☐ | | | |
| 29. Animals. | ☐ | | | |
| 30. Crops - growing or harvested. Give particulars. | ☐ | | | |
| 31. Farming equipment and implements. | ☐ | | | |
| 32. Farm supplies, chemicals, and feed. | ☐ | | | |
| 33. Other personal property of any kind not already listed. Itemize. | ☐ | | | |
| 34. AMOUNTS FROM CONTINUATION SHEETS | | ____ CONTINUATION SHEETS ATTACHED | | |
| | | | TOTAL → | $ |

(Include amounts from any continuation
sheets attached. Report total also on
Summary of Schedules)

| In re | Case No. |
|---|---|
| Debtor(s) | (If known) |

# SCHEDULE C - **PROPERTY CLAIMED AS EXEMPT**

Debtor elects the exemptions to which debtor is entitled under:

**(Check one box)**

☐ 11 U.S.C. §522(b)(1): Exemptions provided in 11 U.S.C. § 522(d). Note: These exemptions are available only in certain states.)

☐ 11 U.S.C. §522(b)(2): Exemptions available under applicable nonbankruptcy federal laws, state or local law where the debtor's domicile has been located for the 180 days immediately preceding the filing of the petition, or for a longer portion of the 180-day period than in any other place, and the debtor's interest as a tenant by the entirety or joint tenant to the extent the interest is exempt from process under applicable nonbankruptcy law.

| DESCRIPTION OF PROPERTY | SPECIFY LAW PROVIDING EACH EXEMPTION | VALUE OF CLAIMED EXEMPTION | CURRENT MARKET VALUE OF PROPERTY WITHOUT DEDUCTING EXEMPTION |
|---|---|---|---|
| **HOMESTEAD EXEMPTION:** | | | |
| **INSURANCE:** | | | |
| **PENSIONS:** | | | |
| **PUBLIC BENEFITS:** | | | |
| **WAGES:** | | | |

| In re | | Case No. | |
|-------|--|----------|--|
| | Debtor(s) | | (If known) |

| DESCRIPTION OF PROPERTY | SPECIFY LAW PROVIDING EACH EXEMPTION | VALUE OF CLAIMED EXEMPTION | CURRENT MARKET VALUE OF PROPERTY WITHOUT DEDUCTING EXEMPTION |
|---|---|---|---|
| **TOOLS OF TRADE:** | | | |
| **PERSONAL PROPERTY:** | | | |
| **MISCELLANEOUS:** | | | |
| **WILD CARD:** | | | |

**Form 6D**

| In re | Case No. |
|---|---|
| Debtor(s) | (If known) |

## SCHEDULE D - CREDITORS HOLDING SECURED CLAIMS

State the name, mailing address, including zip code. and account number, if any, of all entities holding claims secured by property of the debtor as of the date of filing of the petition. List creditors holding all types of secured interests such as judgment liens, garnishments, statutory liens, mortgages, deeds of trust, and other security interests. List creditors in alphabetical order to the extent practicable. If all secured creditors will not fit on this page, use the continuation sheet provided.

If any entity other than a spouse in a joint case maybe jointly liable on a claim, place an "X" in the column labeled "Codebtor" - include the entry on the appropriate schedule of creditors, and complete Schedule H - Codebtors. If a joint petition is filed state whether husband, wife both of them, or the marital community maybe liable on each claim by placing an "H," "W," "J," or "C" in the column labeled "Husband, Wife, Joint, or Community."

If the claim is contingent, place an "X" in the column labeled "Contingent. If the claim is unliquidated, place an "X" in the column labeled "Unliquidated." If the claim is disputed, place an "X" in the column labeled "Disputed." (You may need to place an "X" in more than one of these three columns.)

Report the total of all claims listed on this schedule in the box labeled "Total" on the last sheet of the completed schedule. Report this total also on the Summary of Schedules.

☐ Check this box if debtor has no creditors holding secured claims to report on this Schedule D.

| CREDITOR'S NAME AND MAILING ADDRESS INCLUDING ZIP CODE | CO D E B T O R | H W J C | DATE CLAIM WAS INCURRED, NATURE OF LIEN, AND DESCRIPTION AND MARKET VALUE OF PROPERTY SUBJECT TO LIEN | CONTINGENT | UNLIQUIDATED | DISPUTED | AMOUNT OF CLAIM WITHOUT DEDUCTING VALUE OF COLLATERAL | UNSECU RED PORTIO N, IF ANY |
|---|---|---|---|---|---|---|---|---|
| ACCOUNT NO. _____ | ☐ | | | ☐ | ☐ | ☐ | | |
| ACCOUNT NO. _____ | ☐ | | | ☐ | ☐ | ☐ | | |
| ACCOUNT NO. _____ | ☐ | | | ☐ | ☐ | ☐ | | |
| ACCOUNT NO. _____ | ☐ | | | ☐ | ☐ | ☐ | | |
| | | | Subtotal → (Total of this page) | | | | $ | |
| | | | Total → (USE ONLY ON LAST PAGE) | | | | $ | |

_____ continuation sheets attached.

**(Report Also on Summary of Schedules)**

| In re | | | | | | | Case No. | | |
|---|---|---|---|---|---|---|---|---|---|
| | | Debtor(s) | | | | | | | (If known) |

## SCHEDULE D - CREDITORS HOLDING SECURED CLAIMS
### (Continuation Sheet)

| CREDITOR'S NAME AND MAILING ADDRESS INCLUDING ZIP CODE | CO DEBTOR | H W J C | DATE CLAIM WAS INCURRED, NATURE OF LIEN, AND DESCRIPTION AND MARKET VALUE OF PROPERTY SUBJECT TO LIEN | CONTINGENT | UNLIQUIDATED | DISPUTED | AMOUNT OF CLAIM WITHOUT DEDUCTING VALUE OF COLLATERAL | UNSECURED PORTION, IF ANY |
|---|---|---|---|---|---|---|---|---|
| ACCOUNT NO. _____ | ☐ | | | ☐ | ☐ | ☐ | | |
| ACCOUNT NO. _____ | ☐ | | | ☐ | ☐ | ☐ | | |
| ACCOUNT NO. _____ | ☐ | | | ☐ | ☐ | ☐ | | |
| ACCOUNT NO. _____ | ☐ | | | ☐ | ☐ | ☐ | | |
| ACCOUNT NO. _____ | ☐ | | | ☐ | ☐ | ☐ | | |
| | | | Subtotal → (Total of this page) | | | | $ | |
| | | | Total → (USE ONLY ON LAST PAGE) | | | | $ | |

_____ continuation sheets attached.

**(Report total also on Summary of Schedules)**

| In re | Case No. |
|---|---|
| Debtor(s) | (If known) |

# SCHEDULE E - CREDITORS HOLDING UNSECURED PRIORITY CLAIMS

A complete list of claims entitled to priority, listed separately by type of priority, is to be set forth on the sheets provided. Only holders of unsecured claims entitled to priority should be listed in this schedule. In the boxes provided on the attached sheets, state the name and mailing address, including zip code, and account number, if any, of all entities holding priority claims against the debtor or the property of the debtor, as of the date of the filing of the petition.

If any entity other than a spouse in a joint case maybe jointly liable on a claim, place an "X" in the colum labeled "Codebtor," include the entity on the appropriate schedule of creditors, and complete Schedule H-Codebtors. If a joint petition is filed, state whether husband, wife, both of them or the marital community maybe liable on each claim by placing an "H", "W", "J", or "C", in the column labeled "HWJC."

If the claim is contingent, place an "X" in the column labeled "Contingent." If the claim is unliquidated place an "X" in the column labeled "Unliquidated." If the claim is disputed, place an "X" in the column labeled "Disputed." (You may need to place an "X" in more than one of these three columns.)

Report the total of claims listed on each sheet in the box labeled "Subtotal" on each sheet. Report the total of all claims listed on this Schedule E in the box labeled "Total" on the last sheet of the completed schedule. Repeat this total also on the Summary of Schedules.

☐ **Check this box if debtor has no creditors holding unsecured claims to report on this Schedule E.**

**TYPE OF PRIORITY CLAIMS** (Check the appropriate box(es) below if claims in that category are listed on the attached sheets)

☐ **Extensions of credit In an involuntary case:** Claims arising in the ordinary course of the debtor's business or financial affairs after the commencement of the case but before the earlier of the appointment of a trustee or the order for relief. 11 U.S.C. §507 (a)(2).

☐ **Wages, salaries, and commissions** Wages, salaries, and commissions, including vacation, severance, and sick leave pay owing to employees, and commissions owing to qualifying independent sales representatives up to $4,000* per person, earned within 90 days immediately preceding the filing of the original petition or the cessation of business, whichever occurred first, to the extent provided in 11 U.S.C. §507 (a)(3).

☐ **Contributions to employee benefit plans** Money owed to employee benefit plans for services rendered within 180 days immediately preceding the filing of the original petition or the cessation of business, whichever occurred first, to the extent provided in 11 U.S.C. §507 (a)(4).

☐ **Certain farmers and fishermen** Claims of certain farmers and fishermen, up to $4,000* per farmer or fisherman, against the debtor, as provided in 11 U.S.C. § 507 (a)(5).

☐ **Deposits by individuals** Claims of individuals up to $1,800* for deposits for the purchase, lease, or rental of property or services for personal, family, or household use that were not delivered or provided. 11 U.S.C. §507 (a)(6).

☐ **Alimony, Maintenance, or Support** Claims of a spouse, former spouse, or child of the debtor for alimony, maintenance, or support, to the extent provided in 11 U.S.C. §507 (a)(7).

☐ **Taxes and Certain Other Debts Owed to Governmental Units** Taxes, customs duties, and penalties owing to federal, state, and local governmental units as set forth in 11 U.S.C. §507 (a)(8).

☐ **Commitments to Maintain the Capital of an Insured Depository Institution** Claims based on commitments to the FDIC, **RTC, Director** of the Office of Thrift Supervision, Comptroller of the Currency, or Board of Governors of the Federal Reserve System, or their predecessors or successors, to maintain the capital of an insured depository institution. 11 U.S.C. §507 (a)(9).

* Amounts are subject to adjustment on April 1, 1998, and every three years thereafter with respect to cases commenced on or after the date of adjustment.

| In re | | | Case No. | |
|---|---|---|---|---|
| | | Debtor(s) | | (If known) |

(Continuation Sheet)

TYPE OF PRIORITY

| CREDITOR'S NAME AND MAILING ADDRESS INCLUDING ZIP CODE | C O D E B T | H W J C | DATE CLAIM WAS INCURRED AND CONSIDERATION FOR CLAIM | * C U D | AMOUNT OF CLAIM | AMOUNT ENTITLED TO PRIORITY |
|---|---|---|---|---|---|---|
| A/C # _____ | ☐ | | | | | |
| A/C # _____ | ☐ | | | | | |
| A/C # _____ | ☐ | | | | | |
| A/C # _____ | ☐ | | | | | |
| A/C # _____ | ☐ | | | | | |
| A/C # _____ | ☐ | | | | | |

Subtotal →
(Total of this page) $

_____ Continuation sheets attached.     Total → $
(use only on *last page* of the completed Schedule E)

• If contingent, enter C; if unliquidated, enter U; if disputed, enter D.(Report   total   also   on   Summary   of   Schedules)

| In re | | | Case No. | |
|---|---|---|---|---|
| | | Debtor(s) | | (If known) |

# SCHEDULE E - CREDITORS HOLDING UNSECURED PRIORITY CLAIMS

(Continuation Sheet)

TYPE OF PRIORITY _____

| CREDITOR'S NAME AND MAILING ADDRESS INCLUDING ZIP CODE | C O D E B T | H W J C | DATE CLAIM WAS INCURRED AND CONSIDERATION FOR CLAIM. | * C U D | AMOUNT OF CLAIM | AMOUNT ENTITLED TO PRIORITY |
|---|---|---|---|---|---|---|
| A/C # _____ | ☐ | | | | | |
| A/C # _____ | ☐ | | | | | |
| A/C # _____ | ☐ | | | | | |
| A/C # _____ | ☐ | | | | | |
| A/C # _____ | ☐ | | | | | |
| A/C # _____ | ☐ | | | | | |
| | | | Subtotal → (Total of this page) | | $ | |
| | | | Total → (Use only on last page of the completed Schedule E) | | $ | |

Sheet No. _____ of _____ sheets attached.

**(Report total also on Summary of Schedules)**

| In re | Case No. |
|---|---|
| Debtor(s) | (If known) |

## SCHEDULE F - CREDITORS HOLDING UNSECURED NONPRIORITY CLAIMS

State the name, mailing address, including zip code, and account number, if any, of all entities holding unsecured claims without priority against the debtor or the property of the debtor, as of the date of filing of the petition. Do not include claims listed in Schedules D and E. If all creditors will not fit on this page, use the continuation sheet provided.

If any entity other than a spouse in a joint case maybe jointly liable on a claim, place an "X" in the column labeled "Codebtor," include the entity on the appropriate schedule of creditors, and complete Schedule H - Codebtors. If a joint petition is filed, state whether husband, wife, both of them, or the marital community maybe liable on each claim by placing an "H," "W," "J," or "C" in the column labeled "Husband, Wife, Joint, or Community."

If the claim is contingent, place an "X" in the column labeled "Contingent." If the claim is unliquidated, place an "X" in the column labeled "Unliquidated." If the claim is disputed, place an "X" in the column labeled "Disputed." (You may need to place an "X" in more than one of these three columns.)

Report total of all claims listed on this schedule in the box labeled "Total" on the last sheet of the completed schedule. Report this total also on the Summary of Schedules.

☐ **Check this box if debtor has no creditors holding unsecured non-priority claims to report on this Schedule F.**

| CREDITOR'S NAME AND MAILING ADDRESS INCLUDING ZIP CODE | CODEBTOR | HWJC | DATE CLAIM WAS INCURRED AND CONSIDERATION FOR CLAIM. IF CLAIM IS SUBJECT TO SETOFF, SO STATE | CONTINGENT | UNLIQUIDATED | DISPUTED | AMOUNT OF CLAIM |
|---|---|---|---|---|---|---|---|
| ACCOUNT NO. _____ | ☐ | | ☐ CLAIM IS SUBJECT TO SETOFF | ☐ | ☐ | ☐ | |
| ACCOUNT NO. _____ | ☐ | | ☐ CLAIM IS SUBJECT TO SETOFF | ☐ | ☐ | ☐ | |
| ACCOUNT NO. _____ | ☐ | | ☐ CLAIM IS SUBJECT TO SETOFF | ☐ | ☐ | ☐ | |
| ACCOUNT NO. _____ | ☐ | | ☐ CLAIM IS SUBJECT TO SETOFF | ☐ | ☐ | ☐ | |

Subtotal → (Total of this page) $

_____ **Continuation sheets attached**

Total → (Use only on last page of the completed Schedule F) $

**(Report total also on Summary of Schedules)**

| In re | | | | | Case No. | | | |
|---|---|---|---|---|---|---|---|---|
| | | | Debtor(s) | | (If known) | | | |

# SCHEDULE F - CREDITORS HOLDING UNSECURED NONPRIORITY CLAIMS
(Continuation Sheet)

| CREDITOR'S NAME AND MAILING ADDRESS INCLUDING ZIP CODE | CO D E B T | H W J C | DATE CLAIM WAS INCURRED AND CONSIDERATION FOR CLAIM. IF CLAIM IS SUBJECT TO SETOFF, SO STATE | CONTINGENT | UNLIQUIDATED | DISPUTED | AMOUNT OF CLAIM |
|---|---|---|---|---|---|---|---|
| ACCOUNT NO. _____ | ☐ | | ☐ CLAIM IS SUBJECT TO SETOFF | ☐ | ☐ | ☐ | |
| ACCOUNT NO. _____ | ☐ | | ☐ CLAIM IS SUBJECT TO SETOFF | ☐ | ☐ | ☐ | |
| ACCOUNT NO. _____ | ☐ | | ☐ CLAIM IS SUBJECT TO SETOFF | ☐ | ☐ | ☐ | |
| ACCOUNT NO. _____ | ☐ | | ☐ CLAIM IS SUBJECT TO SETOFF | ☐ | ☐ | ☐ | |
| ACCOUNT NO. _____ | ☐ | | ☐ CLAIM IS SUBJECT TO SETOFF | ☐ | ☐ | ☐ | |
| | | | Subtotal → (Total of this page) | | | | $ |

Sheet No. _____ of _____ sheets attached to Schedule
of Creditors Holding Unsecured Claims.

Total → (Use only on last page of the completed Schedule F)   $

(Report total also on Summary of Schedules)

# SCHEDULE G. EXECUTORY CONTRACTS AND UNEXPIRED LEASES

Describe all executory contracts of any nature and all unexpired leases of real or personal property. Include an timeshare interests.

State nature of debtor's interest in contract, i.e., "Purchaser," "Agent," etc. State whether debtor is the lessor or lessee of a lease.

Provide the names and complete mailing addresses of all other parties to each lease or contract described.

**NOTE:** A party listed on this schedule will not receive notice of the filing of this case unless the party is also scheduled in the appropriate schedule of creditors.

☐ **Check this box if debtor has no executory contracts or unexpired leases.**

| NAME AND MAILING ADDRESS, INCLUDING ZIP CODE, OF OTHER PARTIES TO LEASE OR CONTRACT | DESCRIPTION OF CONTRACT OR LEASE AND NATURE OF DEBTOR'S INTEREST. STATE WHETHER LEASE IS FOR NONRESIDENTIAL REAL PROPERTY. STATE CONTRACT NUMBER OF ANY GOVERNMENT CONTRACT. |
|---|---|
| | ☐ LEASE IS FOR NONRESIDENTIAL REAL PROPERTY.<br>☐ GOVERNMENT CONTRACT<br>CONTRACT NUMBER: |
| | ☐ LEASE IS FOR NONRESIDENTIAL REAL PROPERTY.<br>☐ GOVERNMENT CONTRACT<br>CONTRACT NUMBER: |
| | ☐ LEASE IS FOR NONRESIDENTIAL REAL PROPERTY.<br>☐ GOVERNMENT CONTRACT<br>CONTRACT NUMBER: |

| In re | | Case No. | |
|---|---|---|---|
| | Debtor(s) | | (If known) |

## SCHEDULE H - CODEBTORS

Provide the information requested concerning any person or entity, other than a spouse in a joint case, that is also liable on any debts listed by debtor in the schedules of creditors. Include all guarantors and co-signers. In community property states, a married debtor not filing a joint case should report the name and address of the non-debtor spouse on this schedule. Include all names used by the non-debtor spouse during the six years immediately preceding the commencement of this case.

☐ **Check this box if debtor has no co-debtors.**

| NAME AND ADDRESS OF CODEBTOR | NAME AND ADDRESS OF CREDITOR |
|---|---|
| | |
| | |
| | |
| | |
| | |

| In re | | Case No. | |
|---|---|---|---|
| | Debtor(s) | | (If known) |

## SCHEDULE I - CURRENT INCOME OF INDIVIDUAL DEBTOR(S)

The column labeled "Spouse" must be completed in all cases filed by joint debtors and by a named debtor in a chapter 12 or 13 case whether or not a joint petition is filed, unless the spouses are separated and a joint petition is not filed.

| Debtor's Marital Status: | DEPENDENTS OF DEBTOR AND SPOUSE | | |
|---|---|---|---|
| NAMES | AGE | RELATIONSHIP | |
| | | | |
| | | | |
| | | | |
| | | | |

| Employment: | DEBTOR | SPOUSE |
|---|---|---|
| Occupation | | |
| Name of Employer | | |
| How long employed | | |
| Address of Employer | | |

| INCOME: (Estimate of average monthly income | DEBTOR | SPOUSE |
|---|---|---|
| Current monthly gross wages, salary, and commissions (prorate if not paid monthly.) | | |
| Estimated monthly overtime | | |
| SUBTOTAL | | |
| LESS PAYROLL DEDUCTIONS a. Payroll taxes and Social Security | | |
| b. Insurance | | |
| c. Union dues | | |
| d. Other (Specify) | | |
| SUBTOTAL OF PAYROLL DEDUCTIONS | | |
| TOTAL NET MONTHLY TAKE HOME PAY | | |
| Regular income from operation of business or profession or farm (attach detailed statement) | | |
| Income from real property | | |
| Interest and dividends | | |
| Alimony, maintenance or support payments payable to the debtor for the debtor's use or that of dependents listed above. | | |
| Social security or other government assistance (Specify) | | |
| Pension or retirement income | | |
| Other monthly income (Specify) | | |
| TOTAL MONTHLY INCOME → | $ | $ |

**TOTAL COMBINED MONTHLY INCOME :**      $                                    (Report also on Summary of Schedules)

Describe any increase or decrease of more than 10% in any of the above categories anticipated to occur within the year following the filing of this document.
__ SHEETS ATTACHED.

| In re | | Case No. | |
|---|---|---|---|
| | Debtor(s) | | (If known) |

# SCHEDULE I - CURRENT INCOME OF INDIVIDUAL DEBTOR(S)

The column labeled "Spouse" must be completed in all cases filed by joint debtors and by a named debtor in a chapter 12 or 13 case whether or not a joint petition is filed, unless the spouses are separated and a joint petition is not filed.

| Debtor's Marital Status: | DEPENDENTS OF DEBTOR AND SPOUSE | | |
|---|---|---|---|
| NAMES | AGE | RELATIONSHIP | |
| | | | |
| | | | |
| | | | |
| | | | |

| Employment: | DEBTOR | SPOUSE |
|---|---|---|
| Occupation | | |
| Name of Employer | | |
| How long employed | | |
| Address of Employer | | |

| INCOME: (Estimate of average monthly income | DEBTOR | SPOUSE |
|---|---|---|
| Current monthly gross wages, salary, and commissions (prorate if not paid monthly.) | | |
| Estimated monthly overtime | | |
| **SUBTOTAL** | | |
| LESS PAYROLL DEDUCTIONS   a. Payroll taxes and Social Security | | |
| b. Insurance | | |
| c. Union dues | | |
| d. Other (Specify) | | |
| SUBTOTAL OF PAYROLL DEDUCTIONS | | |
| **TOTAL NET MONTHLY TAKE HOME PAY** | | |
| Regular income from operation of business or profession or farm (attach detailed statement) | | |
| Income from real property | | |
| Interest and dividends | | |
| Alimony, maintenance or support payments payable to the debtor for the debtor's use or that of dependents listed above. | | |
| Social security or other government assistance (Specify) | | |
| Pension or retirement income | | |
| Other monthly income (Specify) | | |
| TOTAL MONTHLY INCOME → | $ | $ |

**TOTAL COMBINED MONTHLY INCOME :**    $            (Report also on Summary of Schedules)

Describe any increase or decrease of more than 10% in any of the above categories anticipated to occur within the year following the filing of this document.
\_\_ SHEETS ATTACHED.

# UNITED STATES BANKRUPTCY COURT
## District of

| In re | Case No. _____ |
|---|---|
| Debtor(s) | (If known) |

## SUMMARY OF SCHEDULES

Indicate as to each schedule whether that schedule is attached and state the number of pages in each. Report the totals from Schedules A,B,D,E,F,I, and J in the boxes provided. Add the amounts from Schedules A and B to determine the total amount of the debtor's assets. Add the amounts from Schedules D,E, and F to determine the total amount of the debtor's liabilities.

### AMOUNTS SCHEDULED

| NAME OF SCHEDULE | ATTACHED (YES/NO) | NO. OF SHEETS | ASSETS | LIABILITIES | OTHER |
|---|---|---|---|---|---|
| A. REAL PROPERTY | | | | | |
| B. PERSONAL PROPERTY | | | | | |
| C. PROPERTY CLAIMED AS EXEMPT | | | | | |
| D. CREDITORS HOLDING SECURED CLAIMS | | | →→→→→→ | | |
| E. CREDITORS HOLDING UNSECURED PRIORITY CLAIMS | | | →→→→→→ | | |
| F. CREDITORS HOLDING UNSECURED NON-PRIORITY CLAIMS | | | →→→→→→ | | |
| G. EXECUTORY CONTRACTS AND UNEXPIRED LEASES | | | | | |
| H. CODEBTORS | | | | | |
| I. CURRENT INCOME OF INDIVIDUAL DEBTOR(S) | | | →→→→→→→→→→→→ | | |
| J. CURRENT EXPENDITURES OF INDIVIDUAL DEBTOR(S) | | | →→→→→→→→→→→→ | | |

Total Number of Sheets of ALL Schedules →

Total Assets →

Total Liabilities →

| In re | Case No.: |
|---|---|
| Debtor (s) | (If known) |

# DECLARATION CONCERNING DEBTOR'S SCHEDULES
## DECLARATION UNDER PENALTY OF PERJURY BY INDIVIDUAL DEBTOR

I declare under penalty of perjury that I have read the foregoing summary and schedules, consisting of _____ sheets and that they are true and correct to the best of my knowledge, information, and belief.      (Total shown on Summary page plus 1 )

Date _____

Signature: _____

Debtor

Date _____
Signature: _____

(Joint Debtor, if any)

[If joint case, both spouses must sign.]

## CERTIFICATION AND SIGNATURE OF NON ATTORNEY BANKRUPTCY PETITION PREPARER
### (See 11 U.S.C. § 110)

I certify that I am a bankruptcy petition preparer as defined in 11 U.S.C. § 110, that I have prepared this document for compensation, and that I have provided the debtor with a copy of this document.

_____      _____
Printed or Typed Name of Bankruptcy Petition Preparer          Social          Security          Number

_____

_____
Address

Names and Social Security Numbers of all other individuals who prepared or assisted in preparing this document:

If more than one person prepared this document, attach additional signed sheets conforming to the appropriate Official Form for each person.

X _____      _____
Signature of Bankruptcy Petition Preparer                              Date

*A bankruptcy petition preparer's failure to comply with the provisions of Title 11 and the Federal Rules of Bankruptcy Procedure may result in fines or imprisonment or both. 11 U.S.C. § 110; 18 U.S.C. § 156.*

## DECLARATION UNDER PENALTY OF PERJURY ON BEHALF OF CORPORATION OR PARTNERSHIP

I, the _____ [president or other officer or an authorized agent of the corporation or a member or an authorized agent of the partnership] of the _____ [corporation or partnership] named as debtor in this case, declare under penalty of perjury that I have read the foregoing summary and schedules, consisting of sheets (total shown on summary page plus 1), and that they are true and correct to the best of my knowledge, information, and belief.

Date _____      Signature: _____

_____

[Print or type name of individual signing on behalf of debtor.]

[An individual signing on behalf of a partnership or corporation must indicate position or relationship to debtor.]_
*Penalty for making a false statement or concealing property: Fine of up to S500,000 or imprisonment for up to 5 years or both. 18 U.S.C. § 152 and 3571.*

# Appendix H

# THE FAIR CREDIT REPORTING ACT

TABLE OF CONTENTS

§ 601. Short title

Fair Credit Reporting Act

§ 602. Congressional findings and statement of purpose [15 U.S.C. § 1681]

(a) Accuracy and fairness of credit reporting. The Congress makes the following findings:

(1) The banking system is dependent upon fair and accurate credit reporting. Inaccurate credit reports directly impair the efficiency of the banking system, and unfair credit reporting methods undermine the public confidence which is essential to the continued functioning of the banking system.

(2) An elaborate mechanism has been developed for investigating and evaluating the credit worthiness, credit standing, credit capacity, character, and general reputation of consumers.

(3) Consumer reporting agencies have assumed a vital role in assembling and evaluating consumer credit and other information on consumers.

(4) There is a need to insure that consumer reporting agencies exercise their grave responsibilities with fairness, impartiality, and a respect for the consumer's right to privacy.

(b) Reasonable procedures. It is the purpose of this title to require that consumer reporting agencies adopt reasonable procedures for meeting the needs of commerce for consumer credit, personnel, insurance, and other information in a manner which is fair and equitable to the consumer, with regard to the confidentiality, accuracy, relevancy, and proper utilization of such information in accordance with the requirements of this title.

§ 603. Definitions; rules of construction [15 U.S.C. § 1681a]

(a) Definitions and rules of construction set forth in this section are applicable for the purposes of this title.

(b) The term "person" means any individual, partnership, corporation, trust, estate, cooperative, association, government or governmental subdivision or agency, or other entity.

(c) The term "consumer" means an individual.

(d) Consumer report.

(1) In general. The term "consumer report" means any written, oral, or other communication of any information by a consumer reporting agency bearing on a consumer's credit worthiness, credit standing, credit capacity, character, general reputation, personal characteristics, or mode of living which is used or expected to be used or collected in whole or in part for the purpose of serving as a factor in establishing the consumer's eligibility for

    (A) credit or insurance to be used primarily for personal, family, or household purposes;

    (B) employment purposes; or

    (C) any other purpose authorized under section 604 [§ 1681b].
(2) Exclusions. The term "consumer report" does not include

    (A) any

        (i) report containing information solely as to transactions or experiences between the consumer and the person making the report;

        (ii) communication of that information among persons related by common ownership or affiliated by corporate control; or

        (iii) communication of other information among persons related by common ownership or affiliated by corporate control, if it is clearly and conspicuously disclosed to the consumer that the information maybe communicated among such persons and the consumer is given the opportunity, before the time that the information is initially communicated, to direct that such information not be communicated among such persons;

    (B) any authorization or approval of a specific extension of credit directly or indirectly by the issuer of a credit card or similar device;

    (C) any report in which a person who has been requested by a third party to make a specific extension of credit directly or indirectly to a consumer conveys his or her decision with respect to such request, if the third party advises the consumer of the name and address of the person to whom the request was made, and such person makes the disclosures to the consumer required under section 615 [§ 1681m]; or

(D) a communication described in subsection (o).

(e) The term "investigative consumer report" means a consumer report or portion thereof in which information on a consumer's character, general reputation, personal characteristics, or mode of living is obtained through personal interviews with neighbors, friends, or associates of the consumer reported on or with others with whom he is acquainted or who may have knowledge concerning any such items of information. However, such information shall not include specific factual information on a consumer's credit record obtained directly from a creditor of the consumer or from a consumer reporting agency when such information was obtained directly from a creditor of the consumer or from the consumer.

(f) The term "consumer reporting agency" means any person which, for monetary fees, dues, or on a cooperative nonprofit basis, regularly engages in whole or in part in the practice of assembling or evaluating consumer credit information or other information on consumers for the purpose of furnishing consumer reports to third parties, and which uses any means or facility of interstate commerce for the purpose of preparing or furnishing consumer reports.

(g) The term "file," when used in connection with information on any consumer, means all of the information on that consumer recorded and retained by a consumer reporting agency regardless of how the information is stored.

(h) The term "employment purposes" when used in connection with a consumer report means a report used for the purpose of evaluating a consumer for employment, promotion, reassignment or retention as an employee.

(i) The term "medical information" means information or records obtained, with the consent of the individual to whom it relates, from licensed physicians or medical practitioners, hospitals, clinics, or other medical or medically related facilities.

(j) Definitions relating to child support obligations.

(1) Overdue support. The term "overdue support" has the meaning given to such term in section 666(e) of title 42 [Social Security Act, 42 U.S.C. § 666(e)].
(2) State or local child support enforcement agency. The term "State or local child support enforcement agency" means a State or local agency which administers a State or local program for establishing and enforcing child support obligations.

(k) Adverse action.

(1) Actions included. The term "adverse action"

(A) has the same meaning as in section 701(d)(6) of the Equal Credit Opportunity Act; and

(B) means

(i) a denial or cancellation of, an increase in any charge for, or a reduction or other adverse or unfavorable change in the terms of coverage or amount of, any insurance, existing or applied for, in connection with the underwriting of insurance;

(ii) a denial of employment or any other decision for employment purposes that adversely affects any current or prospective employee;

(iii) a denial or cancellation of, an increase in any charge for, or any other adverse or unfavorable change in the terms of, any license or benefit described in section 604(a)(3)(D) [§ 1681b]; and

(iv) an action taken or determination that is

(I) made in connection with an application that was made by, or a transaction that was initiated by, any consumer, or in connection with a review of an account under section 604(a)(3)(F)(ii)[§ 1681b]; and

(II) adverse to the interests of the consumer.
(2) Applicable findings, decisions, commentary, and orders. For purposes of any determination of whether an action is an adverse action under paragraph (1)(A), all appropriate final findings, decisions, commentary, and orders issued under section 701(d)(6) of the Equal Credit Opportunity Act by the Board of Governors of the Federal Reserve System or any court shall apply.

(l) Firm offer of credit or insurance. The term "firm offer of credit or insurance" means any offer of credit or insurance to a consumer that will be honored if the consumer is determined, based on information in a consumer report on the consumer, to meet the specific criteria used to select the consumer for the offer, except that the offer maybe further conditioned on one or more of the following:

(1) The consumer being determined, based on information in the consumer's application for the credit or insurance, to meet specific criteria bearing on credit worthiness or insurability, as applicable, that are established

(A) before selection of the consumer for the offer; and

(B) for the purpose of determining whether to extend credit or insurance pursuant to the offer.
(2) Verification

(A) that the consumer continues to meet the specific criteria used to select the consumer for the offer, by using information in a consumer report on the consumer, information in the consumer's application for the credit or insurance, or other information bearing on the credit worthiness or insurability of the consumer; or

(B) of the information in the consumer's application for the credit or insurance, to determine that the consumer meets the specific criteria bearing on credit worthiness or insurability.
(3) The consumer furnishing any collateral that is a requirement for the extension of the credit or insurance that was

(A) established before selection of the consumer for the offer of credit or insurance; and
(B) disclosed to the consumer in the offer of credit or insurance.

(m) Credit or insurance transaction that is not initiated by the consumer. The term "credit or insurance transaction that is not initiated by the consumer" does not include the use of a consumer report by a person with which the consumer has an account or insurance policy, for purposes of

(1) reviewing the account or insurance policy; or
(2) collecting the account.

(n) State. The term "State" means any State, the Commonwealth of Puerto Rico, the District of Columbia, and any territory or possession of the United States.

(o) Excluded communications. A communication is described in this subsection if it is a communication

(1) that, but for subsection (d)(2)(D), would be an investigative consumer report;
(2) that is made to a prospective employer for the purpose of

(A) procuring an employee for the employer; or

(B) procuring an opportunity for a natural person to work for the employer;
(3) that is made by a person who regularly performs such procurement;
(4) that is not used by any person for any purpose other than a purpose described in subparagraph (A) or (B) of paragraph (2); and
(5) with respect to which

(A) the consumer who is the subject of the communication

(i) consents orally or in writing to the nature and scope of the communication, before the collection of any information for the purpose of making the communication;

(ii) consents orally or in writing to the making of the communication to a prospective employer, before the making of the communication; and

(iii) in the case of consent under clause (i) or (ii) given orally, is provided written confirmation of that consent by the person making the communication, not later than 3 business days after the receipt of the consent by that person;

(B) the person who makes the communication does not, for the purpose of making the communication, make any inquiry that if made by a prospective employer of the consumer who is the subject of the communication would violate any applicable Federal or State equal employment opportunity law or regulation; and

(C) the person who makes the communication

(i) discloses in writing to the consumer who is the subject of the communication, not later than 5 business days after receiving any request from the consumer for such disclosure, the nature and substance of all information in the consumer's file at the time of the request, except that the sources of any information that is acquired solely for use in making the communication and is actually used for no other purpose, need not be disclosed other than under appropriate discovery procedures in any court of competent jurisdiction in which an action is brought; and

(ii) notifies the consumer who is the subject of the communication, in writing, of the consumer's right to request the information described in clause (i).

(p) Consumer reporting agency that compiles and maintains files on consumers on a nationwide basis. The term "consumer reporting agency that compiles and maintains files on consumers on a nationwide basis" means a consumer reporting agency that regularly engages in the practice of assembling or evaluating, and maintaining, for the purpose of furnishing consumer reports to third parties bearing on a consumer's credit worthiness, credit standing, or credit capacity, each of the following regarding consumers residing nationwide:

(1) Public record information.
(2) Credit account information from persons who furnish that information regularly and in the ordinary course of business.

§ 604. Permissible purposes of consumer reports [15 U.S.C. § 1681b]

(a) In general. Subject to subsection (c), any consumer reporting agency may furnish a consumer report under the following circumstances and no other:

(1) In response to the order of a court having jurisdiction to issue such an order, or a subpoena issued in connection with proceedings before a Federal grand jury.
(2) In accordance with the written instructions of the consumer to whom it relates.(3) To a person which it has reason to believe

(A) intends to use the information in connection with a credit transaction involving the consumer on whom the information is to be furnished and involving the extension of credit to, or review or collection of an account of, the consumer; or

(B) intends to use the information for employment purposes; or

(C) intends to use the information in connection with the underwriting of insurance involving the consumer; or

(D) intends to use the information in connection with a determination of the consumer's eligibility for a license or other benefit granted by a governmental instrumentality required by law to consider an applicant's financial responsibility or status; or

(E) intends to use the information, as a potential investor or servicer, or current insurer, in connection with a valuation of, or an assessment of the credit or prepayment risks associated with, an existing credit obligation; or

(F) otherwise has a legitimate business need for the information

(i) in connection with a business transaction that is initiated by the consumer; or

(ii) to review an account to determine whether the consumer continues to meet the terms of the account.

(4) In response to a request by the head of a State or local child support enforcement agency (or a State or local government official authorized by the head of such an agency), if the person making the request certifies to the consumer reporting agency that

(A) the consumer report is needed for the purpose of establishing an individual's capacity to make child support payments or determining the appropriate level of such payments;

(B) the paternity of the consumer for the child to which the obligation relates has been established or acknowledged by the consumer in accordance with State laws under which the obligation arises (if required by those laws);

(C) the person has provided at least 10 days' prior notice to the consumer whose report is requested, by certified or registered mail to the last known address of the consumer, that the report will be requested; and

(D) the consumer report will be kept confidential, will be used solely for a purpose described in subparagraph (A), and will not be used in connection with any other civil, administrative, or criminal proceeding, or for any other purpose.

(5) To an agency administering a State plan under Section 454 of the Social Security Act (42 U.S.C. § 654) for use to set an initial or modified child support award.

(b) Conditions for furnishing and using consumer reports for employment purposes.

(1) Certification from user. A consumer reporting agency may furnish a consumer report for employment purposes only if

(A) the person who obtains such report from the agency certifies to the agency that

(i) the person has complied with paragraph (2) with respect to the consumer report, and the person will comply with paragraph (3) with respect to the consumer report if paragraph (3) becomes applicable; and

(ii) information from the consumer report will not be used in violation of any applicable Federal or State equal employment opportunity law or regulation; and

(B) the consumer reporting agency provides with the report, or has previously provided, a summary of the consumer's rights under this title, as prescribed by the Federal Trade Commission under section 609(c)(3) [§ 1681g].

(2) Disclosure to consumer.

(A) In general. Except as provided in subparagraph (B), a person may not procure a consumer report, or cause a consumer report to be procured, for employment purposes with respect to any consumer, unless--

(i) a clear and conspicuous disclosure has been made in writing to the consumer at any time before the report is procured or caused to be procured, in a document that consists solely of the disclosure, that a consumer report maybe obtained for employment purposes; and

(ii) the consumer has authorized in writing (which authorization maybe made on the document referred to in clause (i)) the procurement of the report by that person.

(B) Application by mail, telephone, computer, or other similar means. If a consumer described in subparagraph (C) applies for employment by mail, telephone, computer, or other similar means, at any time before a consumer report is procured or caused to be procured in connection with that application--

(i) the person who procures the consumer report on the consumer for employment purposes shall provide to the consumer, by oral, written, or electronic means, notice that a consumer report maybe obtained for employment purposes, and a summary of the consumer's rights under section 615(a)(3); and

(ii) the consumer shall have consented, orally, in writing, or electronically to the procurement of the report by that person.
(C) Scope. Subparagraph (B) shall apply to a person procuring a consumer report on a consumer in connection with the consumer's application for employment only if--


(i) the consumer is applying for a position over which the Secretary of Transportation has the power to establish qualifications and maximum hours of service pursuant to the provisions of section 31502 of title 49, or a position subject to safety regulation by a State transportation agency; and
(ii) as of the time at which the person procures the report or causes the report to be procured the only interaction between the consumer and the person in connection with that employment application has been by mail, telephone, computer, or other similar means.
(3) Conditions on use for adverse actions.

(A) In general. Except as provided in subparagraph (B), in using a consumer report for employment purposes, before taking any adverse action based in whole or in part on the report, the person intending to take such adverse action shall provide to the consumer to whom the report relates--

(i) a copy of the report; and

(ii) a description in writing of the rights of the consumer under this title, as prescribed by the Federal Trade Commission under section 609(c)(3).

(B) Application by mail, telephone, computer, or other similar means.

(i) If a consumer described in subparagraph (C) applies for employment by mail, telephone, computer, or other similar means, and if a person who has procured a consumer report on the consumer for employment purposes takes adverse action on the employment application based in whole or in part on the report, then the person must provide to the consumer to whom the report relates, in lieu of the notices required under subparagraph (A) of this section and under section 615(a), within 3 business days of taking such action, an oral, written or electronic notification--

---

(I) that adverse action has been taken based in whole or in part on a consumer report received from a consumer reporting agency;

(II) of the name, address and telephone number of the consumer reporting agency that furnished the consumer report (including a toll-free telephone number established by the agency if the agency compiles and maintains files on consumers on a nationwide basis);

(III) that the consumer reporting agency did not make the decision to take the adverse action and is unable to provide to the consumer the specific reasons why the adverse action was taken; and

(IV) that the consumer may, upon providing proper identification, request a free copy of a report and may dispute with the consumer reporting agency the accuracy or completeness of any information in a report.

(ii) If, under clause (B)(i)(IV), the consumer requests a copy of a consumer report from the person who procured the report, then, within 3 business days of receiving the consumer's request, together with proper identification, the person must send or provide to the consumer a copy of a report and a copy of the consumer's rights as prescribed by the Federal Trade Commission under section 609(c)(3).

(C) Scope. Subparagraph (B) shall apply to a person procuring a consumer report on a consumer in connection with the consumer's application for employment only if--

(i) the consumer is applying for a position over which the Secretary of Transportation has the power to establish qualifications and maximum hours of service pursuant to the provisions of section 31502 of title 49, or a position subject to safety regulation by a State transportation agency; and

(ii) as of the time at which the person procures the report or causes the report to be procured the only interaction between the consumer and the person in connection with that employment application has been by mail, telephone, computer, or other similar means.
(4) Exception for national security investigations.

(A) In general. In the case of an agency or department of the United States Government which seeks to obtain and use a consumer report for employment purposes, paragraph (3) shall not apply to any adverse action by such agency or department which is based in part on such consumer report, if the head of such agency or department makes a written finding that--

(i) the consumer report is relevant to a national security investigation of such agency or department;

(ii) the investigation is within the jurisdiction of such agency or department;

(iii) there is reason to believe that compliance with paragraph (3) will--

(I) endanger the life or physical safety of any person;

(II) result in flight from prosecution;

(III) result in the destruction of, or tampering with, evidence relevant to the investigation;

(IV) result in the intimidation of a potential witness relevant to the investigation;

(V) result in the compromise of classified information; or

(VI) otherwise seriously jeopardize or unduly delay the investigation or another official proceeding.

(B) Notification of consumer upon conclusion of investigation. Upon the conclusion of a national security investigation described in subparagraph (A), or upon the determination that the exception under subparagraph (A) is no longer required for the reasons set forth in such subparagraph, the official exercising the authority in such subparagraph shall provide to the consumer who is the subject of the consumer report with regard to which such finding was made--

(i) a copy of such consumer report with any classified information redacted as necessary;

(ii) notice of any adverse action which is based, in part, on the consumer report; and

(iii) the identification with reasonable specificity of the nature of the investigation for which the consumer report was sought.

(C) Delegation by head of agency or department. For purposes of subparagraphs (A) and (B), the head of any agency or department of the United States Government may delegate his or her authorities under this paragraph to an official of such agency or department who has personnel security responsibilities and is a member of the Senior Executive Service or equivalent civilian or military rank.

(D) Report to the congress. Not later than January 31 of each year, the head of each agency and department of the United States Government that exercised authority under this paragraph during the preceding year shall submit a report to the Congress on the number of times the department or agency exercised such authority during the year.

(E) Definitions. For purposes of this paragraph, the following definitions shall apply:

(i) Classified information. The term `classified information' means information that is protected from unauthorized disclosure under Executive Order No. 12958 or successor orders.

(ii) National security investigation. The term `national security investigation' means any official inquiry by an agency or department of the United States Government to determine the eligibility of a consumer to receive access or continued access to classified information or to determine whether classified information has been lost or compromised.

(c) Furnishing reports in connection with credit or insurance transactions that are not initiated by the consumer.

(1) In general. A consumer reporting agency may furnish a consumer report relating to any consumer pursuant to subparagraph (A) or (C) of subsection (a)(3) in connection with any credit or insurance transaction that is not initiated by the consumer only if

(A) the consumer authorizes the agency to provide such report to such person; or

(B) (i) the transaction consists of a firm offer of credit or insurance;

(ii) the consumer reporting agency has complied with subsection (e); and

(iii) there is not in effect an election by the consumer, made in accordance with subsection (e), to have the consumer's name and address excluded from lists of names provided by the agency pursuant to this paragraph.

(2) Limits on information received under paragraph (1)(B). A person may receive pursuant to paragraph (1)(B) only

(A) the name and address of a consumer;

(B) an identifier that is not unique to the consumer and that is used by the person solely for the purpose of verifying the identity of the consumer; and

(C) other information pertaining to a consumer that does not identify the relationship or experience of the consumer with respect to a particular creditor or other entity.

(3) Information regarding inquiries. Except as provided in section 609(a)(5) [§ 1681g], a consumer reporting agency shall not furnish to any person a record of inquiries in connection with a credit or insurance transaction that is not initiated by a consumer.

(d) Reserved.

(e) Election of consumer to be excluded from lists.

(1) In general. A consumer may elect to have the consumer's name and address excluded from any list provided by a consumer reporting agency under subsection (c)(1)(B) in connection with a credit or insurance transaction that is not initiated by the consumer, by notifying the agency in accordance with paragraph (2) that the consumer does not consent to any use of a consumer report relating to the consumer in connection with any credit or insurance transaction that is not initiated by the consumer.

(2) Manner of notification. A consumer shall notify a consumer reporting agency under paragraph (1)

(A) through the notification system maintained by the agency under paragraph (5); or

(B) by submitting to the agency a signed notice of election form issued by the agency for purposes of this subparagraph.

(3) Response of agency after notification through system. Upon receipt of notification of the election of a consumer under paragraph (1) through the notification system maintained by the agency under paragraph (5), a consumer reporting agency shall

(A) inform the consumer that the election is effective only for the 2-year period following the election if the consumer does not submit to the agency a signed notice of election form issued by the agency for purposes of paragraph (2)(B); and

(B) provide to the consumer a notice of election form, if requested by the consumer, not later than 5 business days after receipt of the notification of the election through the system established under paragraph (5), in the case of a request made at the time the consumer provides notification through the system.

(4) Effectiveness of election. An election of a consumer under paragraph (1)

(A) shall be effective with respect to a consumer reporting agency beginning 5 business days after the date on which the consumer notifies the agency in accordance with paragraph (2);

(B) shall be effective with respect to a consumer reporting agency

(i) subject to subparagraph (C), during the 2-year period beginning 5 business days after the date on which the consumer notifies the agency of the election, in the case of an election for which a consumer notifies the agency only in accordance with paragraph (2)(A); or

(ii) until the consumer notifies the agency under subparagraph (C), in the case of an election for which a consumer notifies the agency in accordance with paragraph (2)(B);

(C) shall not be effective after the date on which the consumer notifies the agency, through the notification system established by the agency under paragraph (5), that the election is no longer effective; and

(D) shall be effective with respect to each affiliate of the agency.
(5) Notification system.

(A) In general. Each consumer reporting agency that, under subsection (c)(1)(B), furnishes a consumer report in connection with a credit or insurance transaction that is not initiated by a consumer, shall

(i) establish and maintain a notification system, including a toll-free telephone number, which permits any consumer whose consumer report is maintained by the agency to notify the agency, with appropriate identification, of the consumer's election to have the consumer's name and address excluded from any such list of names and addresses provided by the agency for such a transaction; and

(ii) publish by not later than 365 days after the date of enactment of the Consumer Credit Reporting Reform Act of 1996, and not less than annually thereafter, in a publication of general circulation in the area served by the agency

(I) a notification that information in consumer files maintained by the agency maybe used in connection with such transactions; and

(II) the address and toll-free telephone number for consumers to use to notify the agency of the consumer's election under clause (I).

(B) Establishment and maintenance as compliance. Establishment and maintenance of a notification system (including a toll-free telephone number) and publication by a consumer reporting agency on the agency's own behalf and on behalf of any of its affiliates in accordance with this paragraph is deemed to be compliance with this paragraph by each of those affiliates.
(6) Notification system by agencies that operate nationwide. Each consumer reporting agency that compiles and maintains files on consumers on a nationwide basis shall establish and maintain a notification system for purposes of paragraph (5) jointly with other such consumer reporting agencies.

(f) Certain use or obtaining of information prohibited. A person shall not use or obtain a consumer report for any purpose unless

(1) the consumer report is obtained for a purpose for which the consumer report is authorized to be furnished under this section; and

(2) the purpose is certified in accordance with section 607 [§ 1681e] by a prospective user of the report through a general or specific certification.

(g) Furnishing reports containing medical information. A consumer reporting agency shall not furnish for employment purposes, or in connection with a credit or insurance transaction, a consumer report that contains medical information about a consumer, unless the consumer consents to the furnishing of the report.

§ 605. Requirements relating to information contained in consumer reports [15 U.S.C. § 1681c]

(a) Information excluded from consumer reports. Except as authorized under subsection (b) of this section, no consumer reporting agency may make any consumer report containing any of the following items of information:

(1) Cases under title 11 [United States Code] or under the Bankruptcy Act that, from the date of entry of the order for relief or the date of adjudication, as the case maybe, antedate the report by more than 10 years. (2) Civil suits, civil judgments, and records of arrest that from date of entry, antedate the report by more than seven years or until the governing statute of limitations has expired, whichever is the longer period. (3) Paid tax liens which, from date of payment, antedate the report by more than seven years. (4) Accounts placed for collection or charged to profit and loss which antedate the report by more than seven years.(1) (5) Any other adverse item of information, other than records of convictions of crimes which antedates the report by more than seven years.1

(b) Exempted cases. The provisions of subsection (a) of this section are not applicable in the case of any consumer credit report to be used in connection with

(1) a credit transaction involving, or which may reasonably be expected to involve, a principal amount of $150,000 or more; (2) the underwriting of life insurance involving, or which may reasonably be expected to involve, a face amount of $150,000 or more; or (3) the employment of any individual at an annual salary which equals, or which may reasonably be expected to equal $75,000, or more.

(c) Running of reporting period.

(1) In general. The 7-year period referred to in paragraphs (4) and (6)(2) of subsection (a) shall begin, with respect to any delinquent account that is placed for collection (internally or by referral to a third party, whichever is earlier), charged to profit and loss, or subjected to any similar action, upon the expiration of the 180-day period beginning on the date of the commencement of the delinquency which immediately preceded the collection activity, charge to profit and loss, or similar action. (2) Effective date. Paragraph (1) shall apply only to items of information added to the file of a consumer on or after the date that is 455 days after the date of enactment of the Consumer Credit Reporting Reform Act of 1996.

(d) Information required to be disclosed. Any consumer reporting agency that furnishes a consumer report that contains information regarding any case involving the consumer that arises under title 11, United States Code, shall include in the report an identification of the chapter of such title 11 under which such case arises if provided by the source of the information. If any case arising or filed under title 11, United States Code, is withdrawn by the consumer before a final judgment, the consumer reporting agency shall include in the report that such case or filing was withdrawn upon receipt of documentation certifying such withdrawal.

(e) Indication of closure of account by consumer. If a consumer reporting agency is notified pursuant to section 623(a)(4) [§ 1681s-2] that a credit account of a consumer was voluntarily closed by the consumer, the agency shall indicate that fact in any consumer report that includes information related to the account.

(f) Indication of dispute by consumer. If a consumer reporting agency is notified pursuant to section 623(a)(3) [§ 1681s-2] that information regarding a consumer who was furnished to the agency is disputed by the consumer, the agency shall indicate that fact in each consumer report that includes the disputed information.

§ 606. Disclosure of investigative consumer reports [15 U.S.C. § 1681d]

(a) Disclosure of fact of preparation. A person may not procure or cause to be prepared an investigative consumer report on any consumer unless

(1) it is clearly and accurately disclosed to the consumer that an investigative consumer report including information as to his character, general reputation, personal characteristics and mode of living, whichever are applicable, maybe made, and such disclosure

(A) is made in a writing mailed, or otherwise delivered, to the consumer, not later than three days after the date on which the report was first requested, and

(B) includes a statement informing the consumer of his right to request the additional disclosures provided for under subsection (b) of this section and the written summary of the rights of the consumer prepared pursuant to section 609(c) [§ 1681g]; and
(2) the person certifies or has certified to the consumer reporting agency that

(A) the person has made the disclosures to the consumer required by paragraph (1); and

(B) the person will comply with subsection (b).

(b) Disclosure on request of nature and scope of investigation. Any person who procures or causes to be prepared an investigative consumer report on any consumer shall, upon written request made by the consumer within a reasonable period of time after the receipt by him of the disclosure required by subsection (a)(1) of this section, make a complete and accurate disclosure of the nature and scope of the investigation requested. This disclosure shall be made in a writing mailed, or otherwise delivered, to the consumer not later than five days after the date on which the request for such disclosure was received from the consumer or such report was first requested, whichever is the later.

(c) Limitation on liability upon showing of reasonable procedures for compliance with provisions. No person maybe held liable for any violation of subsection (a) or (b) of this section if he shows by a preponderance of the evidence that at the time of the violation he maintained reasonable procedures to assure compliance with subsection (a) or (b) of this section.

(d) Prohibitions.

(1) Certification. A consumer reporting agency shall not prepare or furnish investigative consumer report unless the agency has received a certification under subsection (a)(2) from the person who requested the report.

(2) Inquiries. A consumer reporting agency shall not make an inquiry for the purpose of preparing an investigative consumer report on a consumer for employment purposes if the making of the inquiry by an employer or prospective employer of the consumer would violate any applicable Federal or State equal employment opportunity law or regulation.

(3) Certain public record information. Except as otherwise provided in section 613 [§ 1681k], a consumer reporting agency shall not furnish an investigative consumer report that includes information that is a matter of public record and that relates to an arrest, indictment, conviction, civil judicial action, tax lien, or outstanding judgment, unless the agency has verified the accuracy of the information during the 30-day period ending on the date on which the report is furnished.

(4) Certain adverse information. A consumer reporting agency shall not prepare or furnish an investigative consumer report on a consumer that contains information that is adverse to the interest of the consumer and that is obtained through a personal interview with a neighbor, friend, or associate of the consumer or with another person with whom the consumer is acquainted or who has knowledge of such item of information, unless

(A) the agency has followed reasonable procedures to obtain confirmation of the information, from an additional source that has independent and direct knowledge of the information; or

(B) the person interviewed is the best possible source of the information.

§ 607. Compliance procedures [15 U.S.C. § 1681e]

(a) Identity and purposes of credit users. Every consumer reporting agency shall maintain reasonable procedures designed to avoid violations of section 605 [§ 1681c] and to limit the furnishing of consumer reports to the purposes listed under section 604 [§ 1681b] of this title. These procedures shall require that prospective users of the information identify themselves, certify the purposes for which the information is sought, and certify that the information will be used for no other purpose. Every consumer reporting agency shall make a reasonable effort to verify the identity of a new prospective user and the uses certified by such prospective user prior to furnishing such user a consumer report. No consumer reporting agency may furnish a consumer report to any person if it has reasonable grounds for believing that the consumer report will not be used for a purpose listed in section 604 [§ 1681b] of this title.

(b) Accuracy of report. Whenever a consumer reporting agency prepares a consumer report it shall follow reasonable procedures to assure maximum possible accuracy of the information concerning the individual about whom the report relates.

(c) Disclosure of consumer reports by users allowed. A consumer reporting agency may not prohibit a user of a consumer report furnished by the agency on a consumer from disclosing the contents of the report to the consumer, if adverse action against the consumer has been taken by the user based in whole or in part on the report.

(d) Notice to users and furnishers of information.

(1) Notice requirement. A consumer reporting agency shall provide to any person

(A) who regularly and in the ordinary course of business furnishes information to the agency with respect to any consumer; or

(B) to whom a consumer report is provided by the agency;

a notice of such person's responsibilities under this title.

(2) Content of notice. The Federal Trade Commission shall prescribe the content of notices under paragraph (1), and a consumer reporting agency shall be in compliance with this subsection if it provides a notice under paragraph (1) that is substantially similar to the Federal Trade Commission prescription under this paragraph.

(e) Procurement of consumer report for resale.

(1) Disclosure. A person may not procure a consumer report for purposes of reselling the report (or any information in the report) unless the person discloses to the consumer reporting agency that originally furnishes the report

(A) the identity of the end-user of the report (or information); and

(B) each permissible purpose under section 604 [§ 1681b] for which the report is furnished to the end-user of the report (or information).

(2) Responsibilities of procurers for resale. A person who procures a consumer report for purposes of reselling the report (or any information in the report) shall

(A) establish and comply with reasonable procedures designed to ensure that the report (or information) is resold by the person only for a purpose for which the report maybe furnished under section 604 [§ 1681b], including by requiring that each person to which the report (or information) is resold and that resells or provides the report (or information) to any other person

(i) identifies each end user of the resold report (or information);

(ii) certifies each purpose for which the report (or information) will be used; and

(iii) certifies that the report (or information) will be used for no other purpose; and

(B) before reselling the report, make reasonable efforts to verify the identifications and certifications made under subparagraph (A).

(3) Resale of consumer report to a federal agency or department. Notwithstanding paragraph (1) or (2), a person who procures a consumer report for purposes of reselling the report (or any

information in the report) shall not disclose the identity of the end-user of the report under paragraph (1) or (2) if--

(A) the end user is an agency or department of the United States Government which procures the report from the person for purposes of determining the eligibility of the consumer concerned to receive access or continued access to classified information (as defined in section 604(b)(4)(E)(i)); and

(B) the agency or department certifies in writing to the person reselling the report that nondisclosure is necessary to protect classified information or the safety of persons employed by or contracting with, or undergoing investigation for work or contracting with the agency or department.

§ 608. Disclosures to governmental agencies [15 U.S.C. § 1681f]

Notwithstanding the provisions of section 604 [§ 1681b] of this title, a consumer reporting agency may furnish identifying information respecting any consumer, limited to his name, address, former addresses, places of employment, or former places of employment, to a governmental agency.

§ 609. Disclosures to consumers [15 U.S.C. § 1681g]

(a) Information on file; sources; report recipients. Every consumer reporting agency shall, upon request, and subject to 610(a)(1) [§ 1681h], clearly and accurately disclose to the consumer:

(1) All information in the consumer's file at the time of the request, except that nothing in this paragraph shall be construed to require a consumer reporting agency to disclose to a consumer any information concerning credit scores or any other risk scores or predictors relating to the consumer. (2) The sources of the information; except that the sources of information acquired solely for use in preparing an investigative consumer report and actually used for no other purpose need not be disclosed: Provided, That in the event an action is brought under this title, such sources shall be available to the plaintiff under appropriate discovery procedures in the court in which the action is brought. (3)(A) Identification of each person (including each end-user identified under section 607(e)(1) [§ 1681e]) that procured a consumer report

(i) for employment purposes, during the 2-year period preceding the date on which the request is made; or

(ii) for any other purpose, during the 1-year period preceding the date on which the request is made.

(B) An identification of a person under subparagraph (A) shall include

(i) the name of the person or, if applicable, the trade name (written in full) under which such person conducts business; and

(ii) upon request of the consumer, the address and telephone number of the person.

(C) Subparagraph (A) does not apply if--

(i) the end user is an agency or department of the United States Government that procures the report from the person for purposes of determining the eligibility of the consumer to whom the report relates to receive access or continued access to classified information (as defined in section 604(b)(4)(E)(i)); and

(ii) the head of the agency or department makes a written finding as prescribed under section 604(b)(4)(A).
(4) The dates, original payees, and amounts of any checks upon which is based any adverse characterization of the consumer, included in the file at the time of the disclosure. (5) A record of all inquiries received by the agency during the 1-year period preceding the request that identified the consumer in connection with a credit or insurance transaction that was not initiated by the consumer.

(b) Exempt information. The requirements of subsection (a) of this section respecting the disclosure of sources of information and the recipients of consumer reports do not apply to information received or consumer reports furnished prior to the effective date of this title except to the extent that the matter involved is contained in the files of the consumer reporting agency on that date.

(c) Summary of rights required to be included with disclosure.

(1) Summary of rights. A consumer reporting agency shall provide to a consumer, with each written disclosure by the agency to the consumer under this section

(A) a written summary of all of the rights that the consumer has under this title; and

(B) in the case of a consumer reporting agency that compiles and maintains files on consumers on a nationwide basis, a toll-free telephone number established by the agency, at which personnel are accessible to consumers during normal business hours.

(2) Specific items required to be included. The summary of rights required under paragraph (1) shall include

(A) a brief description of this title and all rights of consumers under this title;

(B) an explanation of how the consumer may exercise the rights of the consumer under this title;

(C) a list of all Federal agencies responsible for enforcing any provision of this title and the address and any appropriate phone number of each such agency, in a form that will assist the consumer in selecting the appropriate agency;

(D) a statement that the consumer may have additional rights under State law and that the consumer may wish to contact a State or local consumer protection agency or a State attorney general to learn of those rights; and

(E) a statement that a consumer reporting agency is not required to remove accurate derogatory information from a consumer's file, unless the information is outdated under section 605 [§ 1681c] or cannot be verified.

(3) Form of summary of rights. For purposes of this subsection and any disclosure by a consumer reporting agency required under this title with respect to consumers' rights, the Federal Trade Commission (after consultation with each Federal agency referred to in section 621(b) [§ 1681s]) shall prescribe the form and content of any such disclosure of the rights of consumers required under this title. A consumer reporting agency shall be in compliance with this subsection if it provides disclosures under paragraph (1) that are substantially similar to the Federal Trade Commission prescription under this paragraph. (4) Effectiveness. No disclosures shall be required under this subsection until the date on which the Federal Trade Commission prescribes the form and content of such disclosures under paragraph (3).

§ 610. Conditions and form of disclosure to consumers [15 U.S.C. § 1681h]

(a) In general.

(1) Proper identification. A consumer reporting agency shall require, as a condition of making the disclosures required under section 609 [§ 1681g], that the consumer furnish proper identification.
(2) Disclosure in writing. Except as provided in subsection (b), the disclosures required to be made under section 609 [§ 1681g] shall be provided under that section in writing.

(b) Other forms of disclosure.

(1) In general. If authorized by a consumer, a consumer reporting agency may make the disclosures required under 609 [§ 1681g]

(A) other than in writing; and

(B) in such form as maybe

(i) specified by the consumer in accordance with paragraph (2); and

---

(ii) available from the agency.

(2) Form. A consumer may specify pursuant to paragraph (1) that disclosures under section 609 [§ 1681g] shall be made

(A) in person, upon the appearance of the consumer at the place of business of the consumer reporting agency where disclosures are regularly provided, during normal business hours, and on reasonable notice;

(B) by telephone, if the consumer has made a written request for disclosure by telephone;

(C) by electronic means, if available from the agency; or

(D) by any other reasonable means that is available from the agency.

(c) Trained personnel. Any consumer reporting agency shall provide trained personnel to explain to the consumer any information furnished to him pursuant to section 609 [§ 1681g] of this title.

(d) Persons accompanying consumer. The consumer shall be permitted to be accompanied by one other person of his choosing, who shall furnish reasonable identification. A consumer reporting agency may require the consumer to furnish a written statement granting permission to the consumer reporting agency to discuss the consumer's file in such person's presence.

(e) Limitation of liability. Except as provided in sections 616 and 617 [§§ 1681n and 1681o] of this title, no consumer may bring any action or proceeding in the nature of defamation, invasion of privacy, or negligence with respect to the reporting of information against any consumer reporting agency, any user of information, or any person who furnishes information to a consumer reporting agency, based on information disclosed pursuant to section 609, 610, or 615 [§§ 1681g, 1681h, or 1681m] of this title or based on information disclosed by a user of a consumer report to or for a consumer against whom the user has taken adverse action, based in whole or in part on the report, except as to false information furnished with malice or willful intent to injure such consumer.

§ 611. Procedure in case of disputed accuracy [15 U.S.C. § 1681i]

(a) Reinvestigations of disputed information.

(1) Reinvestigation required.

(A) In general. If the completeness or accuracy of any item of information contained in a consumer's file at a consumer reporting agency is disputed by the consumer and the consumer notifies the agency directly of such dispute, the agency shall reinvestigate free of charge and record the current status of the disputed information, or delete the item from the file in accordance with paragraph (5), before the end of the 30-day period beginning on the date on which the agency receives the notice of the dispute from the consumer.

(B) Extension of period to reinvestigate. Except as provided in subparagraph (C), the 30-day period described in subparagraph (A) maybe extended for not more than 15 additional days if the consumer reporting agency receives information from the consumer during that 30-day period that is relevant to the reinvestigation.

(C) Limitations on extension of period to reinvestigate. Subparagraph (B) shall not apply to any reinvestigation in which, during the 30-day period described in subparagraph (A), the information that is the subject of the reinvestigation is found to be inaccurate or incomplete or the consumer reporting agency determines that the information cannot be verified.

(2) Prompt notice of dispute to furnisher of information.

(A) In general. Before the expiration of the 5-business-day period beginning on the date on which a consumer reporting agency receives notice of a dispute from any consumer in accordance with paragraph (1), the agency shall provide notification of the dispute to any person who provided any item of information in dispute, at the address and in the manner established with the person. The notice shall include all relevant information regarding the dispute that the agency has received from the consumer.

(B) Provision of other information from consumer. The consumer reporting agency shall promptly provide to the person who provided the information in dispute all relevant information regarding the dispute that is received by the agency from the consumer after the period referred to in subparagraph (A) and before the end of the period referred to in paragraph (1)(A).

(3) Determination that dispute is frivolous or irrelevant.

(A) In general. Notwithstanding paragraph (1), a consumer reporting agency may terminate a reinvestigation of information disputed by a consumer under that paragraph if the agency reasonably determines that the dispute by the consumer is frivolous or irrelevant, including by reason of a failure by a consumer to provide sufficient information to investigate the disputed information.

(B) Notice of determination. Upon making any determination in accordance with subparagraph (A) that a dispute is frivolous or irrelevant, a consumer reporting agency shall notify the consumer of such determination not later than 5 business days after making such determination, by mail or, if authorized by the consumer for that purpose, by any other means available to the agency.

(C) Contents of notice. A notice under subparagraph (B) shall include

(i) the reasons for the determination under subparagraph (A); and

(ii) identification of any information required to investigate the disputed information, which may consist of a standardized form describing the general nature of such information.

(4) Consideration of consumer information. In conducting any reinvestigation under paragraph (1) with respect to disputed information in the file of any consumer, the consumer reporting agency shall review and consider all relevant information submitted by the consumer in the period described in paragraph (1)(A) with respect to such disputed information. (5) Treatment of inaccurate or unverifiable information.

(A) In general. If, after any reinvestigation under paragraph (1) of any information disputed by a consumer, an item of the information is found to be inaccurate or incomplete or cannot be verified, the consumer reporting agency shall promptly delete that item of information from the consumer's file or modify that item of information, as appropriate, based on the results of the reinvestigation.

(B) Requirements relating to reinsertion of previously deleted material.

(i) Certification of accuracy of information. If any information is deleted from a consumer's file pursuant to subparagraph (A), the information may not be reinserted in the file by the consumer reporting agency unless the person who furnishes the information certifies that the information is complete and accurate.

(ii) Notice to consumer. If any information that has been deleted from a consumer's file pursuant to subparagraph (A) is reinserted in the file, the consumer reporting agency shall notify the consumer of the reinsertion in writing not later than 5 business days after the reinsertion or, if authorized by the consumer for that purpose, by any other means available to the agency.

(iii) Additional information. As part of, or in addition to, the notice under clause (ii), a consumer reporting agency shall provide to a consumer in writing not later than 5 business days after the date of the reinsertion

(I) a statement that the disputed information has been reinserted;

(II) the business name and address of any furnisher of information contacted and the telephone number of such furnisher, if reasonably available, or of any furnisher of information that contacted the consumer reporting agency, in connection with the reinsertion of such information; and

(III) a notice that the consumer has the right to add a statement to the consumer's file disputing the accuracy or completeness of the disputed information.

C) Procedures to prevent reappearance. A consumer reporting agency shall maintain reasonable procedures designed to prevent the reappearance in a consumer's file, and in consumer reports on the consumer, of information that is deleted pursuant to this paragraph (other than information that is reinserted in accordance with subparagraph (B)(i)).

D) Automated reinvestigation system. Any consumer reporting agency that compiles and maintains files on consumers on a nationwide basis shall implement an automated system through which furnishers of information to that consumer reporting agency may report the results of a reinvestigation that finds incomplete or inaccurate information in a consumer's file to other such consumer reporting agencies.
  (6) Notice of results of reinvestigation.

(A) In general. A consumer reporting agency shall provide written notice to a consumer of the results of a reinvestigation under this subsection not later than 5 business days after the completion of the reinvestigation, by mail or, if authorized by the consumer for that purpose, by other means available to the agency.

(B) Contents. As part of, or in addition to, the notice under subparagraph (A), a consumer reporting agency shall provide to a consumer in writing before the expiration of the 5-day period referred to in subparagraph (A)

(i) a statement that the reinvestigation is completed;

(ii) a consumer report that is based upon the consumer's file as that file is revised as a result of the reinvestigation;

(iii) a notice that, if requested by the consumer, a description of the procedure used to determine the accuracy and completeness of the information shall be provided to the consumer by the agency, including the business name and address of any furnisher of information contacted in connection with such information and the telephone number of such furnisher, if reasonably available;

(iv) a notice that the consumer has the right to add a statement to the consumer's file disputing the accuracy or completeness of the information; and

(v) a notice that the consumer has the right to request under subsection (d) that the consumer reporting agency furnish notifications under that subsection.

(7) Description of reinvestigation procedure. A consumer reporting agency shall provide to a consumer a description referred to in paragraph (6)(B)(iii) by not later than 15 days after receiving a request from the consumer for that description. (8) Expedited dispute resolution. If a dispute regarding an item of information in a consumer's file at a consumer reporting agency is resolved in accordance with paragraph (5)(A) by the deletion of the disputed information by not later than 3 business days after the date on which the agency receives notice of the dispute from the consumer in accordance with paragraph (1)(A), then the agency shall not be required to comply with paragraphs (2), (6), and (7) with respect to that dispute if the agency

(A) provides prompt notice of the deletion to the consumer by telephone;

(B) includes in that notice, or in a written notice that accompanies a confirmation and consumer report provided in accordance with subparagraph (C), a statement of the consumer's right to request under subsection (d) that the agency furnish notifications under that subsection; and

(C) provides written confirmation of the deletion and a copy of a consumer report on the consumer that is based on the consumer's file after the deletion, not later than 5 business days after making the deletion.

(b) Statement of dispute. If the reinvestigation does not resolve the dispute, the consumer may file a brief statement setting forth the nature of the dispute. The consumer reporting agency may limit such statements to not more than one hundred words if it provides the consumer with assistance in writing a clear summary of the dispute.

(c) Notification of consumer dispute in subsequent consumer reports. Whenever a statement of a dispute is filed, unless there is reasonable grounds to believe that it is frivolous or irrelevant, the consumer reporting agency shall, in any subsequent consumer report containing the information in question, clearly note that it is disputed by the consumer and provide either the consumer's statement or a clear and accurate codification or summary thereof.

(d) Notification of deletion of disputed information. Following any deletion of information which is found to be inaccurate or whose accuracy can no longer be verified or any notation as to disputed information, the consumer reporting agency shall, at the request of the consumer, furnish notification that the item has been deleted or the statement, codification or summary pursuant to subsection (b) or (c) of this section to any person specifically designated by the consumer who has within two years prior thereto received a consumer report for employment purposes, or within six months prior thereto received a consumer report for any other purpose, which contained the deleted or disputed information.

§ 612. Charges for certain disclosures [15 U.S.C. § 1681j]

(a) Reasonable charges allowed for certain disclosures.

(1) In general. Except as provided in subsections (b), (c), and (d), a consumer reporting agency may impose a reasonable charge on a consumer

(A) for making a disclosure to the consumer pursuant to section 609 [§ 1681g], which charge

(i) shall not exceed $8;(3) and

(ii) shall be indicated to the consumer before making the disclosure; and

(B) for furnishing, pursuant to 611(d) [§ 1681i], following a reinvestigation under section 611(a) [§ 1681i], a statement, codification, or summary to a person designated by the consumer under that section after the 30-day period beginning on the date of notification of the consumer under paragraph (6) or (8) of section 611(a) [§ 1681i] with respect to the reinvestigation, which charge

(i) shall not exceed the charge that the agency would impose on each designated recipient for a consumer report; and

(ii) shall be indicated to the consumer before furnishing such information.

(2) Modification of amount. The Federal Trade Commission shall increase the amount referred to in paragraph (1)(A)(I) on January 1 of each year, based proportionally on changes in the Consumer Price Index, with fractional changes rounded to the nearest fifty cents.

(b) Free disclosure after adverse notice to consumer. Each consumer reporting agency that maintains a file on a consumer shall make all disclosures pursuant to section 609 [§ 1681g] without charge to the consumer if, not later than 60 days after receipt by such consumer of a notification pursuant to section 615 [§ 1681m], or of a notification from a debt collection agency affiliated with that consumer reporting agency stating that the consumer's credit rating maybe or has been adversely affected, the consumer makes a request under section 609 [§ 1681g].

(c) Free disclosure under certain other circumstances. Upon the request of the consumer, a consumer reporting agency shall make all disclosures pursuant to section 609 [§ 1681g] once during any 12-month period without charge to that consumer if the consumer certifies in writing that the consumer

(1) is unemployed and intends to apply for employment in the 60-day period beginning on the date on which the certification is made; (2) is a recipient of public welfare assistance; or (3) has reason to believe that the file on the consumer at the agency contains inaccurate information due to fraud.

(d) Other charges prohibited. A consumer reporting agency shall not impose any charge on a consumer for providing any notification required by this title or making any disclosure required by this title, except as authorized by subsection (a).

§ 613. Public record information for employment purposes [15 U.S.C. § 1681k]

(a) In general. A consumer reporting agency which furnishes a consumer report for employment purposes and which for that purpose compiles and reports items of information on consumers which are matters of public record and are likely to have an adverse effect upon a consumer's ability to obtain employment shall

(1) at the time such public record information is reported to the user of such consumer report, notify the consumer of the fact that public record information is being reported by the consumer reporting agency, together with the name and address of the person to whom such information is being reported; or (2) maintain strict procedures designed to insure that whenever public record information which is likely to have an adverse effect on a consumer's ability to obtain employment is reported it is complete and up to date. For purposes of this paragraph, items of public record relating to arrests, indictments, convictions, suits, tax liens, and outstanding judgments shall be considered up to date if the current public record status of the item at the time of the report is reported.

(b) Exemption for national security investigations. Subsection (a) does not apply in the case of an agency or department of the United States Government that seeks to obtain and use a consumer report for employment purposes, if the head of the agency or department makes a written finding as prescribed under section 604(b)(4)(A).

§ 614. Restrictions on investigative consumer reports [15 U.S.C. § 1681l]

Whenever a consumer reporting agency prepares an investigative consumer report, no adverse information in the consumer report (other than information which is a matter of public record) maybe included in a subsequent consumer report unless such adverse information has been verified in the process of making such subsequent consumer report, or the adverse information was received within the three-month period preceding the date the subsequent report is furnished.

§ 615. Requirements on users of consumer reports [15 U.S.C. § 1681m]

(a) Duties of users taking adverse actions on the basis of information contained in consumer reports. If any person takes any adverse action with respect to any consumer that is based in whole or in part on any information contained in a consumer report, the person shall

(1) provide oral, written, or electronic notice of the adverse action to the consumer; (2) provide to the consumer orally, in writing, or electronically

(A) the name, address, and telephone number of the consumer reporting agency (including a toll-free telephone number established by the agency if the agency compiles and maintains files on consumers on a nationwide basis) that furnished the report to the person; and

(B) a statement that the consumer reporting agency did not make the decision to take the adverse action and is unable to provide the consumer the specific reasons why the adverse action was taken; and
(3) provide to the consumer an oral, written, or electronic notice of the consumer's right

(A) to obtain, under section 612 [§ 1681j], a free copy of a consumer report on the consumer from the consumer reporting agency referred to in paragraph (2), which notice shall include an indication of the 60-day period under that section for obtaining such a copy; and

(B) to dispute, under section 611 [§ 1681i], with a consumer reporting agency the accuracy or completeness of any information in a consumer report furnished by the agency.

(b) Adverse action based on information obtained from third parties other than consumer reporting agencies.

(1) In general. Whenever credit for personal, family, or household purposes involving a consumer is denied or the charge for such credit is increased either wholly or partly because of information obtained from a person other than a consumer reporting agency bearing upon the consumer's credit worthiness, credit standing, credit capacity, character, general reputation, personal characteristics, or mode of living, the user of such information shall, within a reasonable period of time, upon the consumer's written request for the reasons for such adverse action received within sixty days after learning of such adverse action, disclose the nature of the information to the consumer. The user of such information shall clearly and accurately disclose to the consumer his right to make such written request at the time such adverse action is communicated to the consumer.

(2) Duties of person taking certain actions based on information provided by affiliate.

(A) Duties, generally. If a person takes an action described in subparagraph (B) with respect to a consumer, based in whole or in part on information described in subparagraph (C), the person shall

(i) notify the consumer of the action, including a statement that the consumer may obtain the information in accordance with clause (ii); and

(ii) upon a written request from the consumer received within 60 days after transmittal of the notice required by clause (I), disclose to the consumer the nature of the information upon which the action is based by not later than 30 days after receipt of the request.

(B) Action described. An action referred to in subparagraph (A) is an adverse action described in section 603(k)(1)(A) [§ 1681a], taken in connection with a transaction initiated by the consumer, or any adverse action described in clause (i) or (ii) of section 603(k)(1)(B) [§ 1681a].

(C) Information described. Information referred to in subparagraph (A)

(i) except as provided in clause (ii), is information that

(I) is furnished to the person taking the action by a person related by common ownership or affiliated by common corporate control to the person taking the action; and

(II) bears on the credit worthiness, credit standing, credit capacity, character, general reputation, personal characteristics, or mode of living of the consumer; and

(ii) does not include

(I) information solely as to transactions or experiences between the consumer and the person furnishing the information; or

(II) information in a consumer report.

(c) Reasonable procedures to assure compliance. No person shall be held liable for any violation of this section if he shows by a preponderance of the evidence that at the time of the alleged violation he maintained reasonable procedures to assure compliance with the provisions of this section.

(d) Duties of users making written credit or insurance solicitations on the basis of information contained in consumer files.

(1) In general. Any person who uses a consumer report on any consumer in connection with any credit or insurance transaction that is not initiated by the consumer, that is provided to that person under section 604(c)(1)(B) [§ 1681b], shall provide with each written solicitation made to the consumer regarding the transaction a clear and conspicuous statement that

(A) information contained in the consumer's consumer report was used in connection with the transaction;

(B) the consumer received the offer of credit or insurance because the consumer satisfied the criteria for credit worthiness or insurability under which the consumer was selected for the offer;

(C) if applicable, the credit or insurance may not be extended if, after the consumer responds to the offer, the consumer does not meet the criteria used to select the consumer for the offer or any applicable criteria bearing on credit worthiness or insurability or does not furnish any required collateral;

(D) the consumer has a right to prohibit information contained in the consumer's file with any consumer reporting agency from being used in connection with any credit or insurance transaction that is not initiated by the consumer; and

(E) the consumer may exercise the right referred to in subparagraph (D) by notifying a notification system established under section 604(e) [§ 1681b].

(2) Disclosure of address and telephone number. A statement under paragraph (1) shall include the address and toll-free telephone number of the appropriate notification system established under section 604(e) [§ 1681b]. (3) Maintaining criteria on file. A person who makes an offer of credit or insurance to a consumer under a credit or insurance transaction described in paragraph (1) shall maintain on file the criteria used to select the consumer to receive the offer, all criteria bearing on credit worthiness or insurability, as applicable, that are the basis for determining whether or not to extend credit or insurance pursuant to the offer, and any requirement for the furnishing of collateral as a condition of the extension of credit or insurance, until the expiration of the 3-year period beginning on the date on which the offer is made to the consumer. (4) Authority of federal agencies regarding unfair or deceptive acts or practices not affected. This section is not intended to affect the authority of any Federal or State agency to enforce a prohibition against unfair or deceptive acts or practices, including the making of false or misleading statements in connection with a credit or insurance transaction that is not initiated by the consumer.

§ 616. Civil liability for willful noncompliance [15 U.S.C. § 1681n]

(a) In general. Any person who willfully fails to comply with any requirement imposed under this title with respect to any consumer is liable to that consumer in an amount equal to the sum of

(1)(A) any actual damages sustained by the consumer as a result of the failure or damages of not less than $100 and not more than $1,000; or

(B) in the case of liability of a natural person for obtaining a consumer report under false pretenses or knowingly without a permissible purpose, actual damages sustained by the consumer as a result of the failure or $1,000, whichever is greater;
(2) such amount of punitive damages as the court may allow; and (3) in the case of any successful action to enforce any liability under this section, the costs of the action together with reasonable attorney's fees as determined by the court.

(b) Civil liability for knowing noncompliance. Any person who obtains a consumer report from a consumer reporting agency under false pretenses or knowingly without a permissible purpose shall be liable to the consumer reporting agency for actual damages sustained by the consumer reporting agency or $1,000, whichever is greater.

(c) Attorney's fees. Upon a finding by the court that an unsuccessful pleading, motion, or other paper filed in connection with an action under this section was filed in bad faith or for purposes of harassment, the court shall award to the prevailing party attorney's fees reasonable in relation to the work expended in responding to the pleading, motion, or other paper.

§ 617. Civil liability for negligent noncompliance [15 U.S.C. § 1681o]

(a) In general. Any person who is negligent in failing to comply with any requirement imposed under this title with respect to any consumer is liable to that consumer in an amount equal to the sum of

(1) any actual damages sustained by the consumer as a result of the failure; (2) in the case of any successful action to enforce any liability under this section, the costs of the action together with reasonable attorney's fees as determined by the court.

(b) Attorney's fees. On a finding by the court that an unsuccessful pleading, motion, or other paper filed in connection with an action under this section was filed in bad faith or for purposes of harassment, the court shall award to the prevailing party attorney's fees reasonable in relation to the work expended in responding to the pleading, motion, or other paper.

§ 618. Jurisdiction of courts; limitation of actions [15 U.S.C. § 1681p]

An action to enforce any liability created under this title maybe brought in any appropriate United States district court without regard to the amount in controversy, or in any other court of competent jurisdiction, within two years from the date on which the liability arises, except that where a defendant has materially and willfully misrepresented any information required under this title to be disclosed to an individual and the information so misrepresented is material to the establishment of the defendant's liability to that individual under this title, the action maybe brought at any time within two years after discovery by the individual of the misrepresentation.

§ 619. Obtaining information under false pretenses [15 U.S.C. § 1681q]

Any person who knowingly and willfully obtains information on a consumer from a consumer reporting agency under false pretenses shall be fined under title 18, United States Code, imprisoned for not more than 2 years, or both.

§ 620. Unauthorized disclosures by officers or employees [15 U.S.C. § 1681r]

Any officer or employee of a consumer reporting agency who knowingly and willfully provides information concerning an individual from the agency's files to a person not authorized to receive that information shall be fined under title 18, United States Code, imprisoned for not more than 2 years, or both.

§ 621. Administrative enforcement [15 U.S.C. § 1681s]

(a) (1) Enforcement by Federal Trade Commission. Compliance with the requirements imposed under this title shall be enforced under the Federal Trade Commission Act [15 U.S.C. §§ 41 et seq.] by the Federal Trade Commission with respect to consumer reporting agencies and all other persons subject thereto, except to the extent that enforcement of the requirements imposed under this title is specifically committed to some other government agency under subsection (b) hereof. For the purpose of the exercise by the Federal Trade Commission of its functions and powers under the Federal Trade Commission Act, a violation of any requirement or prohibition imposed under this title shall constitute an unfair or deceptive act or practice in commerce in violation of section 5(a) of the Federal Trade Commission Act [15 U.S.C. § 45(a)] and shall be subject to enforcement by the Federal Trade Commission under section 5(b) thereof [15 U.S.C. § 45(b)] with respect to any consumer reporting agency or person subject to enforcement by the Federal Trade Commission pursuant to this subsection, irrespective of whether that person is engaged in commerce or meets any other jurisdictional tests in the Federal Trade Commission Act. The Federal Trade Commission shall have such procedural, investigative, and enforcement powers, including the power to issue procedural rules in enforcing compliance with the requirements imposed under this title and to require the filing of reports, the production of documents, and the appearance of witnesses as though the applicable terms and conditions of the Federal Trade Commission Act were part of this title. Any person violating any of the provisions of this title shall be subject to the penalties and entitled to the privileges and immunities provided in the Federal Trade Commission Act as though the applicable terms and provisions thereof were part of this title.

(2)(A) In the event of a knowing violation, which constitutes a pattern or practice of violations of this title, the Commission may commence a civil action to recover a civil penalty in a district court of the United States against any person that violates this title. In such action, such person shall be liable for a civil penalty of not more than $2,500 per violation.

(B) In determining the amount of a civil penalty under subparagraph (A), the court shall take into account the degree of culpability, any history of prior such conduct, ability to pay, effect on ability to continue to do business, and such other matters as justice may require.
(3) Notwithstanding paragraph (2), a court may not impose any civil penalty on a person for a violation of section 623(a)(1) [§ 1681s-2] unless the person has been enjoined from committing the violation, or ordered not to commit the violation, in an action or proceeding brought by or on behalf of the Federal Trade Commission, and has violated the injunction or order, and the court may not impose any civil penalty for any violation occurring before the date of the violation of the injunction or order.

(b) Enforcement by other agencies. Compliance with the requirements imposed under this title with respect to consumer reporting agencies, persons who use consumer reports from such agencies, persons who furnish information to such agencies, and users of information that are subject to subsection (d) of section 615 [§ 1681m] shall be enforced under

(1) section 8 of the Federal Deposit Insurance Act [12 U.S.C. § 1818], in the case of

(A) national banks, and Federal branches and Federal agencies of foreign banks, by the Office of the Comptroller of the Currency;

(B) member banks of the Federal Reserve System (other than national banks), branches and agencies of foreign banks (other than Federal branches, Federal agencies, and insured State branches of foreign banks), commercial lending companies owned or controlled by foreign banks, and organizations operating under section 25 or 25(a) [25A] of the Federal Reserve Act [12 U.S.C. §§ 601 et seq., §§ 611 et seq], by the Board of Governors of the Federal Reserve System; and

(C) banks insured by the Federal Deposit Insurance Corporation (other than members of the Federal Reserve System) and insured State branches of foreign banks, by the Board of Directors of the Federal Deposit Insurance Corporation;

(2) section 8 of the Federal Deposit Insurance Act [12 U.S.C. § 1818], by the Director of the Office of Thrift Supervision, in the case of a savings association the deposits of which are insured by the Federal Deposit Insurance Corporation;
(3) the Federal Credit Union Act [12 U.S.C. §§ 1751 et seq.], by the Administrator of the National Credit Union Administration [National Credit Union Administration Board] with respect to any Federal credit union; (4) subtitle IV of title 49 [49 U.S.C. §§ 10101 et seq.], by the Secretary of Transportation, with respect to all carriers subject to the jurisdiction of the Surface Transportation Board; (5) the Federal Aviation Act of 1958 [49 U.S.C. Appx §§ 1301 et seq.], by the Secretary of Transportation with respect to any air carrier or foreign air carrier subject to that Act [49 U.S.C. Appx §§ 1301 et seq.]; and (6) the Packers and Stockyards Act, 1921 [7 U.S.C. §§ 181 et seq.] (except as provided in section 406 of that Act [7 U.S.C. §§ 226 and 227]), by the Secretary of Agriculture with respect to any activities subject to that Act.

The terms used in paragraph (1) that are not defined in this title or otherwise defined in section 3(s) of the Federal Deposit Insurance Act (12 U.S.C. §1813(s)) shall have the meaning given to them in section 1(b) of the International Banking Act of 1978 (12 U.S.C. § 3101).

(c) State action for violations.

(1) Authority of states. In addition to such other remedies as are provided under State law, if the chief law enforcement officer of a State, or an official or agency designated by a State, has reason to believe that any person has violated or is violating this title, the State

(A) may bring an action to enjoin such violation in any appropriate United States district court or in any other court of competent jurisdiction;

(B) subject to paragraph (5), may bring an action on behalf of the residents of the State to recover

(i) damages for which the person is liable to such residents under sections 616 and 617 [§§ 1681n and 1681o] as a result of the violation;

(ii) in the case of a violation of section 623(a) [§ 1681s-2], damages for which the person would, but for section 623(c) [§ 1681s-2], be liable to such residents as a result of the violation; or

(iii) damages of not more than $1,000 for each willful or negligent violation; and

(C) in the case of any successful action under subparagraph (A) or (B), shall be awarded the costs of the action and reasonable attorney fees as determined by the court.

(2) Rights of federal regulators. The State shall serve prior written notice of any action under paragraph (1) upon the Federal Trade Commission or the appropriate Federal regulator determined under subsection (b) and provide the Commission or appropriate Federal regulator with a copy of its complaint, except in any case in which such prior notice is not feasible, in which case the State shall serve such notice immediately upon instituting such action. The Federal Trade Commission or appropriate Federal regulator shall have the right

(A) to intervene in the action;

(B) upon so intervening, to be heard on all matters arising therein;

(C) to remove the action to the appropriate United States district court; and

(D) to file petitions for appeal.

(3) Investigatory powers. For purposes of bringing any action under this subsection, nothing in this subsection shall prevent the chief law enforcement officer, or an official or agency designated by

a State, from exercising the powers conferred on the chief law enforcement officer or such official by the laws of such State to conduct investigations or to administer oaths or affirmations or to compel the attendance of witnesses or the production of documentary and other evidence. (4) Limitation on state action while federal action pending. If the Federal Trade Commission or the appropriate Federal regulator has instituted a civil action or an administrative action under section 8 of the Federal Deposit Insurance Act for a violation of this title, no State may, during the pendency of such action, bring an action under this section against any defendant named in the complaint of the Commission or the appropriate Federal regulator for any violation of this title that is alleged in that complaint.

(5) Limitations on state actions for violation of section 623(a)(1) [§ 1681s-2].

(A) Violation of injunction required. A State may not bring an action against a person under paragraph (1)(B) for a violation of section 623(a)(1) [§ 1681s-2], unless

(i) the person has been enjoined from committing the violation, in an action brought by the State under paragraph (1)(A); and

(ii) the person has violated the injunction.

(B) Limitation on damages recoverable. In an action against a person under paragraph (1)(B) for a violation of section 623(a)(1) [§ 1681s-2], a State may not recover any damages incurred before the date of the violation of an injunction on which the action is based.

(d) Enforcement under other authority. For the purpose of the exercise by any agency referred to in subsection (b) of this section of its powers under any Act referred to in that subsection, a violation of any requirement imposed under this title shall be deemed to be a violation of a requirement imposed under that Act. In addition to its powers under any provision of law specifically referred to in subsection (b) of this section, each of the agencies referred to in that subsection may exercise, for the purpose of enforcing compliance with any requirement imposed under this title any other authority conferred on it by law.

(e) Regulatory authority

(1) The Federal banking agencies referred to in paragraphs (1) and (2) of subsection (b) shall jointly prescribe such regulations as necessary to carry out the purposes of this Act with respect to any persons identified under paragraphs (1) and (2) of subsection (b), and the Board of Governors of the Federal Reserve System shall have authority to prescribe regulations consistent with such joint regulations with respect to bank holding companies and affiliates (other than depository institutions and consumer reporting agencies) of such holding companies. (2) The Board of the National Credit Union Administration shall prescribe such regulations as necessary to carry out the purposes of this Act with respect to any persons identified under paragraph (3) of subsection (b).

§ 622. Information on overdue child support obligations [15 U.S.C. § 1681s-1]

Notwithstanding any other provision of this title, a consumer reporting agency shall include in any consumer report furnished by the agency in accordance with section 604 [§ 1681b] of this title, any information on the failure of the consumer to pay overdue support which

(1) is provided

(A) to the consumer reporting agency by a State or local child support enforcement agency; or

(B) to the consumer reporting agency and verified by any local, State, or Federal government agency; and

(2) antedates the report by 7 years or less.

§ 623. Responsibilities of furnishers of information to consumer reporting agencies [15 U.S.C. § 1681s-2]

(a) Duty of furnishers of information to provide accurate information.

(1) Prohibition.

(A) Reporting information with actual knowledge of errors. A person shall not furnish any information relating to a consumer to any consumer reporting agency if the person knows or consciously avoids knowing that the information is inaccurate.

(B) Reporting information after notice and confirmation of errors. A person shall not furnish information relating to a consumer to any consumer reporting agency if

(i) the person has been notified by the consumer, at the address specified by the person for such notices, that specific information is inaccurate; and

(ii) the information is, in fact, inaccurate.

(C) No address requirement. A person who clearly and conspicuously specifies to the consumer an address for notices referred to in subparagraph (B) shall not be subject to subparagraph (A); however, nothing in subparagraph (B) shall require a person to specify such an address.

(2) Duty to correct and update information. A person who

(A) regularly and in the ordinary course of business furnishes information to one or more consumer reporting agencies about the person's transactions or experiences with any consumer; and

(B) has furnished to a consumer reporting agency information that the person determines is not complete or accurate, shall promptly notify the consumer reporting agency of that determination and provide to the agency any corrections to that information, or any additional information, that is necessary to make the information provided by the person to the agency complete and accurate, and shall not thereafter furnish to the agency any of the information that remains not complete or accurate.

(3) Duty to provide notice of dispute. If the completeness or accuracy of any information furnished by any person to any consumer reporting agency is disputed to such person by a consumer, the person may not furnish the information to any consumer reporting agency without notice that such information is disputed by the consumer. (4) Duty to provide notice of closed accounts. A person who regularly and in the ordinary course of business furnishes information to a consumer reporting agency regarding a consumer who has a credit account with that person shall notify the agency of the voluntary closure of the account by the consumer, in information regularly furnished for the period in which the account is closed. (5) Duty to provide notice of delinquency of accounts. A person who furnishes information to a consumer reporting agency regarding a delinquent account being placed for collection, charged to profit or loss, or subjected to any similar action shall, not later than 90 days after furnishing the information, notify the agency of the month and year of the commencement of the delinquency that immediately preceded the action.

(b) Duties of furnishers of information upon notice of dispute.

(1) In general. After receiving notice pursuant to section 611(a)(2) [§ 1681i] of a dispute with regard to the completeness or accuracy of any information provided by a person to a consumer reporting agency, the person shall

(A) conduct an investigation with respect to the disputed information;

(B) review all relevant information provided by the consumer reporting agency pursuant to section 611(a)(2) [§ 1681i];

(C) report the results of the investigation to the consumer reporting agency; and

(D) if the investigation finds that the information is incomplete or inaccurate, report those results to all other consumer reporting agencies to which the person furnished the information and that compile and maintain files on consumers on a nationwide basis.

(2) Deadline. A person shall complete all investigations, reviews, and reports required under paragraph (1) regarding information provided by the person to a consumer reporting agency, before the expiration of the period under section 611(a)(1) [§ 1681i] within which the consumer reporting agency is required to complete actions required by that section regarding that information.

(c) Limitation on liability. Sections 616 and 617 [§§ 1681n and 1681o] do not apply to any failure to comply with subsection (a), except as provided in section 621(c)(1)(B) [§ 1681s].

(d) Limitation on enforcement. Subsection (a) shall be enforced exclusively under section 621 [§ 1681s] by the Federal agencies and officials and the State officials identified in that section.

§ 624. Relation to State laws [15 U.S.C. § 1681t]

(a) In general. Except as provided in subsections (b) and (c), this title does not annul, alter, affect, or exempt any person subject to the provisions of this title from complying with the laws of any State with respect to the collection, distribution, or use of any information on consumers, except to the extent that those laws are inconsistent with any provision of this title, and then only to the extent of the inconsistency.

(b) General exceptions. No requirement or prohibition maybe imposed under the laws of any State

   (1) with respect to any subject matter regulated under

   (A) subsection (c) or (e) of section 604 [§ 1681b], relating to the prescreening of consumer reports;

   (B) section 611 [§ 1681i], relating to the time by which a consumer reporting agency must take any action, including the provision of notification to a consumer or other person, in any procedure related to the disputed accuracy of information in a consumer's file, except that this subparagraph shall not apply to any State law in effect on the date of enactment of the Consumer Credit Reporting Reform Act of 1996;

   (C) subsections (a) and (b) of section 615 [§ 1681m], relating to the duties of a person who takes any adverse action with respect to a consumer;

   (D) section 615(d) [§ 1681m], relating to the duties of persons who use a consumer report of a consumer in connection with any credit or insurance transaction that is not initiated by the consumer and that consists of a firm offer of credit or insurance;

   (E) section 605 [§ 1681c], relating to information contained in consumer reports, except that this subparagraph shall not apply to any State law in effect on the date of enactment of the Consumer Credit Reporting Reform Act of 1996; or

   (F) section 623 [§ 1681s-2], relating to the responsibilities of persons who furnish information to consumer reporting agencies, except that this paragraph shall not apply

   (i) with respect to section 54A(a) of chapter 93 of the Massachusetts Annotated Laws (as in effect on the date of enactment of the Consumer Credit Reporting Reform Act of 1996); or

   (ii) with respect to section 1785.25(a) of the California Civil Code (as in effect on the date of enactment of the Consumer Credit Reporting Reform Act of 1996);

(2) with respect to the exchange of information among persons affiliated by common ownership or common corporate control, except that this paragraph shall not apply with respect to subsection (a) or (c)(1) of section 2480e of title 9, Vermont Statutes Annotated (as in effect on the date of enactment of the Consumer Credit Reporting Reform Act of 1996); or (3) with respect to the form and content of any disclosure required to be made under section 609(c) [§ 1681g].

(c) Definition of firm offer of credit or insurance. Notwithstanding any definition of the term "firm offer of credit or insurance" (or any equivalent term) under the laws of any State, the definition of that term contained in section 603(l) [§ 1681a] shall be construed to apply in the enforcement and interpretation of the laws of any State governing consumer reports.

(d) Limitations. Subsections (b) and (c)

(1) do not affect any settlement, agreement, or consent judgment between any State Attorney General and any consumer reporting agency in effect on the date of enactment of the Consumer Credit Reporting Reform Act of 1996; and (2) do not apply to any provision of State law (including any provision of a State constitution) that

(A) is enacted after January 1, 2004;

(B) states explicitly that the provision is intended to supplement this title; and

(C) gives greater protection to consumers than is provided under this title.

§ 625. Disclosures to FBI for counterintelligence purposes [15 U.S.C. § 1681u]

(a) Identity of financial institutions. Notwithstanding section 604 [§ 1681b] or any other provision of this title, a consumer reporting agency shall furnish to the Federal Bureau of Investigation the names and addresses of all financial institutions (as that term is defined in section 1101 of the Right to Financial Privacy Act of 1978 [12 U.S.C. § 3401]) at which a consumer maintains or has maintained an account, to the extent that information is in the files of the agency, when presented with a written request for that information, signed by the Director of the Federal Bureau of Investigation, or the Director's designee in a position not lower than Deputy Assistant Director at Bureau headquarters or a Special Agent in Charge of a Bureau field office designated by the Director, which certifies compliance with this section. The Director or the Director's designee may make such a certification only if the Director or the Director's designee has determined in writing, that such information is sought for the conduct of an authorized investigation to protect against international terrorism or clandestine intelligence activities, provided that such an investigation of a United States person is not conducted solely upon the basis of activities protected by the first amendment to the Constitution of the United States.

(b) Identifying information. Notwithstanding the provisions of section 604 [§ 1681b] or any other provision of this title, a consumer reporting agency shall furnish identifying information respecting a consumer, limited to name, address, former addresses, places of employment, or former places of employment, to the Federal Bureau of Investigation when presented with a written request, signed by the Director or the Director's designee, which certifies compliance with this subsection. The Director or the Director's designee in a position not lower than Deputy Assistant Director at Bureau headquarters or a Special Agent in Charge of a Bureau field office designated by the Director may make such a certification only if the Director or the Director's designee has determined in writing that such information is sought for the conduct of an authorized investigation to protect against international terrorism or clandestine intelligence activities, provided that such an investigation of a United States person is not conducted solely upon the basis of activities protected by the first amendment to the Constitution of the United States.

(c) Court order for disclosure of consumer reports. Notwithstanding section 604 [§ 1681b] or any other provision of this title, if requested in writing by the Director of the Federal Bureau of Investigation, or a designee of the Director in a position not lower than Deputy Assistant Director at Bureau headquarters or a Special Agent in Charge of a Bureau field office designated by the Director, a court may issue an order ex parte directing a consumer reporting agency to furnish a consumer report to the Federal Bureau of Investigation, upon a showing in camera that the consumer report is sought for the conduct of an authorized investigation to protect against international terrorism or clandestine intelligence activities, provided that such an investigation of a United States person is not conducted solely upon the basis of activities protected by the first amendment to the Constitution of the United States.

The terms of an order issued under this subsection shall not disclose that the order is issued for purposes of a counterintelligence investigation.

(d) Confidentiality. No consumer reporting agency or officer, employee, or agent of a consumer reporting agency shall disclose to any person, other than those officers, employees, or agents of a consumer reporting agency necessary to fulfill the requirement to disclose information to the Federal Bureau of Investigation under this section, that the Federal Bureau of Investigation has sought or obtained the identity of financial institutions or a consumer report respecting any consumer under subsection (a), (b), or (c), and no consumer reporting agency or officer, employee, or agent of a consumer reporting agency shall include in any consumer report any information that would indicate that the Federal Bureau of Investigation has sought or obtained such information or a consumer report.

(e) Payment of fees. The Federal Bureau of Investigation shall, subject to the availability of appropriations, pay to the consumer reporting agency assembling or providing report or information in accordance with procedures established under this section a fee for reimbursement for such costs as are reasonably necessary and which have been directly incurred in searching, reproducing, or transporting books, papers, records, or other data required or requested to be produced under this section.

(f) Limit on dissemination. The Federal Bureau of Investigation may not disseminate information obtained pursuant to this section outside of the Federal Bureau of Investigation, except to other Federal agencies as maybe necessary for the approval or conduct of a foreign counterintelligence investigation, or, where the information concerns a person subject to the Uniform Code of Military Justice, to appropriate investigative authorities within the military department concerned as maybe necessary for the conduct of a joint foreign counterintelligence investigation.

(g) Rules of construction. Nothing in this section shall be construed to prohibit information from being furnished by the Federal Bureau of Investigation pursuant to a subpoena or court order, in connection with a judicial or administrative proceeding to enforce the provisions of this Act. Nothing in this section shall be construed to authorize or permit the withholding of information from the Congress.

(h) Reports to Congress. On a semiannual basis, the Attorney General shall fully inform the Permanent Select Committee on Intelligence and the Committee on Banking, Finance and Urban Affairs of the House of Representatives, and the Select Committee on Intelligence and the Committee on Banking, Housing, and Urban Affairs of the Senate concerning all requests made pursuant to subsections (a), (b), and (c).

(i) Damages. Any agency or department of the United States obtaining or disclosing any consumer reports, records, or information contained therein in violation of this section is liable to the consumer to whom such consumer reports, records, or information relate in an amount equal to the sum of

(1) $100, without regard to the volume of consumer reports, records, or information involved; (2) any actual damages sustained by the consumer as a result of the disclosure; (3) if the violation is found to have been willful or intentional, such punitive damages as a court may allow; and (4) in the case of any successful action to enforce liability under this subsection, the costs of the action, together with reasonable attorney fees, as determined by the court.

(j) Disciplinary actions for violations. If a court determines that any agency or department of the United States has violated any provision of this section and the court finds that the circumstances surrounding the violation raise questions of whether or not an officer or employee of the agency or department acted willfully or intentionally with respect to the violation, the agency or department shall promptly initiate a proceeding to determine whether or not disciplinary action is warranted against the officer or employee who was responsible for the violation.

(k) Good-faith exception. Notwithstanding any other provision of this title, any consumer reporting agency or agent or employee thereof making disclosure of consumer reports or identifying information pursuant to this subsection in good-faith reliance upon a certification of the Federal Bureau of Investigation pursuant to provisions of this section shall not be liable to any person for such disclosure under this title, the constitution of any State, or any law or regulation of any State or any political subdivision of any State.

(l) Limitation of remedies. Notwithstanding any other provision of this title, the remedies and sanctions set forth in this section shall be the only judicial remedies and sanctions for violation of this section.

(m) Injunctive relief. In addition to any other remedy contained in this section, injunctive relief shall be available to require compliance with the procedures of this section. In the event of any successful action under this subsection, costs together with reasonable attorney fees, as determined by the court, maybe recovered.

§ 626. Disclosures to governmental agencies for counterterrorism purposes [15 U.S.C. §1681v]

(a) Disclosure. Notwithstanding section 604 or any other provision of this title, a consumer reporting agency shall furnish a consumer report of a consumer and all other information in a consumer's file to a government agency authorized to conduct investigations of, or intelligence or counterintelligence activities or analysis related to, international terrorism when presented with a written certification by such government agency that such information is necessary for the agency's conduct or such investigation, activity or analysis.

(b) Form of certification. The certification described in subsection (a) shall be signed by a supervisory official designated by the head of a Federal agency or an officer of a Federal agency whose appointment to office is required to be made by the President, by and with the advice and consent of the Senate.

(c) Confidentiality. No consumer reporting agency, or officer, employee, or agent of such consumer reporting agency, shall disclose to any person, or specify in any consumer report, that a government agency has sought or obtained access to information under subsection (a).

(d) Rule of construction. Nothing in section 625 shall be construed to limit the authority of the Director of the Federal Bureau of Investigation under this section.

(e) Safe harbor. Notwithstanding any other provision of this title, any consumer reporting agency or agent or employee thereof making disclosure of consumer reports or other information pursuant to this section in good-faith reliance upon a certification of a governmental agency pursuant to the provisions of this section shall not be liable to any person for such disclosure under this subchapter, the constitution of any State, or any law or regulation of any State or any political subdivision of any State.


Legislative History

House Reports:
No. 91-975 (Comm. on Banking and Currency) andNo. 91-1587 (Comm. of Conference)
Senate Reports:
No. 91-1139 accompanying S. 3678 (Comm. on Banking and Currency)
Congressional Record, Vol. 116 (1970)
May 25, considered and passed House.Sept. 18, considered and passed Senate, amended.Oct. 9, Senate agreed to conference report.Oct. 13, House agreed to conference report.
Enactment:
Public Law No. 91-508 (October 26, 1970):
Amendments: Public Law Nos.
95-473 (October 17, 1978)95-598 (November 6, 1978)98-443 (October 4, 1984)101-73 (August 9, 1989)102-242 (December 19, 1991)102-537 (October 27, 1992)102-550 (October 28, 1992)103-325 (September 23, 1994)104-88 (December 29, 1995)104-93 (January 6, 1996)104-193 (August 22, 1996)104-208 (September 30, 1996)105-107 (November 20, 1997)105-347 (November 2, 1998)106-102 (November 12, 1999)107-56 (October 26, 2001)

Endnotes:

1. The reporting periods have been lengthened for certain adverse information pertaining to U.S. Government insured or guaranteed student loans, or pertaining to national direct student loans. See sections 430A(f) and 463(c)(3) of the Higher Education Act of 1965, 20 U.S.C. 1080a(f) and 20 U.S.C. 1087cc(c)(3), respectively.

2. Should read "paragraphs (4) and (5)...." Prior Section 605(a)(6) was amended and re-designated as Section 605(a)(5) in November 1998.

3. The Federal Trade Commission increased the maximum allowable charge to $9.00, effective January 1, 2002. 66 Fed. Reg. 63545 (Dec. 7, 2001).

# Index

# Q

# R

# S